QUAREIA—THE INITIATE
Book Seven

Josephine McCarthy

For more information and all course modules please visit www.quareia.com

Copyright 2014 © Josephine McCarthy

Published by Quareia Publishing UK

ISBN 978-0-9933480-7-5

Cover illustration by Stuart Littlejohn

Acknowledgements

Thanks to the Quareia team that made this course possible:
Frater Acher, Alex A, Stuart Littlejohn, Aaron Moshe, and Michael Sheppard.

And thank you to all the donors who made this course a reality.

Course Advisory

The Quareia takes a magical apprentice from the beginning of magic to the level of adeptship and beyond.

In order for this course to work, it is wise to work with the lessons in sequence. If you don't, it will not work properly.

Contents

Initiate Module III

Power Dynamics of Creation Part II

Lesson 1

The Deeper Power of Restriction

1.1 Introduction to Module III

In the apprentice section relating to this subject you looked at the powers and beings involved in the process of creation from a magical perspective. We started to look at this deeply powerful process without the usual names and terms that are attributed to these powers and beings. All Kabbalistic and other magical, mystical names were removed: instead, the beings and powers were referred to by what they do.

This was done because there is so much misunderstanding, fantasy, and psychobabble that has developed around these powers, which leads to further misunderstandings and confusion. Also we are looking at these powers without those constructs, so that we can learn about and observe them without preconceived ideas. This way we do not fall into the trap of dipping into religions and systems that are not of our own genuine experience.

Though this subject matter can be thought of as more the realm of mystics than magicians, it is vitally important to know how the creation dynamic works from an inner perspective because the pattern is inherent in all creation, and becomes very active when magic is engaged. Every time you instigate a magical act the deeper dynamics of creation are triggered in one way or another: you are learning the 'software coding' of magic.

In the last module on creation you learned about the powers[1] that are active and perceptible to humans, beings that operate closely with humanity. This is the lowest orbit of creative power and also the one most apparent in magic. In this module we will move closer in and look at the next layer of angelic powers, ones that work deep in the inner worlds in the constant dance of creation and destruction.

These angelic powers are the 'engines' behind the inner realms, the Inner Desert, and the creative life process. They are not angels that can be connected with, and they have little if any human connection: they are the bigger guys who deal with the creation of all life, and though we attempt to put personalities on them, they are impersonal powers that are mirrored in every energetic dynamic in the physical world. As such, we approach these powers as inherent forces, not as angels we can talk to or observe.

As magicians we engage these forces in long-term ritual projects, exorcism, healing, and construction: we work with them as power forces, not as inner contacts. We are too small and they are too big for us to really connect with them as being to being. It would be like a human trying to be aware of every tiny insect under their feet as they walk through a field: the difference in consciousness is that great.

---

[1] Angelic.

10

We will start with the deep power of restriction and through each lesson we will inch a bit deeper into the inner realm and the Inner Desert so that you gain a strong understanding of these powers. Once you understand them, you can then work with them later in your initiate work and also more powerfully as an adept.

1.2 The Power of Restriction

The power of Restriction is a necessary brake for creation. It is one half of two opposing powers. Between them, and with the fulcrum in the middle, they keep the deeper scales of creation and destruction balanced.

Whenever you have a dynamic of creation/birth, there must also be a restriction to ensure that limitless growth does not occur, as such growth in a limited world is very destructive.

When we looked at the lowest expression of creation, we looked at a power called the Unraveller. We learned that it operates through a specific dynamic: either humans mirror creation and learn their own self-restriction, or they unravel and are caught by Restriction that takes their life out of circulation.

This dynamic is not exclusive to humanity: it flows through all creatures, all civilisations, and all patterns. One aspect of Restriction is the cull mechanism: when something overgrows or overpopulates, the cull mechanism starts to kick in. This is the lowest octave of this particular power of Restriction.

The deeper aspect of Restriction is that it limits the creative forging of new paths into life by the Light Bearer. As the Light Bearer carries the Divine Spark on its quest for physical manifestation, it is also the dynamic of the limitless, timeless, and ever-expanding pulse of creative power. Such limitless conscious power cannot take physical form on its own, as there is no vessel large enough to contain it.

The power of Restriction counteracts that quest for a limitless power to be manifest: it restricts that impulse. It limits the amount of creative power and triggers a process that will create a pattern strong enough—a vessel—to contain Divine power. That strong vessel is the physical realm.

Think of Restriction as a large, slowly spinning power that gathers up the souls of the dead and contains or imprisons them. Through its process of slow spinning, along with its natural function of holding, it slows down anything in its orbit.

This power of Restriction also has an action that is very visible in the inner realms, one that can instantly be recognised by magicians. It is an action that is profound, yet it is also something we can observe and consider as magicians: it is the power of Divine Binding or imprisoning.

When something no longer needs to be or should be manifest, it is bound by the power of Restriction. Magicians can observe this in inner vision in a variety of ways. Beings[2] that have physically manifested on earth but no longer have a place there or in the inner realms[3] are bound into the land, where they sink into the Underworld. Eventually they sink deep down into the Abyss and are held there.

Beings that never manifested physically, particularly angelic beings, are bound in the Desert, or upon the present surface of the land, or both. This is something that you will observe for yourself as a magician, and it is also something that you really need to know about.

Where a being has been bound is very important to a magician: where the being is bound will tell you if it is in a temporary holding pattern or if it has been put to sleep.

If the being is restricted in the Abyss, then unless someone powerful enough magically releases it, it is safe to say that it will stay down the Abyss.

If the being is restricted in the land, then it is waiting: the inner powers bind the

---

[2]Human, animal, deity, spirit, dinosaur!

[3]Which always has an aspect of the future.

being into a land feature where it will stay in restriction until its time comes to be released. You have already looked at this in terms of angelic beings bound in rivers and mountains, waiting to be released. If they are bound in land features, then they have been active before and will be active again.

If the being is bound in the Inner Desert, an aspect of the inner realm, then it has as yet not been fully active in the physical world, but it will be at some point. Often the beings bound in the Desert[4] are creative in their impulse, but their unfettered creation brings destruction.[5]

You may also come across very destructive beings held in the Desert: they too will be held there until it is time to do their job.

Quite a few different ancient texts talk about this process, and again it is something you have already looked at in your research. Essentially you learn these various dynamics and aspects in order to recognise them in deep vision so you know not to interfere with them.

If you look back over your work with Egyptian texts and the Scales, you will also see parallels: just as the Scales work with humanity, the deeper scales work with creation. The power of Restriction is one dish of those scales.

This is the big picture of how the power of Restriction works in the process of creation. But, like all other power dynamics, it has many different aspects and levels that are all part and parcel of the power of Restriction. It is these many different aspects that magicians become aware of in their work. To work with such powers requires you to understand fully the relevant counterpoint powers in order for you to keep a power balance as you work. To understand this, let us look at the more magical aspects of this power of Restriction and how it is worked with in magic.

1.3 Binding

When magicians use bindings, they are consciously or unconsciously drawing on the power of Restriction in their work. Tapping into such power unconsciously and without thought is how magicians often get themselves into a mess, or end up unintentionally doing untold damage.

Simple folk binding spells are unlikely to have any great pull on this power simply by nature of the magic used. But once a ritual magician who also works in vision begins to use such methods, they would be wise to know what they are actually doing, working with, and why, before they dive into it.

Magicians love binding things: it's that simple. They love to bend and bind power to 'their will,' to bind things or people whom they dislike, and to bind beings or people whom they personally perceive as being 'wrong.'

Then, hopefully, they eventually grow up…usually as the result of bitter experience. Either they leave magic alone altogether,[6] they slowly degenerate, or they move on and learn a deeper layer of magic with more experience to guide them. So what goes wrong?

You have already looked at the outer magical longer-term consequences of unbalanced binding in your apprentice work; now we will look at the various angles of the deeper dynamics from a power perspective.

1.4 Triggering overgrowth and limiting growth

For sheer technical reasons, working with the power of Restriction when it is not needed or is unbalanced will trigger overgrowth. Something which appears unbalanced on its surface, when looked at deeper as a long-term dynamic, can often turn out to be part and parcel of a longer process of rebalancing. If this process is interfered with in the wrong way, it upsets the balance and everything spins out of control.

This is why short-term, conditional magic so often makes a situation worse in the long term, rather than better. And this dynamic

---

[4]Usually angelic, sometimes deities.
[5]Through too much creation.
[6]They are essentially bound out of magic.

runs through everything that lives: certain viruses may seem bad, but the virus can often restrict another illness or infection that left unchecked could wreak havoc on the body. Causing restriction in the wrong place or in the wrong thing can trigger, by nature of the fine balance of power, an overgrowth of something else.

But when there is an initial unbalanced overgrowth, the application of the power of Restriction can limit that overgrowth and restore balance. Most things in nature have the power of Restriction hard-wired into their species. When overgrowth happens, eventually the natural restriction kicks in and cuts back the overgrowth through death, disease, aggression and so forth.

As humans we have learned how to dodge around this in many different ways. Because we have done this for so long, we have forgotten about the positive aspect of restriction. As a result we now live in a world which is ripe for Divine Restriction. If nature, the expressive vessel of life, cannot cope or implement the restriction, then the deeper powers that flow out of the inner worlds will.

Taking this back to magic, the inherent dynamic of self-balance in nature is a powerful force that also expresses itself in magic. When Restriction is placed on a person or place that does not in truth need it, how it will affect the person or place largely depends on the level of magic used and the level of balance or imbalance that the place or person actually has, not what it is perceived to have.

If a person or place has as much balance as is possible in an imbalanced world, the magic will have little effect other than to cause a slight disturbance that is soon dissipated.

If the person or place has a bit of imbalance, the magic will trigger or speed up events that will bring about as much balance as is possible: it will engage the power of the Grindstone. The Grindstone power will flow into the place or person, which will manifest as a series of difficulties that polish them and move them towards balance, should they choose to engage with it.

If the person is pretty unbalanced and they have been bound by the power of Restriction, then the power of the Unraveller will trigger, and what happens next will depend on their ability to learn from experience. They will either totally unravel, or they will understand what is happening and make a decision to sort themselves out.

This would engage the Grindstone, which could happen by direct magical engagement or by fate triggering this power subtly. It is one of those life situations where someone feels that everything is falling apart around them and they make the decision to change their own choices and actions.

If they do not make that choice, they are slowly unravelled to the point of destruction, at which point the power of Restriction kicks in with full strength: the person is locked down in every way possible, either by their life circumstances or by illness.

Finally, if whatever is being bound by Restriction is truly out of balance and destructive, then the power of Restriction kicks in immediately and the person is bound out of action.

How these dynamics work is poorly understood in a lot of magical communities, and often a magician cannot understand why some of their applied magic works and other bits do not.

What they are not getting is that magic is essentially a force of nature: it flows through all the same dynamics that everything else in creation does. Magic cannot stop a force of nature, but it can trigger various dynamics like a catalyst.

Magic cannot be successful if it flies in the face of nature, simply because inappropriately applied magic is the same as using the wrong tool for a job: if it doesn't fit, it will not work.

So you cannot in truth fully bind something if it does not actually need binding. And how the magician approaches such an action will determine how that magical act affects them.

If the magician engages the power of Restriction in a forceful way when it is not needful,[7] then it is more likely that the magician will find themselves restricted than the intended target. All magic flows through the magician and affects the magician just as it affects the intended recipient. We have talked about this before.

When you apply magic you step into a stream of complex, alternating forces. Those forces simply seek their natural outlet. The magician directs the forces into the vessels (situations) that have need of that force. If the vessel is not in need of that force, then the force simply flows over the top and keeps seeking its vessel. If the magician is in actual need of that force and does not realise it, then they will become the vessel to be filled.

It is the simple, impersonal aspect of power seeking its vessel that so many magicians do not understand. The power of Restriction will not restrict something that does not need restricting, not because it has any thought or emotion or sense of judgement/compassion towards the intended victim, but because it cannot fill or hold a vessel that does not need it: the vessel is the wrong 'shape' for that power at that time.

If the magician feels that someone or something needs binding in order to restore balance, first they must look to themselves and ensure that they too do not need restriction. When they are clear about what they are doing and why, and where they stand in the picture of the dynamics, then releasing the power of Restriction will trigger a flow of power that seeks balance. If they release such power with the intention of it flowing into whatever vessel in the situation needs filling, then it will seek expression and fill whatever needs filling.

Just remember that all these deeper and more powerful creative forces will only flow where they are meant to flow. They can be triggered, they can be observed and worked with in your own development, and they can be worked with in powerful magic; but they will only do their own intended job. They will

---

[7]For example binding a person with the power of Restriction because they piss they magician off or the magician doesn't agree with them.

not pander to the imbalanced or immature thinking of a scorned magician. If as an adept you ever release such power and aim it at a person or place, and it is unsuccessful, it is most likely because the intended recipient in truth does not need restricting. That is when the magician must think very carefully about their real motives, ideas, and opinions, because the universe is telling them they got it wrong.

If the intended recipient begins to display difficulties in their lives but they continue what they are doing, then they are likely going through a rebalancing process as a result of the magic.

Remember: working with these Divine Powers means to stand amongst them and work with them in harmony, not to use them as your own personal armoury.

1.5 Strength

The power of Restriction can be a force to work with to strengthen something, or yourself. When the power of Restriction is engaged in order to strengthen, it flows as a higher octave of the Grindstone. In some mystical/magical systems, the power of Restriction is called Strength.

Working with the power of Restriction in this way enables the magician to call upon these deeper powers of creation to flow through them and restrict them in whatever way is needed in order to strengthen and balance themselves. This magical action speeds up the natural process for the magician. Restriction will flow through any aspect of the magician's life, actions, health, and body, and in whatever way is needful, in order to strengthen, mature, and rebalance them.

However, inviting these deeper powers to engage with an individual human can be folly if the power of the Grindstone has not already been worked with to its full completion. We work our way inwards in the inner worlds in slow steps, working with each power in turn as necessary: the trick is to become as balanced as possible so that you can pass by and through these powers without being torn apart or filled with them.

Once the magician has worked with the Grindstone as much as they are capable of, then the power of Restriction is triggered. Then anything not polished by the Grindstone is sought out by the power of Restriction and is limited. It becomes a powerful barrier, but instead of fighting it we work with it as a boundary, as a limitation: we ensure that we focus on what needs to be dealt with, and that we learn from it. This in turn strengthens the magician, as the restriction of weights on a muscle will strengthen it if worked with wisely.

The magical sword, the Limiter, is connected to both the Grindstone and the power of Restriction: the sword is the lowest octave of this power. By first learning the power of the Limiter and then working with the Grindstone in our magical lives, we eventually reach a place where it is wise to be open to the power of Restriction. But it is a choice that must be thought about carefully, as sometimes our greatest magical strength comes from death: the ultimate restriction.

1.6 Vessels and Restriction

In your apprentice work you worked a lot with vessels, which are a form of restriction: a vessel restricts a power or substance and contains it. The same is true of a temple. A temple is also a vessel with boundaries that contain power and contact: the directions and thresholds define a contained space into which power can flow in a limited way in order to achieve something.

In adept magical construction, the power of Restriction is triggered within the substance of the building or within the thresholds of the temple. First the magician learns to build up thresholds, work with directions, and contain power within that setting. Later the magician learns to reach further into the inner worlds and bring the power of Restriction into the pattern, both in themselves and in the temple space.

By engaging this deeper creative power the temple becomes a living vessel of Divine Consciousness. Any magic done within it that flows with the forces of nature will be powerful and far reaching. Any magic done in such a temple that is not in harmony with the natural forces will trigger the various power dynamics to jostle until the magic is either brought into harmony or becomes tightly restricted and closed down.

As you will have started to realise, the deeper into the inner powers you go, the higher the stakes become. This is why a true adept is called an adept: they become adept at working carefully and powerfully with the true forces of creation.

To begin the process of understanding the force of Restriction, you will start with the simple steps of recognising this power, understanding its dynamic, and passively incorporating its power into your ritual work. You will not actively try to work 'face to face' with it: that would be insane at this stage of your training. But simply keeping an awareness of it, flowing with it, learning its lessons, and applying them under your own steam will prepare you for direct interaction with Restriction at a later stage of your magical life and work.

1.7 About the practical work

In this practical work you will learn the first step of incorporating the power of Restriction passively into your ritual patterning. Because of the necessity for balance in such work, you will also incorporate two other deeper Divine creative powers that you will read about in the next few lessons of this module.

Because you will incorporate them before reading about them, do this vision ritual once; then once you have read and worked with the next few lessons you will be directed to come back to this working and do it again in the light of what you then will know.

After that, how you work with this is up to you. You can fully incorporate these dynamics in your usual ritual work, or use them only when you need to pull on deeper creative powers of rebalance.

The stone temple room where you will work is itself an expression of the three creative powers. While you will be aware of the powers as separate angelic presences, you should also be aware that in fact you will be working within these three powers. Don't try to understand beyond that for now, just keep that awareness: the room is the junction of the consciousness of these three vast angelic beings.

1.8 *Task:* **The ritual expression of human balance**

Set up your working space, put out the tools, light the lights and open the gates. Go round the directions, acknowledge the contacts on the thresholds, bow to them, and tell them you are learning about the deeper powers of creation.

Place the sword in its position by the central altar, place the cord around your right wrist, the vessel on the altar, and the stone by your feet. Put on your stole.[8]

Stand for a moment in silence to still yourself. Close your eyes. Be aware of the sword and hold out your left arm. Make the sigil of the Limiter in the air with your left hand and then the sigil of the vessel with your right hand. With your arms stretched out to the side, be aware of the stars, the future and the Star Father above you; and be aware of the Mother, the earth, the stone, and the past beneath you.

Cast your mind to your feet, and be aware of the power of the Grindstone beneath your left foot and the power of the Threshing floor beneath your right foot.

Be aware of the flame within, and that your centre is where everything comes together: you are the fulcrum. Everything you do in life flows from the Grindstone and the Limiter, and everything is harvested on the Threshing Floor and weighed in the vessel.

---

[8]Do this from now on in ritual to charge it.

Fix in your mind the image of yourself standing with these powers around your body. Take as long as you need to fix the image of this stance in your head.

For this next part, keep an awareness of yourself standing within the powers, surrounded by the directions: you are leaving the pattern hanging there in space. Sit down facing south, with the central altar before you, and close your eyes.

Go to the Inner Library, and go straight to the stone temple room. As you walk towards it you will notice that many beings and people from the Inner Library are following you. As you reach the stone temple room, the people fan out and surround the outside of this place, but none follow you in.

Once inside, go round the directions of the stone altars starting in the east. Bow to the directions, and then stand in the centre of the directions.

Remember the image of yourself standing in your own work room with the powers around your body. Merge the two together so that you are standing in the stone temple room and also your own work space at the same time.

Once you have a good sense of yourself in both places, turn your focus back to the stone temple room and, and in vision, hold out your left arm. As you take the arm out, work very deliberately, unfolding the arm with focus. When the arm reaches its extension, see the sigil of the Limiter appear by your hand.

An angelic being steps out of the east, the angel connected to your sword, and stands by your left shoulder. As the angel touches your shoulder, a sword appears in your left hand. Your hand and the hand of the angel on your shoulder both uphold the inner Limiter.

Now unfold your right arm, carefully and deliberately, with focus. When the arm reaches its full extension, see the sigil of the vessel appear in your right hand.

An angelic being steps out of the west, the angel connected to the vessel and scales, and stands by your right shoulder. As the angel touches your right shoulder, a brightly shining vessel appears in your right hand. Your hand and the hand of the angel together uphold the power of the vessel.

Turn your attention to your right hand holding the vessel. Look at your cord: you will notice it is moving. The cord has become a snake, a cobra, and it is slowly winding its way up your arm. Do not be afraid of it: this cobra is the guardian of Ma'at, and it will protect you. The snake winds its way across your shoulders to the back of your head, and rears its head over your head, its eyes staring straight forward.

Once the cobra is in place, you become aware of a pulse beneath your feet. The stone floor is slowly pulsing like a heartbeat: you are feeling the heartbeat of the land, of the Mother, of the earth itself.

As you feel into the heartbeat, you realise that each foot feels it differently. In the left foot it is vigorous and strong: the Grindstone that marches you forward into the future. In the right foot the heartbeat feels gentler, as though fading away: the Threshing Floor that sifts and weighs.

Stand for a movement in that awareness of everything around you. Feel into your centre, into your inner flame, your vital force. You are at the centre of all things: of all times, all worlds, and all forces that flow through nature. From that centred place, you feel the balance between the two powers of east and west.

As you stand in that balance, the angel that initiated you in this place steps out of the south altar and stands before you, looking at you. Then the angel looks beyond you and lifts a ram's horn. The angel blows on the horn. The sound reverberates round the room and makes your body shake.

The room falls away and you find yourself out in the stars, the two angelic beings upholding you at each shoulder, the flame within keeping your balance, and the cobra with its hood extended over the back of your head guarding you. The angel before you with the horn turns slightly to your left and sounds the horn once more. Keep your eyes on the angel with the horn and do not look around you.

Behind your left shoulder and behind the angel at your left shoulder, you feel a vast force building up, a force that shines a brilliant light. It fills the left side of your body with light and vigour. It fills your sword, which starts to hum with power and becomes bright with light.

As you fill with the power you will begin to feel invincible: check that feeling straight away. Cast your mind to your left hand and remember the name of the sword: the Limiter. Engage that power of limitation and understand that the power is not your own power; it is the Divine Power of creation, the Light Bringer.

The Light Bringer is the power of creation, the impulse to forge into the future, into life. It flows through your left hand, through the sword, through your heart, your left eye, and through your left foot.

As you keep your eyes on the angel before you, a bright road, too bright to see in detail, opens up before you. The angel with the horn stands on that road and you understand that it is your road forward into the future, and also into timelessness.

Your sword fills with power and light and becomes too heavy for you to hold up. The angel at your left shoulder reaches out and takes the sword from you and holds it in position for you. Let it go willingly, but keep your arm out.

As soon as you relinquish the sword, the angel before you turns slightly to your right and blows the horn one more time. A power begins to build up behind your right shoulder, behind the angel that is standing at your right shoulder. It is a power of darkness and of stillness. The dark stillness fills the right side of your body and you begin to feel a sensation of restriction on your right side. Your right arm and leg become very heavy, and your right eye begins to blur.

Your first instinct might be to struggle against this, but do not. Let its power fill you.

The darkness is a powerful force that weighs you down on your right side, and it is darkness so intense that you can barely understand it. The angel to your right shoulder places a hand upon your right hand and helps you hold up the vessel, as it seems to get heavier and heavier; yet you know instinctively that you must not release your hold of it.

Once you stop resisting the darkness, a deep peace fills you. The vessel in your right hand draws your attention more and more, and you begin to realise that it is filled with everything you have done so far in your life, good and bad. As you keep your attention on the vessel you become aware that it also holds everything you have ever done in any of your lives, past, present, or future: it is the sum total of your deeds while you have been in physical manifestation.

The vessel gets heavier and heavier until you think you are going to drop it. Just as you feel you can no longer hold it, the angel on your left shoulder places the sword back in your hand.

It is then that you realise that your sword initiates actions, and your vessel holds the completion of those actions: you limit the use of the sword so as not to put too much weight in the vessel. You begin to become balanced.

As soon as you realise this, the flame within turns to a bright, beautiful spark. It is a spark full of power and beauty, a spark so intense and wondrous that it fills your heart with joy: you are filled with a brief glimpse of perfect balance. The joy builds until you think you will burst, until both angels at your shoulders remind you of the tools you hold.

As soon as you become aware of your tools again, the spark within you becomes a focused point of light: a fulcrum. The tools weigh equally in your hands. You are filled with light and dark, with forward momentum and yet restriction: you are in balance.

With this realisation, the angels vanish, the tools disappear, and you are left drifting in the stars. You are at total peace, in total stillness, and in harmony with the stars around you. This is where you belong, where you come from, and where you will return to.

Physically lie down while keeping the vision and spend some time just being in that stillness and silence among the stars. Don't worry about falling asleep, as you may well do. Just let go and drift.

When you wake up, sit quietly in your work space for a short while before closing the space down and putting things away. Write up everything you can remember straight away in your journal and type up a summary into a computer file for your mentor (if you are being mentored).

1.9   What happened?

In this vision you encountered the next layer of powers that you will learn to work with. As you begin to work with deeper and more powerful forces, you must learn to understand how those forces work by first experiencing them directly in your own body in vision.

This vision takes you a step deeper in while still keeping you on 'this side of the threshold,' which in turn allows you to experience a tiny fraction of those powers.

You may have noticed that the deeper powers switch sides: the Limiter and Grindstone, the two powers which limit, condense, and encourage restriction are on the magician's left side. These are the powers closest to humanity. As we go further into the inner realms, that power of limitation becomes pure Restriction and darkness[9] and is perceived to be on the right side of the magician. The powers work in opposition, with the lower octaves in the active left hand and the higher octave to the right side, behind the magician.

Similarly the power of the vessel, which both weighs and holds completed action, but is also the dispenser of life, is to the right of the magician. But the Light Bearer, a deeper power of life that flows into the vessel, appears behind and left.[10] The Bearer of Light seeks the south, the future, and the Power of Restriction oversees everything that has been

---

[9]The darkness of density and restriction.

[10]It lights the future action of the magician.

completed and is therefore, in our human time, in the past.

All these powers revolve round the central spark, the fulcrum of the power which is perfect balance. Though we cannot achieve perfect balance in life, it is what we strive to achieve, and by working towards that achievement we learn to connect in a small way to these vast powers. The closer to balance we come, the more deeply we can connect with these powers.

By experiencing these powers in vision, out in the stars, we can remember at a deep level: we touch base with who we really are as eternal souls. Yet because we are in life we cannot stay within that experience. It triggers, and our deeper selves remember: we carry that experience back into our magical and mundane lives. Our minds may forget as the memory of the experience fades, but our deeper consciousness does not forget: it is a subtle awakening.

In turn this influences at a subtle level how we work with power, how we wield the tools, and how we view the world around us. The opposing powers of limitation and release, of action and result, and then of the impulse to manifest in life (the Light Bearer) and to withdraw from life (Restriction), all dance around the magician, which triggers the next stage of the maturation of the magician.

Once we gain an understanding of these opposing features with stillness in the centre, and are able to work from that understanding, then we are able to step into the deep and powerful flow of magic that works in harmony with creation and destruction.

Lesson 2

The Light Bearer

The Light Bearer is a power that sits in a pattern of opposition to Restriction. It is a power that propels the potential for time, substance, and life into creation. The Light Bearer is the light that shines in the darkness, the light that falls from Divine consciousness as it seeks physical expression. It is a Divine power that expresses through angelic power;[1] a vast power that left unchecked would facilitate limitless creation.

Fragments of knowledge of this being can be found in very ancient texts and creation myths like the story of the Ogdoad in Ancient Egypt, where this power is known as the god/goddess Heh/Hauhet: a complete deity[2] who is time. Heh/Hauhet is connected with fire that brings life, the length of time while also keeping an aspect of infinity: limitless creation.

Heh/Hauhet is kept in check and slowed down by Kuk/Kuaket, another male/female power of creation that is the darkness but which has the potential for dawn and dusk.[3]

The Light Bearer and Restriction also are referred to in Genesis:

> "And God said: 'Let there be light.' And there was light. And God saw the light, that it was good; and God divided the light from the darkness."

In that story we have the fragments of the deep inner truths of creation. However from a magical perspective this is not talking about the light of day and the dark of night, as those all belong in the completed creation: it refers to the impulses of inner power, of Divine expression before we reach a completed creation.[4]

Momentum is initiated into action, and restriction is introduced to limit that momentum so that it does not cascade out of control. We are looking at the very deep inner powers at work that come together with the other powers that result in a physical world.

And this is not something that happened a long time ago; it is something that is in constant motion: creation is a constantly turning wheel in balance with destruction. As the magician learns to tread deep into the inner worlds, they can observe this for themselves.

So let us take a closer look at the Light Bearer.

2.1 The Light Bearer

The nature of this vast power is one of impulse and the creative fire. It is filled with the potential of time and manifestation. It forges a path in the inner worlds that is a path for

---

[1] Threshold.
[2] Male and female.
[3] Restriction and thresholds.

[4] The physical world.

20

potential of time, and it carries the creative fire in a forward impulse as it barrels towards physical expression. It is limitless in its power. If left unchecked, its physical expression would be a sudden explosion of power that would destroy.

In its forward motion it is balanced by restriction that slows it down and gives it boundaries. Also this is the first point in inner creation where there is a positive and negative power in a perpetual struggle: both are equal in their power and keep each other in check. That is the deepest and most technical aspect of this power.

To mystics and magicians, this power can appear as a vast angelic being of light and power that is unconscious of mere mortals. These vast powers of creation have many octaves to them, and we can learn a lot about the dynamics of magic and the physical world by looking at these powers, as such dynamics run through everything that manifests in the physical world. Such powers as these have many other powers and dynamics in their orbit, and it is these clusters of power, rather that the Light Bringer itself, that magicians have the most interaction with.

2.2 The Inner Temples and Library

The area in the inner worlds in which the inner temples and Inner Library can be found is in the wider orbit of the Light Bearer. The dynamics of time and the creative fire find expression in the collective consciousness of the knowledge, skills, and wisdom that is the inner temples and Inner Library.

The tide of time potential that the Light Bearer emits enables these inner places to contain the collective knowledge and wisdom from temples that existed in the deep past and also in the far future: they are containers out of time that nevertheless hold deep inner expressions from past, present, and future. This potential in turn allows all the knowledge, wisdom, and experience that expressed in

time in physical temples to be collected and held in an orbit.

The dynamic of time, light, and creative fire, held in limitation by restriction, creates a fertile environment for these inner structures to reside in. While ever there is the faintest connection with something manifest in the physical realm, these structures are held in the orbit of the Light Bringer. Once there no longer exists any connection whatsoever in the physical realm with these inner structures, they begin to degrade and vanish into the sands of the Inner Desert/inner worlds, or they slowly descend into the Abyss.

The connection with the physical world[5] is like an elastic tension that holds the structures in this power orbit. Once this band of tension no longer exists, the structures break away and begin to fragment and dissolve, just as the tension between the Light Bringer and Restriction enables each of them to exist in an active holding pattern.

By understanding this overall dynamic, we start to understand the connections between these inner structures, the mysteries, and the power we call the Light Bringer. We start to see fragments of this connection in the use of language in ancient texts: knowledge and wisdom is 'light'; the Light that falls into manifestation[6] brings true knowledge of Divinity to the physical world; the Light resides in all substance... these and other examples all point to the relationship between the Light Bringer and the inner temples/Library. We also see the connection with the sacred flame, the creative fire, and the inner flame that connects us to Divinity.

This is also the same power that is referred to in Ancient Egyptian texts when the term "a million years" is used in texts. The tension between the infinite Light Bearer and Restriction gives us time as we understand it. It is a long time, but is also a limited time. Through a limitation of time, we have

---

[5]A fragment of knowledge, a crumbling physical temple, a human connecting with them.

[6]Lucifer.

existence; we have substance, a physical expression; we are born, we die, we have generations—but not infinitely so. This was one of the mysteries behind Heh/Hauhet.

Now we will take this complex understanding down a few octaves so that we can see how it applies in magic and the inner worlds.

2.3 Magical Application

The very low resonances of the Light Bringer's power are active in magic, and the deeper into magic you go, the more powerful this power's resonance becomes—which is why it is important to understand it in all its different expressions.

At its lowest resonance in magic, it is the power of the south, the creative power that forges a path into the future while sourcing its roots in the present and the past. The power forges the future from the 'present' patterns created in magic. This in turn is a mirror of the process of Divine Creation, which is why it can be so powerful.

The magical pattern[7] is created in the east and set in motion into the south via the central flame.[8] The magical pattern itself is limited by nature of its creation: the pattern is given boundaries and form (Restriction), a task as a focal point, and is then released into the stream of power which is a low octave of the Light Bringer.

The creative power of the future (Light Bringer) then carries the pattern of magic into the future to unfold its action. How that action expresses itself depends on the creative power dynamics that are low octaves of the deeper powers of creation.[9]

This weave of complex forces takes the magical pattern and essentially fits it to the task ahead so that it will unfold in as balanced and useful way as possible. This formation of the expression of the magic ensures that it fits with the fate patterns of everything it will touch, so that everything works in a harmonic way.

This is the dynamic at play when we hand magic over to the south powers once it is formed. We do this because this process is far better at making sure that the pattern works properly than we would be if we attempted to control it ourselves.

An interesting side effect that crops up when we allow magic to flow in this way is that every pattern of magic that flows down the route of the Light Bringer ends up recorded in the Inner Library. Everything orbits round everything else, and as the inner temples/Library orbit the Light Bringer, as magic flows with the power of the Light Bringer, it also becomes imprinted in the inner temples as they are so deeply connected with each other.

These recordings appear in the Inner Library and can be accessed with the right techniques and knowledge. We are able as magicians to tap into ancient patterns of magic that were set in motion and observe them in order to learn. As apprentices and initiates, we access these inner structures via the east, but as adepts, we can also step into the stream of creative fire flowing into the magical direction of south to access these magical patterns in order to learn for the future. The deeper we flow into magic, the more our linear ideas of time, existence, and expression start to fall apart. We begin to understand time and consciousness as an 'all-encompassing now.'

2.4 The need for limitation

When we cast magic into the path of the Light Bringer in order for it to unfold in the future, we also have to engage the power of Restriction to ensure that the magic has an end as well as a beginning, so that it does not wander out of control or overexpand.

This is done in the early stages of the magical patterning: the magic is given a focal point, a purpose, a time limit, and a conclusion. It is also wise to ensure that there is also a

---

[7]Ritual or vision or both.

[8]Which is a mirror of perfect balance.

[9]You learned about these in the apprentice section: the Grindstone, the Unraveller, the Fates, and so forth.

composting process so that when the magic is spent, its remaining energies are recycled and held out of time.

We do this by working with the contacts and powers in the magical directions: each of them places their own influence and power into the magical pattern. So for example the magical stone and the powers that flow through it anchor the magic in physical manifestation; the contacts in the west and north insert into the magic the breakdown process.

This is why the magician works in cooperation with the inner beings and directional contacts: between the team, everything that needs to be in the pattern is included. This in turn mirrors the Divine act of creation where the Divine impulse crosses into the inner realms and is changed, shaped, and affected by the various dynamics and powers with which it connects.

Just as the Divine impulse for manifestation flows in the orbit of the Light Bearer and the other dynamics of creative power in the inner realms on its journey to manifestation, so too the magical pattern created by the magician flows into the orbit of the directional powers and contacts that mould and shape it as it seeks expression in the south/future.

When a magician works within this method, he or she draws on all of these different powers and dynamics in order to achieve magic. And by working in conjunction with these powers, the magician does not fully fuel the magic themselves: the burden is shared by collaboration. This ensures that powerful and longer-term magical patterns can be successful, properly contained, and have finality to them.

2.5 Magical Construction

Many ancient temples and some magical lodges/temples were constructed with the power of the Light Bearer infused into the substance of the building. When magical construction is undertaken, many different threads of power, beings, and magical patterns come into play: together they ensure the building's spiritual and magical integrity.

They also ensure the long-term survival of the temple's inner pattern, the temple's mirror in the inner worlds, and the enlivening of the building's very substance: the temple becomes a living vessel of Divine Power.

Any fragment of the building will hold the power of the Light Bringer: it becomes transformed from mere stone to the living DNA of a magical pattern.

Many ancient temple/religious buildings around the world hold this pattern, the only difference between them being each culture's expression of the powers. The powers may be called angels, deities, demons, spirits, messiahs... The labels are irrelevant: the powers themselves are universal and unchanging. In your apprentice training you looked at the beginnings of magical construction from various angles. The understanding of the Light Bringer in a physical construction is the next stage.

The Light Bringer brings a particular quality to a temple building: it creates a pathway for the future and ensures that all the different powers that come together in the substance walk the same path. The Light Bringer forges the long-term future existence of the power pattern, enlivens and enlightens it, and embeds the creative fire within the substance. This in turn creates a sacred substance that can then be worked with by priest-magicians in order for the building to be become a sacred entity in its own right. The building becomes the canvas, and the drawings, sculptures, inscriptions, and symbols become the voice of the entity.

The builders of many Ancient Egyptian temples clearly understood this deeply: the inscriptions not only narrated a story or dynamic, but by nature of the sacred substance they were painted on, they themselves were sacred filters and the utterance of magic.[10]

---

[10]Recognise the story of Moses and the stone inscription of the Ten Commandments? The stones themselves were said to hold the power of divinity.

The Light Bearer is one of the last powers to be brought into a magical or sacred construction. This power seals the pattern, sets the future, and fills the vessel with creative fire. Because it is brought through in such a way, it is rarely depicted in visual or sculptural form in a temple unless it has some inner restriction incorporated into it.

This does sometimes happen: it can be seen in Indian temples where the deity representing the Light Bringer has an image and mythology that tells of adjustment, tension, and change. Ganesh is a good example of that dynamic in action, and you will look at this as a part of your practical work.

Bringing the Light Bearer into substance is not something a magician would normally do unless they are involved in creating a physical structure that is meant to last a very long time and travel down through history.

Constructing a magical lodge from an inner aspect is a type of construction that may only last a few decades: such is the nature of magic. Such a construction has no need of the Light Bearer. But should a magician somehow become involved in the construction of a stone church, temple, or other long-term sacred structure, this skill can be brought into action. We can see remnants of this in some churches in the West that were built in the Norman era, but by the end of the fifteenth century the knowledge was lost in that culture.

2.6 On the practical work

When an adept works with the Light Bearer in magical work they normally use a fusion of ritual, vision, and working directly with substance. The ritual aspect draws all the lines of power together and sets the pattern in shape and time. The vision opens the gates fully and brings the power through. Finally the adept bridges the power through into stone substance.[11]

The pattern that is woven creates a first boundary for the power and also creates a limitation of time.[12] The pattern also gives the power a specific filter: it is in the form that the religious or magical expression of the power will take.

The pattern is the lines in and out to the various inner contacts, priesthoods, powers, angelic beings, and deities. The vision opens the contact and states the path to be taken. The visionary ritual then begins the externalisation process. The bridging into stone blocks is the completion that sets the power in substance and places it in the stream of time.

This work is not done by an individual but by a group of adepts or magical priests and/or priestesses. This is because the power is too much for one body to cope with: the lines that are worked with in the weaving are aspects of angelic beings. Just carrying one line is a massive physical burden: building is hard work!

During the initiate phase of your training, you only need an overview of the weaving in action. You can choose to simply read the following vision through so that you understand the inner dynamics of the process during construction, or you can go and observe this process in action by working in vision. To do this, go to the Inner Library and ask the contact there to take you to a place where you can safely observe this in action.

2.7 *Task:* Vision of Temple Construction

Stepping over the threshold, you find yourself standing on a ledge looking out on a scene of construction. The outer shape of a temple is complete, but it is yet to be magically constructed: it is the pattern of the shape that has been set. Once the magical construction is completed, the building will be physically finished.

---

[11]Wood or any other type of material is not suitable for holding such power.

[12]Hence the Egyptians used the term "a million years" as their limitation of time for the power.

All around the temple shape you can see men and women weaving power back and forth, and their weave has a flow of angelic beings going into it and filling up the weave. These beings appear as bodies of light with many eyes and wings, forming themselves into the shape of the pattern.

Inside the shape, the people are weaving threads and connecting them from one end of the building to another. They are pulling threads from one corner of the building (the keystone) and weaving an inner matrix for power to pass through. At the point in the building where the directions come together, two cubic blocks of stone appear laid side by side. They appear where the stone altar is. The people are pulling the threads from the keystone and running them into the two blocks of stone and back out again, spreading them round the building shape. When all the threads are full of angelic beings, one of the people steps forward to the east of the building with the two blocks of stone behind them. They stand facing east, put their heads back, and utter a loud cry.

The building shape's east wall falls away and is replaced by light. As you adjust to the light, you realize that it is coming from a woman who stands on the threshold of the East. At her head are the stars and at her feet is the moon. She stretches out her arms and her robe falls open. The opened robe reveals the void within her.

Out of the light step two large Angelic beings that move to the cubic stones and stand opposite each other, face to face. They stretch out their wings to touch, reaching beyond the building's ceiling. They reach out and touch hands, crossing their arms at the wrist. They each move their left foot forward (with the stones between them) until their left feet touch the stone. They create a figure of eight pattern with their bodies, which upholds the building and enlivens the web pattern.

You observe power flowing through these two beings in a constantly moving figure of eight shape that flows above, beneath, and around the stones. All the threads around the building spring to life and appear as threads of fire. One of the stones begins to burn brightly with light; the other one becomes very dark.

Once the angels are in place, another being steps out of the East. You see the faint outline of a human shape, but this being's inner fire is so bright that you cannot see any detail: it is the Light Bearer.

The Light Bearer goes to the two cubes and lies upon the cold stones. His body sinks into the stones, becoming one with them: the light within substance, the light shining in the darkness. The two stones fuse into one cube of light and darkness (a double cube that is now one).

The stone becomes the living altar that will travel down through time: the sacred substance, the vessel that carries light into darkness and triggers life.

The person who gave the call stands before the cube altar and places their hands lightly on the stone.

As you look closely, you notice that their left hand is filled with light, and their right hand is filled with darkness: they are in balance.

The person puts their face to the stone and breathes across it. As they breathe, you watch as light and darkness flows through them, through their breath, and into the stone.

A whirlwind develops round the person until it obscures them. The whirlwind seeks a home, and flows through the person and into the stone. Suddenly there is stillness. The pattern of the building shines brightly, the people are still and silent, and the person standing by the stone cube appears to be in deep communion with the stone.

The person then draws a small knife, cuts their hand, and squeezes drops of their blood onto the stone. As the blood touches the stone, look closely: the stone begins to move and pulse as though it had a heartbeat.

The heartbeat gets stronger and begins to pump the flow of power and energy around the threads of power that make up the shape of the building: the whole shape and pattern of the building becomes a living being. The blood of the priest or priestess triggers life, and also creates a bloodline of priests:the angelic powers create the deep octave of power, and the human mirrors that action at a lower octave, and also gives completion.

A priest from the Inner Library touches you lightly on the shoulder and tells you that it is time to leave. As you turn to go, the priest tells you to turn back for one last look.

As you turn back, the scene has changed: the temple is now physically finished. It is full of people working within it: they chant, they are decorating the walls, and impressing the words of the chant into pictures and symbols.

The building pulses with light and dark, and the two cubic stones fused into one have become a cubic stone altar: the heart of the temple buried deep in its body. You can see deities, angelic beings, spirits, and people all interacting with the flow of power that is the building.

The priest leads you away, but before he or she parts with you in the Inner Library, they turn to face you to make sure you are paying attention. The priest does not speak, but they hold their right index finger to their lips in a sign of "silence, speak not of what you saw."

The priest then leaves you. You may now either return to your work space or stay in the Inner Library for a while to absorb learning from what you just witnessed.

If you do the vision, write down your experiences and observations, and make a computer summary. If you have just read through it, do a bit of research around some of the imagery, as there are things in this vision that refer back to mysteries surrounding the roots of Western magic. Write up your findings in a computer file.

2.8 *Task:* **Research**

Look up the Mundeshwari Temple, Kaimur, India. It is dedicated to Shiva and Shakti, the male and female Divine principles. It has been in continuous use for 2,300 years and has gone through many changes in its time, but the basic principles still apply.

Note the shape, the deities it is dedicated to (two who are balanced together), and Ganesha on the threshold as the clearer of obstacles, protector of the way, and the lord of all living beings.

Ganesha is an Indian deity who has the principles of the Light Bearer flowing through him. Look up his story, and read more than one version, as each version has its own bits to add. Look at how he was 'restricted' by having his form changed, and look at how he is a deity that governs so much of creation.

You will find this a good exercise for learning how to spot the creation dynamics in other cultures: the same power, different titles, names, appearances But the main ingredients are all there. He is the product of two main Divinities: male and female. He is a threshold guardian, and an opener of the way.

Look at websites from India, look at anthropological and archaeology sites, but avoid New Age or Western popular sites, as they tend to slant the information towards what they understandor have made up, and leave out what they do not.

Overall, what you are looking at is the whole vessel of the temple, what is poured into it, and what power dynamics operate through it.

2.9 *Task:* **More research**

Look up references to the Masonic black and white floor, and also look up the cubic altar in different religions and systems.

Also look up the tale of the plague that hit Delos in the fourth century BC. The people consulted the Oracle, who told them that Apollo was angry that his altar was a single cube and that it should be doubled. This led to many years of trying to work out a geometric puzzle.[13]

---

[13]Thanks to the wrong advice from Plato.

Look back over the construction vision, and figure out what they had missed which so angered Apollo.

Lesson 3

Perfect Balance

The power of balance is the third dynamic of the three core powers of creation. This power, *Perfect Balance*, sits between the power of Restriction and the Light Bearer with its inclination towards creative physical manifestation.

It keeps the two opposing powers in balance. As the Divine impetus for creation pulses in to the inner worlds from Divine source, it is guided through Perfect Balance: the tension between Restriction and the Light Bearer forces it to flow down the middle of the tension. As it passes through Perfect Balance, it receives equal measures of power from the two opposing powers.

This forms a pattern of balance, of creation and restriction (destruction) equally embedded in the creative impulse so that it can manifest into time. The creative fire is enough for it to manifest in physical form, and the Restriction ensures that the fire does not burn too brightly and has a time limit on its manifestation.

The orbit of Perfect Balance is where we find root deities and primal deities, all of which have a measure of creation and destruction, of light and dark. When as magicians we work with subdivided deities but wish to find the true, balanced, and complete source of that sub-deity, this is where we track back to find the source of that power.

It is the last of the deeper creative powers before we start to encounter the lower powers of creation, the ones which are directly active in the formation of the creation into a person, place, being, or thing. All the powers of creation that you learned about in the apprentice section have their roots in this power.

Before the creative power can manifest into something physical, it must pass through a variety of filters that essentially split its power into dynamics. Those dynamics are things like the Grindstone, the Unraveller, the Threshold, the Wheel of Fate, and so forth.

As magicians, understanding this dynamic and the three core powers of creation lets us work with fragments of these powers as they manifest in life. They are inherent in all magic, from the smallest act to the most powerful, and working with them in gnosis enables the magic to reach as balanced and harmonic a state as possible.

Nothing can manifest in Perfect Balance, but neither can anything manifest physically if it does not have the resonance or influence of this power: it is a paradox.

3.1 The Thresholds

There is a lot of talk in magic about thresholds, yet few people really understand what this means. Thresholds when crossed in magic take the magician from one quality of power/energy to another.

These thresholds are usually guarded, and will repel those who should not cross. Each threshold in magic and inner vision allows a crossing from one level of power and energy to another, and the guardian of the threshold ensures that those who cross it are compatible with the power they are attempting to step into.

This dynamic of *compatibility* became degenerate in the minds of many cultures and devolved down into whether you are *worthy* to cross. This in turn led to guilt tripping, power grabbing, and ego bolstering: people believed that if they were 'good' or worthy, they would cross a threshold unharmed.

What is deemed 'good' depends entirely on the culture's standard of 'goodness' which did and still does vary widely. This in turn led to the development of various kinds of magic in an attempt to dodge around the guardians. We have already looked at some examples of this in some later Ancient Egyptian texts which contain spells to dodge the threshold guardians in death. Humans always seem to have this lowest common denominator of manipulation. Declarations of: "I am righteous," "I am pure," "I am worthy," "I deserve it," and so forth.

All this is a complete misunderstanding of the real dynamics of the thresholds and displays a stunning lack of inner connection and understanding of power. The threshold guardians are not there to *kick out the unworthy*; they are there to *reject the unbalanced*.

Each threshold is a stage of power where energy shifts from one state to another. If your inner and outer body can deal with the shift of power and is compatible with the power levels over the threshold, the guardian will let you pass unharmed.

When we learn the basics of magic as you learned them in the apprentice section, we learn not only about the nuts and bolts of magic and its techniques, but we also take small steps towards understanding the different worlds around us, what drives them, and how we flow and back and forth energetically with everything around us. This learning process changes the magician at a very deep level, causing shifts in energy/consciousness which in turn changes how we are, what we do, and how we see the world. These changes are the result of shifts in consciousness.

It is not how we are and how we behave as a result of those shifts that interests the guardians, it is the energetic shifts themselves. They are not judges, they are *weighers of the scales*, which is to say they perceive how our balance of light and dark, spirit and substance is at that time. This in turn tells them whether we can withstand the shift in power/energy when we cross a threshold. They are there to keep us and the worlds beyond the threshold safe.

There is no bolt of lightning that will come out of the sky if you cross a threshold that you are incompatible with, and there will be no heavenly punishment. One of two things will happen: either you will be suddenly kicked out of vision and be bruised, or if you manage to push through the guardians or bypass them, the impact of the incompatible energy will likely trigger a cascade response in the mind or body, which will result in the unravelling of your mind or body over a span of time.

I did not realise this for quite a while and when I used to teach groups; I would sometimes take a few people in vision and place them in deep centres of power so that they could experience them for themselves.

I thought I was doing a good thing: I could get there with no problem, and I could take them there with me, with no problem; but by the action of me carrying them to an inner state *to which they should have walked themselves,* I bypassed their own personal interaction with the guardian. I carried them over the threshold, thus disengaging the natural action of the guardian.

Some people dealt with this just fine, some blanked out and became disorientated, and others seemed okay but then went on to have total mental or physical breakdowns. I did not realise the harm I was doing to people...and there is no sorry in the inner worlds.

It is for this reason that I do not teach face-to-face practical magic any more. I will show the way and give the information, but ultimately the student has to make the steps themselves and have their own experiences—which is how this course works. This time I have learned to guide a student a step at a time!

Essentially, when you reach a threshold a guardian perceives your weighing of light and dark, spirit and matter, and how your deeper spirit/soul flows back and forth between these two states. If the flow is compatible with the power beyond the threshold, you will be able to cross unharmed.

If the flow is almost compatible, you will still be given access, but you may have some kickback or struggle with its energy for a while. This is caused by a catalyst process that happens in the inner worlds: if you are almost compatible with a power, being in its presence or orbit will trigger the incompatibility to move towards balance.[1]

The closer in the inner worlds you tread, the more powerful this dynamic becomes. If you cross over the directional threshold into a magical direction, you are crossing a wide threshold into a place that has a multitude of different energies: it is very likely you will be compatible with the energies there: it is a safe sandbox to learn in.

If you forge deeper and attempt to stand in the orbit of the Light Bearer, Restriction, or Perfect Balance, then you have to be directly compatible with those powers. If you are not, the tension between those powers will at best kick you out and leave you bruised and exhausted. At worst it would tear you apart so that your world starts to fall apart around you. Anything between those two extremes could certainly cause problems in your life and health for quite some time.

Why does this happen? Resonance. When you come into the energy orbit of these larger powers, they deeply affect everything around them, including you. The power of Restriction will resonate powerfully with your own restriction, the Light Bearer will resonate with your creative fire, and the power of Perfect Balance will resonate with your scales. All these inherent life powers within you will be amplified, and if they are out of balance with each other within you, it will cause an energy conflict within you as they each seek to find their own balance.

So for example if you have a simple cold or virus, your immune reaction will be overtriggered to the point that your immune system will have gone into overdrive. It can be dangerous to attempt such work in such circumstances: your cold could turn into a major battle for survival, or a latent immune imbalance may be heavily triggered—everything becomes more powerful than it needs to be, and everything fights itself.

In the same way, if the magician has a mild mental imbalance, that will be amplified. If the magician has a slow-growing cancer, it will suddenly become virulent.

The human body and spirit works through its imbalances in a way that it can cope with, and if we support the body and spirit in that process it will strive to find its own balance. However if the body and spirit is exposed to power that is beyond its capacity to accommodate, it will go into meltdown in an effort to process it.

Think of this as a house's electrical system with its fusebox. If too much power flows through the cables to the washing machine, the appropriate fuse will trip to stop the flow.[2] If there is no proper fuse in place, too much power could flow into the appliance and cause a fire. The washing machine does not set on fire because it is unworthy, but because too much power has flowed into its circuits, some of which may be faulty and therefore weak points.

---

[1] An energetic healing crisis.

[2] The threshold.

A major part of the magician's training is making sure that their circuits are strong and healthy, that their fuses are in place, and that no circuitry is weak, damaged, or faulty. This part of training is far more important that learning the words of a ritual, or learning fancy sigils, or gaining keys to an inner realm: a solid, grounded magician will find these things out for themselves regardless. What is important is that they understand what they find and are strong and balanced enough to cope with the power of what they work with.

All of this comes down to knowing the powers of creation, destruction, and balance, and knowing how to navigate or orbit these powers. The 'knowing' is not about skill but about development. If the inner and outer muscles are developed and the right balance of restriction and creation is held, then everything is in place for the magician to work powerfully and safely.

So let us look at how this boils down into practicalities for the magician.

3.2 Finding magical balance

A lot of what you learned in your apprentice training was about stepping you towards understanding the various forms of balance in stages. You learned the basis of balance for your actions, of your instincts, your tools, your practice, and your inner senses, while being protected by boundaries as you worked. Your magical ritual and vision work took you to some simple, wide thresholds where you could practice the outer actions and inner impulses of moving from one energy state to another.

By starting to learn balance from the simplest outer magical actions, you mirror a deeper pattern: balance begins from the densest part of us and evolves outwards. We do not reach out of ourselves to achieve balance; it starts within the body's substance and actions, and then moves out to the mind, the deep consciousness, and then our deeper selves that are connected to everything around us.

Many magicians work endlessly in deep and powerful rituals and visions to reach 'up' to find balance and harmony from outside of themselves. They will do rituals to gain strength, balance, wisdom and so forth, and all is destined to fail. The powers of balance, restriction, and creation are all fostered in the magician from within themselves in the most practical terms. And I am not talking about abstractions, but real, solid, physical practicalities.

You cannot understand how balance works if you do not know how to balance. Inner and magical balance works the same way physical balance does: everything is mirrored in everything else.

When you look at balance in terms of scales, energies, and so forth, you are working in abstractions; and in truth you cannot guess the weight of something by looking at it. Learning how to balance is an important skill: the body's very substance learns the process before the mind and consciousness learns it, because the powers of restriction, creation, and balance all reside within the substance of the body: *these powers express in the bones, muscles, organs, nerves, and skin of the body.* This was understood in many cultures and is also the foundation of things like Yoga and Tao Yin.

Balance and the distribution of substance versus mind is critical to working with deeper power dynamics. It starts with the physical understanding of the distribution of weight, of balance, then expands into learning the balance and coordination of movement. From there it moves to understanding the upkeep of balance in the body through nutritional and medicinal care.

Once the body is moving towards an understanding of balance, the person's attention is spread out to their living conditions, how they maintain their own environment, and how they interact with everything around them.

This passively starts to trigger changes in perception, which in turn begins to catalyse change in the mind. To start with the mind is folly: always start from the substance and work out from there.

Physical training like Yoga, Tai Chi, martial arts, ballet, gymnastics, and so forth all bring these elements together in order to create a vessel that can process creative fire. The ancients knew this, and many successful mystical and spiritual schools had an element of these disciplines in their training.

Just as a ballet dancer uses visualisation to physically balance, so the magician uses physical balance dynamics in order to use their minds in a balanced way. We will look at this in a small way in the practical work. Working with physical/mental balance teaches you about magical balance in ritual; working with balance in ritual teaches you the balance of energies in the inner worlds.

3.3 Balance in working magical practice

The overall principle of balance flows through magical practice by way of the magician's techniques. If balance is not incorporated into the practice and actions, the unbalanced force and element of the magic is likely to spin out of control in its actions. This is a major dynamic that some magicians fail to understand to their detriment—and also to the detriment of those affected by their magic.

Too often magic is influenced by emotion, be that compassion, wanting, hate, anger, or fear. Magic fuelled by emotion tends to have only an end point (the result wanted) and emotion (and often beings) to drive it. Such magic is a loose cannon that can trigger all sorts of imbalance in the magic's energy. Unforeseen results and consequences are often the end of this tale. Emotion, just like belief, has no place in magic.

Balanced magic has a creative point, a peak of completion, an unravelling, and a death/end.

It is like engineering. You would not build a car out of anger or with wishful thinking; you build it using the principles of engineering. At every stage of the unfolding of magic there should be a counterpoint, an anchor, a destination, and a place in time—all of which have elements that balance each other.

The use of a central flame creates a fulcrum that everything else balances round. The use of the various combinations of directions in ritual brings in forces that are in tension with one another: east/west, north/south, east/south/west/north/centre, light/dark, and so forth.

In vision, the central stillness within the person triggers the fulcrum within them, and either the use of a tool[3] or a visionary construct[4] creates a foundation: a tension of opposites, and the magical action creates a future.

Past and future balance each other, fast and slow, angel and human: all these and many other combinations create a pattern that relies on balance.

This in turn enables the three deep creative powers to find expression in the magic, which fuels it, strengthens it, and makes sure that it stays on track in a way that is conducive to all the patterns of fate, creation, and destruction that run inherently through all things: it makes the magic compatible throughout the worlds.

Later as an adept the magician roots themselves with their feet deep in the Underworld, with their heads in the stars, and their centre as the fulcrum. Without tools or temples, the magician becomes the scales, with their consciousness as the central pillar and their arms and minds as the creative action/compost dynamic. What keeps it all balanced is the left hand creative dynamic and the right hand completion/weighing/composting dynamic: the birth, culmination, and death of the magic are all entwined in the magical action.

To work like this without an exteriorisation[5] the magician themselves must be

---

[3]For example a foot on the stone.

[4]For example the Inner Library, landscapes, or temples.

[5]No tools, no work space, no words, no actions.

balanced—and I mean literally able to balance. As I said earlier, the physical ability of the magician's body to maintain balance allows the deep inner powers to flow around and through the magician: the magician stands within the vortex of magic as he or she works.

As the power hits the physical body, if the body has a good ability to balance, the substance of the body itself will distribute the power flows evenly through the body's energy channels and release them accordingly.

The energy that does not need to flow through the magician flows around them in orbit before it releases—and again, the strength of that power can knock the inner integrity of the magician unless they can counterbalance it: the knowledge that the body has regarding balance is triggered and the inner and outer body shifts accordingly to counterbalance the force of the magic.

And this brings me to another point that is important to understand and work with: the knowledge of the inner body, the energetic body, is directly influenced by the knowledge and health of the outer body, and vice versa.

The magician's inner and outer bodies are inextricably linked. Even though we try to think of them as separate units, they are not. By teaching the outer body the principles of balance, the inner body learns them too. When the inner energetic body is aligned, so too is the outer body. First you teach the substance, and what the substance learns, everything else learns.

Not only does this adherence to balance affect the inner dynamics of power and energy in magic, but it can also protect the magician from certain levels of impact. When a force is projected towards the magician, if they have no inherent balance and their body does not know the principles of balance, the force will knock them off-centre both energetically and physically.

It is far easier to magically attack and seriously damage a magician who has poor balance than a magician with good balance. And it is more likely that an adept with poor balance will get a nasty impact if they work with strong inner powers.

This can be seen when groups of magical adepts come together for a round of work. As the adept stands silently in a flow of power, the body of an adept with poor or damaged balance can be seen to be constantly swaying and may actually tip over during the mediation of a force.

As apprentices, the basic principles of counterpoints were built into your training actions so that you learned the principle of balance in a passive way without realising it. There were counterpoints in the substance around you (tools, directions), and as you moved round the directions and moved the tools around, you were subconsciously learning the principles of magical balance.

As an initiate the principles of balance are to be learned in your body and joined with the balance of action/tools/space; and as an adept the principle of balance will be learned by joining your energetic body with everything around you.

The practical work for this lesson is quite intensive but allows you to pull together the three principles you have just been learning about in this module, which in turn will prepare you for what will come next.

3.4 *Task:* Revisit the vision of balance

Go back to the vision in Lesson 1 of this module. Redo the vision, but this time when you are out in the stars, when you have finished observing the actions, instead of drifting in the stars you are going to forge a path.

While you are out in the stars, look down at your feet. Your left foot is filled with the light of the Light Bearer, and your right foot is filled with the darkness of Restriction. Before you is a path of light that is the trail of the Light Bearer. Beyond the path, if you look carefully, you will see the planet Earth, your home.

Feel yourself balanced with the Divine spark within you, the light of your left side, and the dark of your right. Take a step forward with your left foot onto the bright path of the Light Bearer.

As you step out on to the path, a bright white cube appears under your foot. Stand on that bright cube with your right foot suspended off the path. Now place your right foot down on the path and lift your left foot off the bright cube: a dark cube of black appears under your right foot.

Step forward one foot at a time. Alternating bright white and dark black cubes appear under your feet as you step forward towards the Earth. As you walk and the cubes appear, the Earth gets closer and closer: you are forging a path of light and dark towards physical manifestation.

As you walk you can feel the difference in power between the cubes, and as you speed up to walk at a normal pace you become aware that your right heel is placed down on the dark cube before your toes lift off of the bright cube: through your action of forward movement, the two opposites of light and dark become linked in your body. Your human body and your forward momentum link these two powers in a moving balancing act as you forge forward towards physical existence.

As you walk you become aware of the continent that you live on, the country, the city, town, neighbourhood, house, and finally room where your body is sitting in vision. The closer you come to your home/building, the more you realise that you are vast in size and may not fit into the building, let alone the body sitting in vision.

Cast your mind to your right foot as you walk; the darkness of the cube, the density of substance. The more you focus on the density of substance, the more your etheric body shrinks and restricts itself until it can be accommodated in its physical form. The more restricted your etheric body becomes, the more it intensifies the brightness of the

light within you and beneath your left foot: the two powers become intensely polarised.

Stand before your body and look at it. As you stand there you realise that you stepped through the south wall of the work room, passing through the south altar.

Turn and look beyond the south altar: a long path of black and white squares, made up of the light and dark cubes, forms a path into the south, into the future, and out into the stars. Look at it and realise that this is your path as a magician and as a human. It will take you into the future and ultimately to the stars: your path is defined by your balance between the creative light and the harvest of Restriction. Your eternal consciousness is the bright Divine spark within.

3.5 *Task:* **Associated Research**

Look up the history of chequerboard floors in temples and ritual structures. You will have to plough your way through lots of conspiracy and other silly websites, but if you do an image search you may be more successful at least in seeing the depictions through time.

If a site makes a claim without a direct historic reference, discount it and in general ignore the text, as it will tend to devolve down into 'good and evil' rather than 'light and dark' energy.

Just look at the images, where they are, when they were, and in what context they belong. One useful site has an e-version of an old book called *Pompeii: Its Life and Art*. Look at Chapter Ten: the Temple of Apollo, figure 28. It will show you the cubic white and black floor in the temple of Apollo.[6]

www.gutenberg.org/files/42715/
42715-h/42715-h.htm

3.6 *Task:* **Threshold practice**

Set up your working room with all your tools in the directions, open the gates, and welcome the

---

[6]The light bearer and god of the south.

contacts to the thresholds. Still yourself by the central altar with the south altar beyond you.

Recover the sense and vision of the light and dark, your left side and right side, and of the path of light and dark flowing from you. Be aware of the your body filled with light on the left side and darkness on and right side, and be aware of the angelic presences at your shoulders.

Go to the east altar and stand in silence. Close your eyes and in vision, walk through the altar and over the east threshold. Do it slowly and be aware of any change in how you feel as you cross the thresholds: you are learning to 'feel' into each threshold so that you can be aware of its power and how it affects you as you cross. It will be a subtle shift, like a whisper, as it is a wide threshold and is one of the lowest level thresholds you can cross in vision.

Once over the threshold turn back and look into the room. Look at the floor, look at the pathway your footsteps have made, and then look at your feet. Look at whether the threshold is bright or dark.

When you are ready, step back into your body, open your eyes and repeat in the south, west, and north.

When you have finished stand before the central altar, close your eyes, and in vision step into the central flame. Stand in the flame and wait until your own inner spark, the creative fire within, resonates exactly with the power of the central flame.

When you feel that harmony, in vision look beyond the flame to the south altar. Look at the floor that leads to the south altar, and look at the path into the south beyond. Now turn round and look at the floor leading to the north altar, and look at the path that flows from the north altar and into the north beyond.

Open your eyes and go to the east altar. Look at the sword and close your eyes. Now pass into the sword and pay attention to how it feels to cross the threshold into the sword.

Come back out again and repeat with the cord in the south, the vessel in the west, and the stone in the north. Pay close attention to how the threshold of each tool feels as you cross into it and back out again.

Open your eyes, and sit and meditate for a short while. Think about how each threshold felt and presented itself. Before you close the room down, write up your notes in your journal, and later type them out on computer. Write up how they felt, any resistance or forward momentum that you felt, any shift in balance, any sense of confusion or focus, and any surge in energy.

3.7 *Task:* Physical balance exercise

When you move your body in balance, the powers follow you and flow with you in harmony. Trying to write specific physical exercises without a physical demonstration is difficult, so I will try to keep things as simple as possible. For those of you who already do some physical discipline that uses balance, adjust what follows as is necessary for you to work with what you know.

When you raise a leg off the ground, the shift in weight needs a counterbalance to compensate. Usually we fling out our arms out and move our torso to try and rebalance. In certain physical disciplines, like yoga, ballet, and gymnastics, we learn to isolate different parts of the body and shift weight accordingly, so that balance in the body can be pushed to the extreme.

For magicians, who are of different ages, weights, and physical levels of fitness, such heavy training is not always possible; but the techniques important for magic are possible for anyone to work with, and those techniques use the mind.

I discovered this by accident when training as a dancer[7] and as I advanced in magic, I

---

[7] And rediscovered a well-known wheel of which I had been unaware.

35

realised it had application in magic: using the mind to balance the body. It is something you can experiment with or incorporate into your own physical discipline, and is something you should try to keep up with, as it will really help the body adjust to magic.

Everyone has a dominant side to their body in terms of balance, so when you figure out which is your stronger side, work the weaker side more. Always start with the weaker side, and always do more on that side.

Stand up and put your feet together. Now turn them out, both at the same time, to a comfortable position with the heels together. Don't turn out one and then the other, as this pushes the rotation of the hip on the dominant side more, which will unbalance you.

Your centre/fulcrum runs from the crown of your head, down through the centre of your torso, down between your legs, and lands at the point where your heels meet when your feet are turned out. We use turned out feet because this frees up the hips to join in the balance exercise. When the feet are together pointing forward, the centre of balance is different, which is why most classical dance forms work with feet turned out. You do not need to work with the extreme turnout that dancers do, but you do need to find your own natural turnout, which is found by turning both feet out at the same time.

Now be aware of where your head is and what it is doing. Normally when an untrained person turns out their feet, they sway back a bit, stick their chin out, and also stick their ribcage out in order to balance. This disengages a lot of the body's structure that can be utilised in balance.

Your aim is to keep your weight ever so slightly forward rather than back, and not to move the head or the ribcage at all: you isolate the feet so that only they move. It's harder than it sounds! Just trying to turn out the feet without moving anything else will teach you about how your body handles weight distribution and balance. Practice this simple movement until you can do it without moving

anything else. Learning a simple isolation will really help you when processing magic.

If your hands involuntarily turn out at the same time as your feet, then it is a sign that as an adult you need to do a lot more physical work that uses isolation.[8] Hands and feet connection is normal in young children, but should not be present in adults: if you are doing that, your brain needs rewiring by learning isolation.

Once you can turn out without moving anything else, then it is time to test the balance of the body's fulcrum. Do this first by holding on to something, then once you have a good idea of the movement, do it without support.

Start by raising one leg in front of you, but instead of letting the toe lead the action, have the heel lead the action. Your foot will be slightly turned out already: lift the foot slowly, with your focus on the heel leading the movement and your toes pulled back. Keep both legs straight.

Your body will want to move in order to compensate. Don't allow your legs to bend at all, as it will throw the focus back to the body. Take note of what happens to your body: what wants to move and where does it want to move to? What is wanting to counterpoint the movement? Is it your arms? Is it your head? Is it your torso?

Now try this: do the action again, but before you start imagine that a hand comes down from the ceiling and grabs your hair by the crown and holds you up. Really focus on it so that your body responds: your neck will lengthen and you will feel a lift out of your hips. Now lift your leg while feeling the grip on your crown.

If your arms want to go out, just imagine your arms out the sides: use your inner vision to imagine your arms, head, and so forth out instead of physically moving them out: counterpoint with your mind and not your body.

Do the same raising the leg to the side, toe up facing the ceiling and heel pointing to the

[8]Like martial arts, tai chi, or yoga.

ground.[9] First see what wants to fly out,[10] and instead of using your body parts to balance, use your mind. Then do the same to the back without tipping the body forward.

Now do the other leg. Once you have gotten good at this, up the game a bit by doing it on one leg on tiptoe. Use something to hold on to. Raise the leg in the position, then rise onto tiptoe. Everything in your body now has to balance on the bridge of one foot, so then you really start to learn about body balance.

Once you are up on tiptoe, let go of what you are holding on to, and try to balance. Use your arms and use your head[11] this time, and instead of imagining the arms, you are going to imagine an orange ball.

Imagine an orange ball hanging in the air on the opposite side of the body to the raised leg when you try to balance. Keep your mind on that visual. If you raise the leg to the front, see it behind you; if the leg is raised to the side, see it on the opposing side; if the leg is raised to the back, see it before you. See how long you can hold the balance for.

Experiment with where you place this ball: if the leg is low, see the ball high so that you could draw a line from your foot through the body to the ball in an acute or opposite angle. As you try to balance on one foot on tiptoe, use your arms and the orange ball to focus your balance. The better you get at it, the less you will need to use your arms, and the more you will be able to rely on the orange ball: move it around you in order to learn how to counterbalance.

And if you feel silly standing in your living room on one leg imagining an orange ball moving around you, remember this: as a magician when you step into the flow of power, your body will seek to counterpoint the balance. If it knows how to balance, it will utilise that knowledge and act accordingly. If it doesn't you are more likely to get energetic knocks, bumps, and scrapes.

This is a tiny fraction of a huge body of knowledge that involves the crossover between the body and magic, and learning to balance, counterpoint, compensate, hold weight, shift weight, and move power around. If you have not still taken up a physical discipline, now would be the time to do it. You need to do a discipline that uses subtle shifts of energy and balance, one that teaches you how to move power around you and how to isolate and focus certain aspects of the body. Weightlifting is pointless for this type of work, as is running: it is not about muscle or endurance, it is far more subtle and complex than that.

Yoga, Tai Chi, soft martial arts, ballet, or gymnastics[12] would be good ones: anything that makes you learn how to balance, transfer weight around, and use your mind as well as your body.

Start with the above simple balancing exercise and do it a few times a week until you get good at it, then do it once a week at least. I do it to this day: while I am waiting for the kettle to boil or something to cook, or when I have a few spare minutes, I practice a balance routine.

3.8 *Task:* Researching Ardhanarishvara

Look for an image of Ardhanarishvara (the composite). The best image, if you can find it, is one from the British Museum. It shows Shiva and Durga as Ardhanarishvara. Note on this image in particular which hand holds the sword (left) and on which side runs the river of Shiva (right).

Ardhanarishvara is a complete root deity of balance. This will give you a good idea of how important complete balance is/was in ancient religions. You can also search out other deities that are composites of male and female and read about them.

---

[9]That position uses hip rotation.

[10]Arms, usually!

[11]The heaviest part of you, very useful for balance and counterpoint.

---

[12]For the younger ones among you.

3.9 *Task:* **Researching Hexagram use in India**

Look up the use of the Hexagram in India, as it is a symbol of Perfect Balance. Look at where and why it appears.

Lesson 4

The Weave

"Even the gods don't fight against Ananke."
—Simonides

The Weave and weaving (our human description) is a creative force that has two major octaves in the act of creation and destruction. The higher octave is deeper into the inner realm and sits beyond the three main creative powers that you have just looked at.

The higher octave is a creative angelic pattern that captures the first impulse of Divine Creation in its 'weave.' As the impulse flows it joins with the weave and begins to lay down the first structure that holds all forms of manifest expression.

The impulse is transformed from pure light/energy/air into a form that holds all potential for life: it becomes the 'DNA' of the manifest world. In this state the Divine impulse has the potential for all of creation and becomes the first building block of life.

When adepts reach deep into the inner realms they perceive this weave as a vast pattern like a complex and beautiful web out of which everything flows. It is the root pattern for the angelic beings that you encountered in previous lessons as they wove between the planets. It is also the root pattern for the Metatron Cube and the Flower of Life: these are all octaves of the same weave.

The strands of the weave are made up of angelic consciousness. Hopefully by now you have lost the idea that all angels look like humans and wear long white robes. The majority of angels that appear in the deep recesses of creation are anything but: they are lines of power, wheels of power, rods of power... Each angel is a single focused consciousness that bridges and transforms. To observe them in action in vision is literally mindblowing.

Like everything else in creation these angels have lower octaves that act as tensions and counterbalances. The power octaves of this power are deities of fate and weaving, angelic beings that pattern fate, and the pattern of life itself. Our DNA[1] is the lowest octave of this power, as is the harmonic patterning we find in everything when we look under a microscope.

When the creative impulse flows into the highest octave of the weave it is separated out into strands. Each of these strands of energy is affected by the counter-forces of Restriction, The Light Bearer, and Perfect Balance. This spreads out the threads into positive, negative, and the fulcrum. As these threads progress further they are affected by the lower powers of creation: the Grindstone, the Unraveller, and the Threshold. The threads are then taken up by the Fates and Weavers and woven into a life form.

---

[1] And the DNA of every living thing.

I talk in terms of threads of energy because that is how they are often perceived by us when we work in vision in the depths of the inner realms: the imagery becomes a vocabulary that we can understand and work with. But to know these powers in their true form is beyond our current comprehension. And to try to understand them without practical visual and vocal vocabulary risks us devolving down into incomprehensible abstracts. The understanding of these vast powers is best approached through images and words that we understand from our everyday life: *the revelation of meaning comes from simplicity.*

The Weave's lower octaves are powers that you were slowly introduced to as an apprentice in obvious and not-so-obvious ways. These lower octaves present to us as angelic beings and deities that are involved solely in the weave of the planet, the solar system, living beings, a personal fate, and so forth. It is this lower level of the octaves that we as magicians work with magically.

The higher octaves, though, are simply experienced.[2] Through such experience the adept begins to understand truly and fully the relationship between the deepest weave and the lower fates. One resonates with the other. As one vibrates, so does the other. The two are inextricably linked to one another.

What is initiated as an action in the higher weave profoundly affects how the lower weave expresses itself. And when the lower weave is acted upon, so to the higher weave begins to vibrate at the same frequency: they are the light and dark of each other.

When you change something in the expression of the lower weave, the higher weave also adjusts to compensate. This in turn then affects how the Divine impulse flows into the next pulse of the power weave. It is a constantly changing, evolving, and interactive relationship.

It is because of this that any magic to do with fate or the future must be compatible with everything around it. The more compatible it is, the less of a shift the magic causes at the higher octave, and the less of a disturbance it makes in the continual, harmonic flow of Divine power into creation.

If the magic is incompatible with the higher weave harmonic it will either fail or, if the magic is powerful enough, it will cause a ripple of disturbance through the inner worlds that in turn will change how the Divine impulse expresses itself.

The dynamic of a subtle action which sometimes has a great effect and at other times has no effect at all is something our physicists are currently grappling with in the outer world.

The same dynamic teaches us magicians to pay very close attention to our magical actions. When we engage in magic that steps outside a pattern's current flow in order to initiate the flow of a new pattern, such an action is likely to have wide-ranging effects in many unforeseen directions.

In order to avoid this as much as possible, we magicians work within structures and patterns that are already strongly embedded in physical manifestation, and we work with a line of fate that is still making its way along its fate weave.

Changing something with magic that is already patterned and working towards its endpoint means *changing how it achieves its endpoint.*

For example a magician may work to avoid a hotspot in someone's life by protecting them from immediate danger. To do this the magician works with the person's fate weave. Since the event on the horizon is a hotspot and not an end point, it is safe to go ahead and divert the oncoming event round the person. This saves them from a possible major accident.

But note that the magician has not altered the person's overarching fate pattern. They will still go on to have their key experiences and die when they are supposed to die. The person's weave of fate has not been changed; the magician has simply altered *how that person's fate expresses.* The overall harmonic

---

[2]As an adept.

pattern remains and continues to vibrate with the highest octave of the weave in an unbroken line of communion.

Now let us look at a different example. Say the magician decides to help a woman conceive by pulling a new life into her body using magic, a life that would not normally have been conceived had magic not intervened. If the magic is successful, it will trigger feedback in the higher creative weave. This will change how the higher weave expresses itself.

We cannot predict how this changed expression will manifest for us in the physical world. It may be good, it may be bad, it may be neither. We just don't know: the variables are outside our current ability to understand. What we do know is that it does change things on a very deep level, and as the change passes down through the powers towards manifestation it seeks to rebalance itself. If that rebalance can come through destruction, then that it how it will express. If that rebalance can come from creation, then that is how it will express.

And notice that the problem came from magically inducing a *conception*. This is different from using magic to change whether a baby lives or dies. It is also different from using magic to help a woman's body regenerate so she becomes fertile (because she still might not get pregnant). *Directly triggering a conception using magic creates a new pattern and that is when major problems can kick off.*

There are so many different levels and variables within this aspect of creation that it can sometimes become overwhelming. Often the magician becomes frozen from fear of acting in a way that will trigger unintentional destruction. It is better simply to bear in mind that we do not truly understand all the variables and dynamics. We do know that working with already active fate patterns tends to avoid the worst of the potential creative imbalances.

You looked at some of the on-the-ground aspects of this tightly knotted weave in your apprentice training when you looked at cause and effect in magic in general. The dynamics of the higher and lower aspects of the creative weave of life are a deeper resonance and a deeper octave of that cause and effect dynamic.

As initiates this essentially boils down to the following: use your common sense, think before you act, and be very clear about what you are doing and why. Only then will you be ready to thrust your hands into the cooking pot of magic.

Also work within what you know until you fully understand it: this enables you to spot the subtleties in magic that you would otherwise miss. These subtleties are often the quiet indicators that point us to the particular patterns that we can work within powerfully and effectively without screwing everything up.

So now let us look at the weave in magic and the beings magicians work with.

4.1 Weaving in ritual

In previous lessons you worked a few times on picking up threads and either passing them on or anchoring them into things. This was very obviously magical weaving.

Yet every time you work in a ritual pattern you are in fact weaving magic. When you work in a direction you are picking up or connecting with strands of power that then link in with and join strands from other directions and beings that you are working with. This is how a magical pattern is built.

When you work with the lower powers of creation they automatically trigger fates within the pattern you are weaving, adding in their own dynamics that in turn trigger latent fate patterns, nudge other fate patterns to adjust themselves, and so forth. This is how a lot of magic works.

Understanding this as you work will give you insight into the deeper powers that flow through your magic. This in turn will teach you to work carefully and with forethought. Too many people rush into magic and stick their hands into all sorts of cooking pots without giving any thought as to how the bigger pattern will change as a result of their magic. Changing patterns when appropriate is not a problem, so long as you know that is what you are doing and why.

So the next time you work with ritual action keep in mind that everything you do weaves threads of power. The more you keep this in mind, the more your deeper self will engage with the pattern as you travel within the weave through time.

4.2 Weaving in vision

Working in vision on a weave is another major aspect of magic and fate. You have experienced this in some ways in your work with threads and when you left a path or trail behind you. All these things create change in a pattern, which is essentially what magic is all about. *Magic happens when a weave is altered or interacted with.*

This dynamic comes into sharp focus when you work with the lower powers of creation and/or the deities of fate: when these powers are worked with directly in vision the patterns are revealed to you and your actions trigger a cascade of change in the pattern.

Visionary work on weaves is more powerful than working with ritual patterns, so the method is chosen according to the task. Often both techniques are used together so that the inner and outer actions come together in harmony to create a powerful shift in something.

The one vital thing to remember with magical weaving at any powerful level is that it must not be done with a sense of total control: it should be done along with deities or angelic beings and in the spirit of cooperation, not control.

The magician triggers the focus of the magic, but does not control how the magic will fully express itself. This enables all the many unforeseen twists and turns of fate to match up in the pattern to the magic.

A magician may open up a potential path, but they should not define how the power makes its way down that path. Nor should

they control how it finally expresses itself. A magician who needs to transform their own future or another person's may trigger that transformation; but exactly how the change should express is best left to the fates.

Often in such cases the magician would really like A to happen, and triggers the pattern to change, but the end result is B. In hindsight they realise that B was really the better option. The inner dynamics, if left to do their job, find the best possible solution that will bring about balance and forward momentum to a fate.

There are also passive and more natural ways to work with the power of fate that are very traditional or 'shamanic' ways of working. Let me give you an example. I have written about it before in one of my books. I don't think I have mentioned it so far in the course, but forgive me if I am repeating myself—old age!

In my early forties I had to make a decision, and whatever choice I made was going to have far-reaching consequences for my two daughters. I could not actively use magic at the time for magical reasons, and I was afraid that I would make the wrong decision. I sat out in a field and asked the land for help and guidance, and explained to the wind that the wrong decision would most likely wreck the futures of my two girls. I had no problem living with the consequences of my own bad decisions, but I did not want to inflict them on others. I had an instinct as to the right way forward, and I asked for simple feedback from nature on that decision.

As I sat, a beautiful spider crawled up in front of me and started spinning a web between two stones. I didn't get the message at first until an inner contact whispered for me to pay attention. As the spider spun her web, I watched in fascination. I marvelled at how she could build such a complex weave without being able to see the whole thing. Then I got the message:

> "Your fate is being spun and you
> cannot see the overall picture, so you
> have to rely on your instincts and

keep focused on the task immediately in front of you. Then the web will be spun without complications."

It was one of those moments when suddenly everything becomes bright and beautiful, and nature pulses with deep, inner creative life. Then I knew my instincts were right and that I had to stop worrying about an overview: my job was to focus on the immediate task in hand and go with the decision my deeper instincts indicated.

And it was indeed the right decision. Everyone I knew thought I was nuts to make the choice I did, but it was the right one and as far as my girls were concerned it changed their lives for the better in so many extraordinary ways. And yet on the face of it the decision appeared to those around me as stupid and self-defeating.

By passively invoking the powers of fate in nature and calling for help when I was in real need, nature responded with a message. But the magician has to be able to spot those responses, be able to read nature, and be able to communicate with such a huge collective power. The ability to communicate directly with nature in a passive and exteriorised way[3] is an important skill, which is one of the reasons there is a lot of nature work in this course.

If a magician is in a position where they cannot use magic for one reason or another, then the passive triggering of communion with the powers in an externalised way is a method that can get the magician help when they truly need it without causing any magical waves or energy signatures.

There are a lot of reasons why an adept may be unable to use magic in a given situation. They may need to stay invisible from a destructive force. There may be a vulnerable child in their immediate family. Or they may be under a direct attack that will take time to dismantle.

At such times the magician needs to be invisible and not make any major changes to their fate pattern, at doing so could make them visible. Working passively with nature in call and response is an excellent solution. The deeper the magician has worked in the inner worlds, the more powerful the call and response becomes.

You have already begun learning the methods of working with your own fate pattern, working with the Measurer, She Who Holds The Measure of your life and who measured your cord for you. She is the fulcrum of fate work. Now it is time to begin looking at the other deities[4] who work with fate patterns and the weave of fate and time. They are from different cultures and virtually every culture had/has some version/s of these powers.

When it comes to choosing which deity to connect with the choice is theirs, not yours. You cannot decide on the basis of what interests you or what current stream of magic you are interested in. The female power of fate weaving finds you on the basis of your own current fate pattern, the fate of your other lives, the complex weave of fates that run in your bloodlines, and *the necessity of where you path needs to go for whatever reason*.

This is very important for all magicians to understand, particularly in the area of fate: *necessity is paramount and desire is of no importance*. If the magician works towards necessity in fate patterns then their magic will be successful as it will follow the natural, powerful tide of creation: everything flows and should flow towards what is necessary.

This was deeply understood in the ancient world, which is why the goddess who is the mother of the fates in Greek and Roman mythology is called *Ananke*, which means necessity. We will look at her and her daughters in more depth in a moment.

Understanding—and I mean *really* understanding—this vital dynamic of necessity

---

[3]No vision, no ritual, no direct magic.

[4]Almost exclusively goddesses/female powers.

within fate magic is a major key for adepts to powerful and successful magical work. When you work in true necessity, all of fate comes up behind you and works with you. If you work from desire rather than necessity and the two are not compatible, then the full force of fate works in *opposition* to whatever magic is being produced. Understanding the difference between desire and necessity is what separates a dabbler from a true adept.

When a magician wishes to connect with a goddess/female power of fate, knowing which one they are standing before in vision can help them understand how this particular power works with fate. This in turn tells the magician what powers are to be woven into a fate pattern, which is pretty important. It also tells the magician which octave of the weaver they are being presented with.

If a lower octave of a fate power connects with the magician, it is likely that the necessity of such work lies in more mundane changes to a fate pattern. However if a higher octave of the fate power connects with the magician, it is a signal that the necessary magical work is more likely to change nations, cultures, or the evolution of a populace.

Or it can indicate that though the shift in fate may appear mundane to the magician, in the long term it will have far-reaching consequences. It may be that the magician is working on the fate pattern of an individual, but if a higher octave of fate power turns up and presents themselves then it is likely that the individual will go on to trigger vast changes in the world that will reverberate for a long time after they have died.

Often this cannot be seen by the magician through divination, particularly if the fate of the individual will trigger changes that will last for millennia, which is why the magician works within necessity and trusts the fates to do their job.

4.3   Some of the Goddess of fate/weaving

As we go through this small selection of fate goddesses you will notice that some of them are concerned simply with the fate of humans or individual humans: they are lower octaves of the fate power and will have a deeper octave that lies behind their power. If the fate goddess is also linked to creation then you know you are reading about a deeper power of creation and the weaving of the creative fire into life.

Neit/Neith

Origins: first dynasty/predynastic Ancient Egypt (before 3000 B.C.)

> "I am All That Has Been, That Is, and That Will Be. No mortal has yet been able to lift the veil that covers Me. The fruit which I brought forth was the sun."
>
> —Inscription from the adyton of the temple of Neith in Sais

Neith is said to have been "born the first, in the time when as yet there had been no birth." Known as an "Opener of the Ways" and also as "North of her Wall."[5] Her priestesses hold titles such as: *"Priestess of Neith who opens all the paths,"* and *"Priestess of Neith who opens the way in all her places."*

She is often depicted holding the *was* staff and an *ankh* sign (dominion and life). The ankh is held in her left hand (opening the path to life), and the *was* (staff of dominion, the power of Set/destruction in balance) in her right hand.[6]

Neith is a virgin battle goddess and the weaver of creation. As such she is depicted with two arrows and a shield, and also with a loom: she is the personification of the primordial waters of creation but she

---

[5]Think about that in terms of what you know of the magical directions.

[6]As an aside, Set is depicted with the same power tools but held in reverse–think about that.

also holds the power of destruction. As the goddess of creation and weaving, she was said to reweave the world on her loom daily.

From her inscriptions, power tools, and depictions, we are told that Neith is a higher octave of fate: she is the power that weaves the whole of creation. As a higher octave of fate she is not easily nor immediately contacted: we must go through other, lower octaves of fate to commune with and connect with this power.

In modern magic she can present to a magician as a goddess with her signs and attributes *who does not speak*. Her voice is that of all creation, and as such her utterance is profound. When Neith shows up in the life of a magician, she often presents with a quiet presence that radiates power, but she usually does not ask for the more usual immediate connections that deities often expect when they connect with humans. She will often appear[7] as a presence that is powerful but one that will not communicate directly: she keeps a silent presence within the realm of the magician. She will often repel direct contact, but will guide the magician through their deeper instincts.

Ananke

Ananke (Greek: "force, constraint, necessity") is the goddess of necessity and fate. She marks the beginning of the cosmos along with Kronos (time). She was seen as the powerful director of the fate of both humans and gods, and was the higher octave of the three fates.

She emerged self-formed at the very beginning of time–an incorporeal, serpentine being whose outstretched arms spanned the breadth of the universe. Ananke entwined in the serpentine coils of her partner Kronos and together they surrounded the primal egg of solid matter in their constricting coils and split it into its various parts (earth, heaven and sea) and so triggered the birth of creation, and brought order from chaos.

---

[7]In vision or physically turn up as an unexpected statue or image.

Ananke and Kronos remain entwined as the cosmic orbiting forces of fate and time, upholding the rotation of the heavenly orbits and the constant flowing passage of time.

Think about this mythic pattern in terms of what you have learned so far in this module: a dividing of the primal Divine Impulse, a higher octave of fate that is also deeply affected by Restriction and the Light Bearer, and how these powers start to form patterns that encompass balance, restriction, and creation. The bringing of deep creation patterns from the threshold of Divinity to the various octaves of creation and weaving them into form was something clearly understood in classical Greece.

Figure 4.1: Museum Collection: Pushkin State Museum of Fine Arts, Moscow, Russia. c. 470–460 B.C. (Common Usage)

And look at the image of her above. Note the wings (angelic power), the torch held in the darkness (the Light Bearer), the left foot forward (going into life). The concept of her as the higher weave in Greek mythology is connected to the Metatron Cube and the Flower of Life, along with the trunk of the sacred Tree of Life. With what you have learned so far you should be able to make connections between the concepts and depictions.

Figure 4.2: Ananke and the Moirae (Public Domain)

The above depiction of Ananke clearly demonstrates the dynamic of the higher and lower octaves of fate, and it is one that shows Ananke as the overarching power of fate (the higher octaves) with the Three Fates, the Moirae underneath her.

Just as Ananke weaves the fate of all of creation, that power then resonates with the lower octaves of fate, which are involved more with the fates of nations and individuals.

Notice in this image the dynamics of orbits, of the turning of time and the weaving of fate.

Here we start to see classical depictions of these deep inner dynamics of higher and lower octaves that work through the inner realms of creation.

The classical understanding of this higher power of fate also includes the deep mystical understanding that this high octave was in orbit with and a part of the dynamic of the Light Bearer and Restriction/constriction, of time (Kronos), and how these powers all came together to restrict, divide, and weave the raw power of Divine Creation into the physical world. They often presented in Orphic texts as two snakes (Ananke and Kronos) wrapping around and constricting the expansion of creation to form the physical world.

The Moirae

In Greek mythology, the Moirai,[8] who were also known as the Fates and in Roman mythology as the Parcae, were the lower octave of Ananke. The Three Fates were part of both Greek and Roman mythology and were:

Clotho/Nona	(spinner/creator)
Lachesis/Decima	(allotter/measurer)
Atropos/Morta	(cutter)

Clotho/Nona took the thread of creation and began spinning a life; Lachesis/Decima allotted a specific life span to each creation; and Atropos/Morta set the time of death and ensured it was adhered to.

They controlled the creation, the span of life, and the time of death of every mortal. They were independent of the other gods, linked only to Ananke and Kronos, and they directed fate, making sure that the fate pattern assigned to every being might take its course without obstruction.

At the birth of a human the Moirai span out the thread of their future life, following the human's steps and directing the consequences of his or her actions according to the counsel of the gods.

In Greek mythology Zeus had the power to intervene in order to shift a fate or to rescue someone from a specific fate. The Fates themselves did not directly interfere in the details of a human's fate, but they intervened

---

[8]In Classical Greek it means "apportioners."

with junction points and help when absolutely necessary[9] and when creation was in need of a certain course of fate.

In general it was understood that the Fates set patterns and boundaries, but how the human navigated within those boundaries was a matter of their own choice and free will. The human's choices decided how the pattern would express itself and whether the pattern would be lived to its full potential or not.

Because they were weavers of individual fate, they were also seen as deities of prophecy and often their priestesses were oracles. And as the cutter of fate, Decima was also often perceived as being a deity of death and the underworld.

The Moirai were often depicted as ugly old women who were stern and inflexible. Clotho carried a spindle or a scroll of fate, Lachesis carried a staff[10] and Atropos carried a pair of scales or a cutting instrument. At the birth of each human they appeared spinning, measuring, and cutting the thread of life.

This concept of female weavers of fate and bringers of the time of death can be found in many different cultures. By looking at the different versions you start to see how different peoples were aware of these powers and worked with them in different ways. Often the main theme is battle, as the outcome of a battle not only defined the fate of a person but the fate of tribes and nations.

Often different animals appear in the myths and legends of these fates, and these tell the magician what particular creatures are connected to fate. This in turn helps the magician in terms of augury and dreams. The most common ones are horses,[11] bees, swans, and ravens. In your practical work you will research for yourself the various forms of the fates.

4.4 *Task:* Research

The Fates of Nordic and Germanic cultures were depicted as female weavers and spinners, and also as spirit female warriors. A Viking form of magic called *Seidr* was heavily involved in the altering of fate, particularly in relation to battle, and was a form of magic used by the Völva who were female shamanic magicians. Seidr (seething) was the fire power of rage that was used to fuel magic aimed at enemies.[12] Remnants of it have remained in communities with Viking roots.

For example when I was a child, when a woman became very angry (usually at an errant husband) she would poke the fire to give it air so that it became strong. Then she then would rant and spit into the fire, sending curses streaming towards the hapless individual on the receiving end.

I guess it is less seen these days since central heating and electric fires are now the norm… But to this day in areas that were once Viking,[13] a woman will still say that she is seething with anger at someone.

What I would like you to do for your task is first to look up Seidr, and if at all possible approach it by looking at the poems that have survived. There are modern day revivals of Seidr but I have not looked at them in any depth, so I cannot comment on them as to whether they would be a good source or not. The one thing to keep in mind is that the weaving of fate and the destruction by seething was female, not male.

The power of weaving fate was exclusively female and it appears to also be that way in most ancient cultures. The same goes for seething: it is a power that comes from the raging mother whose child is threatened, a power that is far more terrifying when unleashed than a male warrior in battle. This same connection with the female destroying power can be read in the story of Sekhmet

---

[9] The power of necessity-the power of Ananke.

[10] Look up the connection to Egypt with the *djed* staff of Ptah, which is a staff of stability/life.

[11] Particularly the White Horse.

[12] I am being very broad here, just to keep it simple.

[13] Yorkshire, where I grew up, for example.

and also of Kali. It is a power that destroys everything in its path.

This destructive female power is part and parcel of the weaving of fate: creation and destruction are the two threads of power that are woven to make the fate: a woman can 'create' a new life and give birth, and that power is equalised on the scales by the power of total destruction. In today's world a lot of that side of feminine power is heavily suppressed in various cultures, but in ancient cultures it was often (not always) tapped into and female warriors were a major resource for a kingdom. The mixture of female magic, working with fate, and working with rage are all themes that crop up in a variety of ancient writings. Men had the strength and brute force, and woman had magic, fate weaving, and uncontrolled rage. So keep all this in mind as you look at these various forms of fates, as the themes will keep repeating.

Look up and read about Frigg, Dísir, Idis, and the Norns. Look up the Völva and seething.

Look up Valkyries and the poem Darraðarljóð, from Njal's Saga. Pay close attention to the Valkyries' appearance before the Battle of Clontarf.

There is also a comment in the Saga of the Volsungs that describes looking into the face of a Valkyrie as being like looking into fire. When you research these various topics, look for the connections of fire, the animals, fate, and battle.

Look up and read about Bean Sidhe

The Bean Sidhe[14] is often referred to as the Woman of the Barrows. This is not a direct translation, but is rather a poetic one. Bean (pronounced "ban") means *woman* in Gaelic and Sidhe ("shee") means *faery*. They are known as dwellers of the hills, duns, or barrows because of the faery connection: hills, duns, and barrows were known for their faery 'infestation.' The Bean Sidhe and Bean Nighe

appear in prophetic visions or dreams when people, particularly warriors, were about to die.

Look up and read about spiders, fate, and weaving

Spiders often appear in myths, legends, and visions in connection with fate. Look up tribal stories of 'grandmother spider.' The spider and fate connection also shows up in various Abrahamic texts in terms of protecting the future of a prophet or future king. If you search for mentions of Jesus, Mohammed, and David, and spiders spinning webs for protection, you will find a variety of legends around the theme.

4.5 *Task:* **Think about the Metatron Cube**

With all that you have read about the mythic personalities of fate, cast your mind away from the mythologies and legends and think back to the Metatron Cube. Remember that is it a pattern of creation that sits right on the threshold where the Divine Breath crosses the Abyss and begins its journey into creation. It is a weave of angelic consciousness, a template for creation, and is for magicians and mystics the deepest source of hidden knowledge: it is the DNA of creation.

The Metatron Cube is our human depiction of that pattern rather than the true pattern itself, which is beyond normal comprehension. Knowing what you now know, you will realise how much silly stuff there is out in the world about the Metatron Cube, and you will also start to realise how powerful it can be to work with this human reflection of the weave of creation. It is not a puzzle to be solved; it is a pattern to be absorbed and eventually experienced directly.

Redrawing the Metatron Cube each time you learn something new about it will help you to absorb its secrets at a deep level.

---

[14]Or Bean Nighe in Scottish mythology, also known as the Washer by the Ford.

Lesson 5

The Breath

In the beginning was the Word, and the Word was with God, and the Word was God.

—*John* 1:1

The Breath of Life and the power of Utterance are the greatest powers a magician can work with. The pure power of creation flows through the human voice and breath when used mystically or magically. And the further into adeptship a magician goes, the more the line blurs between mysticism and magic, as they spring from the same source.

Many people think that mysticism is specific to a religion and is about being 'pure' in a religious sense, but nothing could be further from the truth. Mysticism is an understanding of *that which remains hidden*. It is the understanding of the deepest mysteries of Divine creation and destruction. Without that understanding the magician is merely a turner of tricks. An adept of magic is one who flows in the current of Divine power and takes an active role in that process. And what plugs the magician into that current of Divine power is the understanding of the power of breath and the Word.

To step towards the adept understanding of such raw power, the initiate begins the process of learning, practice, and reflection. This can never be just an intellectual or philo-sophical form of study, but must relate to direct experience.

To start you on this journey, in this lesson we will look at the mystical writings and understandings that our forebears left us. We will also work with the direct experience of this power.

From the very beginning of your training you have worked with the breath in a variety of forms; and each time we visit this subject your practice and understanding will take you a step deeper into this profound mystery. Such steps teach you the power of the breath and the voice, while also aligning you with the vast power that lies behind the Utterance. It is a journey that takes a lifetime.

When you first started working with ritual you used your voice a lot. For most of you those rituals would have been powerless, as you were simply learning a pattern. But for an adept plugged into the powers of creation, those words take on a different dynamic which brings the individual to the threshold of *speaking the worlds into being*. Words have power when the one who utters them stands fully in the stream of Divine Impulse.

Each religious and mystical system understood this; yet in each of them the use of the breath and the voice degenerated quickly into pompous recitals and intellectual exercise. We can see this right at the birth of Christianity, where great profundity and power was set in words. Within a generation or two it had already become simply words on paper or words in ritual to be debated, argued, and amended according to agenda. The power in the words was quickly lost as people focused on the meanings and interpretations, and not on the power.

So let us look first at the dynamic of this power. Then we will look at various mystical texts that leave crumb trails, and then we will look at the magical application.

5.1   The Breath of Life

The Breath of Life refers to the Divine Breath that breathes out of the nothing to create every-thing. It is the first pulse of power in creation: the *breath*, then the *sound*, and then the *Word* that brings everything into being. It is the breath that hits the first pattern of creation as it begins its journey into physical manifestation.

The Breath of Life is also the first sound: the vibration that causes everything else to vibrate and that triggers life in substance. The Divine breathes life into us, and the magician breathes life into magic.

We think of breath as being air—atmospheric gases that we breathe in order to survive. But the Breath of Life is what is *behind* the atmospheric gases: it is the magical and Divine element of power that enables the atmospheric gases to manifest. So think of the Breath of Life, the Utterance, and the Word as being a raw power that can manifest as anything: it is pure power and vibration. That is its highest manifes-tation. At its lowest octave, which is what magicians work with, it is the power that brings something to life.

The action of using the breath to bring something to life can be *mediated breathing* or *bridging*, it can be *blowing*, it can be *vibrating a sound using the voice*, or it can be *actual words*.

Without being immersed in the power of the Breath of Life the sounds and words are just that: noises. But when the magician learns how to bridge and mediate the pure power of the Breath of Life then they can stand in the flow of creation and mediate it into the magical act. There is nothing more powerful in magic, nothing so simple, and yet nothing else that is so hard to do.

You began to work with this power in your apprentice training. In your initiate and adept training you will continue to revisit deeper layers and different understandings—with practical experience—until one day you can breathe, and the whole of creation breathes through you.

Ancient and religious texts are littered with references to the Breath of Life. Usually the phrase is found either in creation myths or in magic that brings something to life. Before we move on from thinking about the highest expression of the breath, let us look at some texts that feature this foundational power. As you read through them you will start to see how connected they are.[1] The more of your own reading and research you do, the more references to the Breath of Life you will find. We will look at Jewish, Christian, and Egyptian texts that all express the same creative dynamic.

Read through these snippets of text. Then we will look in more detail as to what exactly is going on from a magical perspective.

Ezekiel 37:1-10

(From the Jewish Publication Society Old Testament)

> 37:1 The hand of the LORD was upon me, and the LORD carried me out in a spirit, and set me down in the midst of the valley, and it was full of bones;

> 37:2 and He caused me to pass by them round about, and, behold, there were very many in the open valley; and, lo, they were very dry.

> 37:3 And He said unto me: 'Son of man, can these bones live?' And I answered: 'O Lord GOD, Thou knowest.'

---

[1] They all sprang from the same source.

37:4 Then He said unto me: 'Prophesy over these bones, and say unto them: O ye dry bones, hear the word of the LORD:

37:5 Thus saith the Lord GOD unto these bones: *Behold, I will cause breath to enter into you, and ye shall live.*

37:6 And I will lay sinews upon you, and will bring up flesh upon you, and cover you with skin, and put breath in you, and ye shall live; and ye shall know that I am the LORD.'

37:7 So I prophesied as I was commanded; and as I prophesied, *there was a noise, and behold a commotion*, and the bones came together, bone to its bone.

37:8 And I beheld, and, lo, there were sinews upon them, and flesh came up, and skin covered them above; *but there was no breath in them.*

37:9 Then said He unto me: 'Prophesy unto the breath, prophesy, son of man, and say to the breath: *Thus saith the Lord GOD: Come from the four winds, O breath, and breathe upon these slain, that they may live.*'

37:10 So I prophesied as He commanded me, and the breath came into them, and they lived, and stood up upon their feet, an exceeding great host.

Note the commanding of the four winds to bring the breath, so that the breath would breathe upon the slain. Note also that the human is instructed to say "thus saith the Lord God." This is one of these vital little hidden details: you speak with the flow of Divine creation flowing through your words.

Trimorphic Protennoia/Codex XIII

(Second century A.D. Sethian gnostic text.)

I am the Invisible One within the All. It is I who counsel those who are hidden, since I know the All that exists in it. I am numberless beyond everyone.   I am immeasurable, ineffable, yet whenever I wish, I shall reveal myself of my own accord. I am the head of the All. I exist before the All, and I am the All, since I exist in everyone.

I am a Voice speaking softly. I exist from the first.   I dwell within the Silence that surrounds every one of them. And it is the hidden Voice that dwells within me, within the incomprehensible, immeasurable Thought, within the immeasurable Silence.

I descended to the midst of the Underworld, and I shone down upon the darkness. It is I who poured forth the water.   It is I who am hidden within radiant waters. I am the one who gradually put forth the All by my Thought.   It is I who am laden with the Voice. It is through me that Gnosis comes forth. I dwell in the ineffable and unknowable ones. I am perception and knowledge, uttering a Voice by means of thought. I am the real Voice. I cry out in everyone, and they recognize it,[2] since a seed indwells them.

I am the Thought of the Father, and through me proceeded the Voice, that is, the knowledge of the everlasting things.   I exist as Thought for the All—being joined to the unknowable and incomprehensible Thought.   I revealed myself—yes, I—among all those who recognize me. For it is I who am joined with everyone by virtue of the hidden Thought and an exalted Voice, even a Voice from the invisible Thought.   And it is immeasurable, since it dwells in the Immeasurable One. It is a mystery; it is unrestrainable by the Incomprehensible One. It is invisible to all those who are visible in the All. It is a Light dwelling in Light.

---

[2] The voice.

51

It is we also who alone have separated from the visible world, since we are saved by the hidden wisdom, by means of the ineffable, immeasurable Voice. And he who is hidden within us pays the tributes of his fruit to the Water of Life.

The Cosmology of Neith

The full text is at the end of the lesson for you in case you wish to read it all, as it is difficult to find on the internet in English.

The Primeval Hill:

She spoke then:

"This place where I am shall become an earthen hill within the First Waters, it will be a support for all the powers":

And that place where Neit spoke became the Place within the First Waters, that place became Ta-Senet, the Land of the Waters, and also Sau. *The Word of Neit took flight from that which had emerged* and with that Per-Neter and Buto came into being also:

She spoke again:

"I spoke well on that which emerged."

5.2 Breath and creative power

You will notice that in all these texts the breath and the voice is an *initial impulse power* for the creation of life. This is the breath in its highest Divine octave. Understanding this deeply within yourself—and standing within that understanding as a magician as you resonate that power of the breath into your magical work—is the beginning of learning how to be a threshold for energy and power.

Many magical texts that have been left to us by the ancients and our forebears are full of magical recitations, yet they are essentially useless and meaningless if they are not worked with while standing within that creative power. We can track the degeneration of magic over the last thousand years when we look at the words used, the words to be spoken; words that have moved from being ones that open the gates for the creative power to being words of command and control for a limited purpose.

At this stage you need to understand that the breath and the voice—sound and air—are the root powers that all magic revolves round. The full use of that power comes with great responsibility. Each time you work with this power you recreate the act of creation, and thus you stand within that Divine stream of power.

This is the stage at which the magician guards his or her magic from the stupid and profane. This is also the stage where the magician begins to understand that even mundane words have power when spoken from a place of power.

Once the magician begins to work with the breath and the Utterance, the power cannot be switched on or off. The magician becomes a living threshold for the Divine breath. As such their words can have far-reaching consequences. The power flows through a spoken comment just as much as it flows through a magical Utterance. That is not to say that the magician must never speak 'bad words' to someone, but it does mean that any word, be it an insult, a teaching, or a compliment, must come from a balanced place.

5.3 The breath and Utterance as a catalyst

The action of breathing into something, and the act of uttering something magically, has three main root dynamics: *fate, the elements,* and *enlivening.* Magical utterance *awakens and directs* something, and the breath *triggers life* in something. This collection of root dynamics is the basis of creation itself, and the pattern repeats in many different octaves throughout life, magic, and time.

The breath gives life to something. The Utterance directs that life or triggers it into action. From those two root actions magic forms, weaves, and directs to focal points in order for something to be achieved. For a magician to be able to do this, they must understand the dynamics fully within themselves and be able to connect with the stream of raw creative power in order to trigger the magical action in full power.

The first step towards this skill is learning how to breathe without any power connected to it, something you started in your apprentice training. Then you must learn to make sound with that breath through the use of speech and sound vibration. Learning these primary steps is like developing basic muscles before the athlete-to-be learns specific techniques.

Learning the basics of breath and Utterance while also learning the powers of the inner worlds and visionary magic bring two strands together that weave into becoming magic. One without the other is useless in terms of adept, or even initiate, magic.

Some people can tap straight into these power dynamics and do it naturally, but the majority have to learn the basic steps before they can learn to bridge power. Many magicians make the mistake of believing that reciting particular words—spells—will give them power. This is a dead end designed to keep those hungry for power busy and out of trouble, just as buying a computer but not turning it on, not having software, and not knowing how to work it will leave people back where they started.

The power in the spoken word comes from the breath, and before that from the deep inner connection within the magician to the Divine patterns, powers, and beings. So let us take a look at these dynamics in more detailed and practical forms.

5.4 The magical use of breath

The use of the breath in magic permeates virtually all aspects of magic in one form or another.

When a magician bridges the threshold of the inner and outer worlds and breathes the power of the whirlwind into something, it brings it to life. This can be a deity form,[3] a sword, a fate pattern...any vessel that can be breathed into. The one thing to remember with such work[4] is that when you breathe life *into* something, you are then responsible for it. You have birthed it, so you will have to guard it as a parent.

When you breathe life *over* something, you awaken it. 'Into' and 'over' are two separate things that look the same from outside, but are magically very different. When you breathe magically *into* something—a vessel—you are bridging life into something that previously had no life within it. When you breathe *over* something you awaken a preexisting potential that was only sleeping. The deeper into this profound magical practice you go, the more the differences will become apparent.

When you began working with your magical sword, both physically and in vision, you breathed *over* it. A magical sword, properly connected to inner power and pattern, becomes an expression of *one specific sword* that simply manifests itself in many different places. Just as the enlivened statues of a deity are all connected to the same specific deity, this is a single power with many expressions. Breathing along the blade of a magical sword, done properly, triggers the deep inner aspect of the sword into awareness: it wakes up. It becomes a *living outer expression of a deeper sword power* that has many outlets for that expression through time.

When you breathe magically *into* a sword as part of a creative process, it creates a whole new pattern of consciousness that pours into the vessel that was previously a mundane sword: you birth a new sword with both an inner and an outer expression. Obviously it takes more than just breathing to birth a whole new magical sword, but the last act that triggers the completion is the breath. The magician's ability to do this comes from their ability to stand in the stream of creative

---

[3] Statue or image.

[4] Which you are training for adept-level magic.

power and weave/direct the power through the breath and into a waiting vessel.

This use of breath is also employed when the magician wishes to awaken a dormant fate pattern. We do not use up every strand of our fate patterns in a life: our choices narrow down the paths we walk. This concentrates all our creative energy in one part of the weave. This is often how most lives are lived—in a small corner of their web.

Some individuals, however, through the choices they make, expand out across their web and "live many lives in one life." That is to say they step out into the unknown in life and have many varied and colourful experiences. Such individuals rarely need to breathe across their fate to enliven a path within it; they are usually tearing up the road themselves through their adventures.

But when a magician has found themselves locked into a segment of their fate pattern which seems to be limiting them—they get stuck in a tangle—one of the things that can open their fate back up is identifying a path that could have been walked but which has become dormant from disuse: the magician works with the web of fate and breathes an awakening.

Of course, unless the magician has identified why they got stuck in a rut and are willing to take the necessary steps to forge forward, using their breath magically will create only a temporary window into their wider fate path. It is our actions and choices that keep those opened paths alive and awake.

5.5   Blowing

Blowing is a variant of the magical breath. Blowing is used to move things from one place to another or one world to another, and is often used to send decaying or unhealthy patterns into the Void or to dispatch magical attacks.

Blowing can also be used to connect with the winds and to mediate the whirlwind of the inner worlds to the outer winds. When blowing is connected to sound—such as blowing through a horn—it heralds a power

out into the world, usually as a wake up call or as a call to destroy something.

The magical action of blowing into a particular horn with magical intent bridges a power of resonance that shakes things into unbeing. Look at these excerpts from Joshua 6 in the Torah. Notice the use of withholding the voice until the right time[5] and how the priests mediated the whirlwind through the horn.

Excerpts from *Joshua* 6

> 6:9 And the armed men went before the priests that blew the horns, and the rearward went after the ark, the priests blowing with the horns continually.
>
> 6:10 And Joshua commanded the people, saying: 'Ye shall not shout, nor let your voice be heard, neither shall any word proceed out of your mouth, until the day I bid you shout; then shall ye shout.
>
> 6:11 So he caused the ark of the Lord to compass the city, going about it once; and they came into the camp, and lodged in the camp.
>
> . . .
>
> 6:20 So the people shouted, and the priests blew with the horns. And it came to pass, when the people heard the sound of the horn, that the people shouted with a great shout, and the wall fell down flat, so that the people went up into the city, every man straight before him, and they took the city.

The use of the horn/blowing can also *flatten an area* in terms of frequency or drive low-level beings away: the deep resonant vibration of the horn creates an energy environment that is not conducive to a lot of low-level beings. This is particularly true of parasitical and destructive Underworld beings found in mountainous areas.

---

[5]Letting the power back up.

Horns can be worked with like magical swords: beings can be connected to them, and their own pattern can be brought forth form the inner worlds to reside in the outer horn. They become vessels in their own right.

5.6 The magical use of Utterance

The use of the voice in magic has many varied applications, many of which tend to pass by the magician who relies solely on ritual speech in magic. The voice and the Utterance are so much more than that.

The magical use of the voice and Utterance is about *sound, frequency, language, breath,* and *words* that can *awaken, instruct, create,* and *form* patterns that the magician fills with energy and power.

The simple use of words is only the start of the use of the voice: reciting a ritual text as an exteriorised ritual act does not in itself fill anything with power or energy. As an apprentice you learned some simple, basic rituals using the voice. Those rituals are upheld by the larger body of energy that is the course. But as an apprentice magician, for the most part there was no power and minimal energy behind the ritual: you were learning the system, not really operating it.

Once the magician has worked in the inner worlds and gone through the various inner and outer changes that accompany that work, the door of magical energy and power slowly starts to open. Learning to work in vision and ritual at the same time starts to widen that doorway so that power and consciousness beyond your own can engage through your actions to trigger magic.

The use of the voice becomes the endpoint of the magical action: it is the act of exteriorising that has a large pattern of magic behind it, and the voice sets it off into the future in order to act. This is why a person off the street and a magician could utter the same words, and one will not trigger magic while the other will trigger a whole slew of magical action. It is not the words so much as the power *behind* the words uttered.

In the early part of your apprentice training you were instructed to talk to everything around you. This is an important first step in the use of the voice in magic. It is also the first step where the magician prepares to grow into the magical understanding that everything around them has a form of consciousness, some of which can communicate back to you.

This also prepares the magician for being a part of an inner and outer community: by talking to everything you begin the slow process of opening up lines of communication with all the different layers of consciousness that can talk back to you.

It teaches you to be part of the pattern of creation. On a lower octave it indicates to the beings around you that you are willing to reach out.

It also prepares you at a deep level for using your voice to trigger things: your voice becomes a catalyst for change. Let us look at the different ways the voice can be used in magical action.

5.7 Creating patterns through voice

Previously you learned to take threads of energy and anchor them or release them in another direction: this was the beginning of learning how to create an energetic pattern. When done in vision and in ritual movement at the same time, this starts to trigger the deeper powers of the inner worlds; and when the voice is added into that action it completes and directs it.

The voice is not used much early on in the training of such action. This is because the use of words can easily go wrong, and when you are weaving a magical pattern it is important to get it right. Not having too much control, but having accurate direction and care over the words used—these are all very important in order to succeed at whatever you are trying to achieve.

Too much control in the verbal direction limits the magic. Inaccurate direction disorders the magic and can make it fail entirely. Knowing how to direct accurately is a whole skill set in itself, and harder than it sounds.

The other issue magicians often face when using the voice/speech is speaking in a language they do not understand (like Hebrew). There are many instances in magical rituals and grimoires where the use of such language is incorrect, and thus the direction is incorrect. Such use of language is generally only useful for names, and those names have to have a genuine source with proper understanding behind it.

If you are working in your own language there is a much better chance that you will understand fully what you are saying and why you are saying it.

However, there are instances where specific chants or recitations in another language carry a great deal more power because they have been used for millennia that way: the recitation builds up its own pattern. When the chant or recitation is in a sacred language, this also adds a great deal more power to the working. The problems arise with bad translations, missing words, the *wrong* words, or incorrect pronunciations: it does not fit exactly with the pattern. To avoid these issues, the magic in this training course uses other languages in ritual only minimally.

As you progress it may be good for you to experiment with different languages. You will learn a great deal from your failures and mistakes, and have wonderful surprises as a result of your successes. It is best, though, to approach this as a specific future experiment, done just for its own sake, rather than relying on it when you really need it to work.

And if you do choose to experiment with language/recitation, be very careful what you do: I have come unstuck a couple of times from using foreign recitation that worked too well...I then had a mess to clean up.

5.8   Instructing through words

When you instruct with words it is usually the end point of a magical working: you do it when the patterns are being drawn together and you are working with an inner contact to bring something to fruition. Over the span of your training you will develop this skill more and more. We will work with it in this lesson in the practical section.

It is vitally important that your words are *specific, correct,* and *to the point.* If you dress magical actions with flowery words and prolonged, unnecessary sentences the magic will likely fail: there will be no true focus or instruction. Let's have a look at three examples, one flowery and overcooked, one that is straight to the point, and one that is just plain stupid. Let's assume this recitation is directed at an angelic being in a direction and that the magician is working on a pattern to create a new pathway for a magical action.

Example one: flowery and overcooked

> Oh wonderful angel of the east whose power is beyond all greatness, how thy great bounty is. I beseech you to offer your power in this endeavour to link forth thy power and greatness into this work; and I command you to flow the threads of power into my hands so that I may open the gateway for the future of this magic for it to be successful.

First, flattery gets you nowhere with angels. You need to be clear and specific so that they know who you are addressing and what you need. The recitation both asks and commands...so which is it to be? The recitation also asks the angel to link power into the work—what part of the work? The whole thing? This specific action?

It also asks the angel to flow power into the hands of the magician so that they may "open a gateway." Now, do you really want all the power of the angel in your hands? Not a great idea. And what gateway do you want opening? And is it not already open?

Nor has the recitation actually told the angel what you are doing and what you want it to do, and the open-ended request for "power in the hands" still does not tell the angel exactly what you are doing.

Let us have a look at version two.

Example two: straight to the point

> Angel of the east, angel of air, I ask for a thread of air power that will carry my words of magic into the south, into the future, to clear blockages in my fate path if it is necessary. I give you my left hand that I may receive that thread of air power. I anchor it in the central flame of the Void, where it will be joined by other elemental threads. And I release the woven pattern into the future in the south.

The first difference is the magician not only specifies the magical direction but also the element from which they wish to obtain a power thread.

The request asks specifically for an angel of air, as the thread worked with is needed to carry the *words* of the ritual and also to initiate the *breath* of that future—birthing it. So the thread that will be handed over will be specifically to carry Utterance within the pattern.

The magician tells the angel what they are trying to achieve, and also specifies that it is only for if it is really necessary: sometimes a blockage is there for a real purpose that will ultimately help you. The angel is far more able to assess what is needful and what is not from their standpoint than you are from yours.

The magician then specifies with which hand they are working (left, future) and that they want only a *thread* of power to weave with, not the whole body of power that the angel carries—you don't use a nuclear bomb to crack a nut.

Then it is stated where the thread is going and what will happen to it: it will be anchored in the central flame of the Void, woven in with other threads, then released into the south. This tells the angel how much power the thread needs, and that it should also be compatible with other elemental threads.

Knowing that it will go in the central flame also tells the angel that you are submitting to the powers of creation, so you are working within a stream of power with which they are compatible, and one with which you are less likely hurt yourself. This in turn allows the angel to put as much power as necessary into the thread to achieve the end goal without you blowing yourself up.

The end result will be that the angel indeed hands you a thread full of air power, one which will safely and effectively carry the Utterance of the magical pattern into the future and birth it. Everyone is clear on what they are doing, there is minimum control on the part of the magician, and the angel is free to give you what you need, including things/energy you had not thought of. The magic will work in harmony with the fate patterns around it as well as the fate pattern it is to be inserted into.

Example three: the really stupid version

> I call on Raphael, angel of the east, Light Bearer and healer to clear my fate path of obstacles so that I may live in peace, light, and abundance.

Seriously?

For starters the name Raphael is a bit problematical in magic: it has been very badly misunderstood, misappropriated, and misrepresented over time.

Many people seem to think that Raphael is mentioned in the Torah and is an ancient name for the angel (i.e. 1500 B.C. or older). Wrong. The name Raphael does not appear anywhere in the Torah; rather it began to appear during the period of 200 B.C. to A.D. 600, scattered in a small section of apocryphal and prose texts. It is now thought by scholars to have seeped into the texts via Babylonian influence, but the foundations for the use of this name are shaky. When we look at the tales that outline this angel's actions, then look at the name's meaning in Hebrew, we immediately start seeing a total disconnect, probably due to a scholar. Once a mistake or new thing is introduced, it spirals slowly out of control.

Where Raphael is mentioned (in apocryphal texts) this angel's power is exhibited as one that *binds and releases*:

> And again the Lord said to Raphael: "Bind Azazel hand and foot, and cast him into the darkness…"
>
> —*Enoch* 10:6

In *Tobit* 3:17 Raphael binds a demon and restores sight. The book of Tobit is not a mystical account of occurrences; it is a fictional story that is meant to teach by example. Similarly Raphael does not appear in the Quran, but does appear in the Hadith as Israfil, where he blows the horn for Judgement Day.

None of these actions have any bearing on magic connected to direct healing, nor to fate patterns—so why use it in fate magic? This is a good example of someone somewhere attributing a name to a nameless angel/s and everyone subsequently running with it. The action of the angel who has been named Raphael is one of *withholding and binding*. Similarly the mentions of healing in the text are ones of *binding to restore*, not directly to heal.

The Torah does not mention angelic names for a reason: they do not *have* names, they have functions. Humans make up names for angels, and by doing so begin to limit the interface with the angel. Working with angels in specific reference to element, land, or function is usually far more efficient.

The next issue with the silly invocation is the use of the name *Light Bearer* which is a totally different type of angelic being again. Then we get to the "please do this for me" mentality. The words ask the angel to clear obstacles in the fate path so that everything will be happy, abundant, and peaceful. Good luck with that one.

The magical clearing of obstacles should only be done if the person has done everything in their power to move forward and yet still cannot; or if they have been magically locked down by an attack.

Life is one continuous job of overcoming obstacles, learning new skills, and developing: there is no such thing as peaceful, happy stasis for anyone who wishes to progress in anything. If you are not prepared to do everything you can in an outer sense before trying magic, you will get no inner response. And you will certainly not get any inner response from a "please do this for me" or a "love and light" attitude.

So how you use your words, what is behind those words, and why the appeal is there is as important as knowing who you are addressing, what they do, and why they do it. And once these techniques have been mastered with the inner connection, the magician also has to be careful how they use their everyday voice, as the two become fused: the saying "words have power" takes on a wholly different meaning.

5.9 Reading ancient texts out loud

The development of the voice in magic when used with inner power and vision becomes a very powerful tool. This tool can be used to recite ancient and sacred texts out loud which, if it is the right text spoken for the right reasons, opens many gates and brings power in.

Some ancient and sacred texts tell you something, some record events, and some mirror the voices of the deities.

When the texts which are the words of the deity are spoken in power with deep inner connection, it brings the power of that deity into the space and triggers that power into action. This deity utterance can be spoken to bring the deity into the ritual, or it can be used to trigger nature, which is its most powerful application.

The mistake that magicians make when uttering the words of the deity is connecting with those words as if they were their own. This triggers the 'god complex' in humans and often the magician begins to spin out on a power trip and believe themselves to be a god. This is an ego trap that wraps the magician up in their own minds and shuts their power down. However if such recitation is used to *give voice to the gods,* the magician becomes a mediator of the deity power and allows the deity to spring to life through the voice of the magician.

Recitations of deities come in two forms: *composed* by man, and *written down* by man—two very different things. These recitations can come from various sources and when looking at ancient text it can be hard to figure out which is which: the golden test is to recite them magically while standing in a flow of magical power.

Some of the recitations were written down by people who just made them up in the hope of flattering the deity, or in order to manipulate the priesthood or a community. Others wrote them down in inspiration, and these utterances can be a mixture of deity and human: the deity power inspires the writer, but the writer gets in the way of the deity who is announcing and instead fills in their own words and meanings.

Then there are writers who 'hear', and write what they 'hear.' This too can get sticky depending on who they are and what system they are operating...not to mention 'who' is actually talking to them.

Some writers who are unbalanced or who do not operate within a balanced system sometimes get a parasite or low-level being trying to talk through them. Other writers who are balanced but are not operating within any system hear the words of a being that touches them deeply: that is often a deity or angelic recitation. Then there are those who are balanced and working within a balanced system, and words just stream through them.

There are many variables and just because a text sounds like a deity talking does not necessarily mean that it is so. It takes discernment to tell the difference. It often takes years of working in the inner worlds before one can tell the difference between an invalid voice and a valid one.

Angels and deities talking through humans is as old as humanity itself, and once you have touched on a true recitation you will realise it has a certain 'feel' to it, along with what is actually said.

More recently 'channeling' has become a fashion in the West. This is basically a combination of people who are unbalanced, people wanting attention, people listening to parasites, and so forth. I have yet to come across anything truly meaningful from the voice of a 'deity' or 'angelic being' talking through a channeller.

Sometimes you will come across a writer who is writing text about something and dropped right in the middle of the writer's text will be a deity or angelic being speaking through the person. Once you have fully experienced reciting a sacred deity or Divine Utterance, you will spot these inadvertent mediations straight away: they have a certain feel to them. Poets were often gateways for these deity voices, and throughout history there are some very powerful poems with a couple of stanzas in them that is the voice of an inner being, deity, or angelic being.

Getting to the stage where you can spot—and understand—such recitation is akin to learning literature. As the student delves deeper into the subject, they slowly learn to discern what 'good' literature is and is not, above and beyond personal taste.

5.10 Use of voice to instruct the elements

This is really an adept skill that we will work with later in the course, and it takes a long time to learn. Not all magical adepts can grasp this skill, which ultimately comes down to them misunderstanding creation and/or the flow and power of the elements.

In history we can spot when this type of magic is used; both when it worked and when it did not.

Because of the advanced nature of this technique you began the first steps of it in your apprentice training. You will continue to take small steps until you are ready to engage it fully and truly start to learn how moving and affecting the elements forms part of your work as an adept.

You will begin to notice that certain core skills (not techniques) in magic have to be developed over time and with practice. These core skills have many different outer applications, but they track back to the same foundation.

When the voice is used to affect an element[6] a series of skills come together to effect change. It is not only a matter of skills, but how, why, and where they are used. No amount of reciting spells from a grimoire will effect serious change or have any powerful effect because the words themselves have no effect or meaning if they do not come from a place of balance, understanding, and inner power.

When a magician utters to the elements it must be for a really good reason and be done in the full flow of the power of creation. It becomes a mediated utterance that mimics the flow of creation from the Word/sound/breath to the substance itself. Such utterance is used to calm, put to sleep, wake up, or focus or direct an element to a specific level of power and expression.

Really bad reasons for doing such a thing would be things like: "to brighten up the weather for our outdoor ritual," "to flare up fire to attack someone who slighted me," "to show off to gain something," "to use earth to attack someone," or "to alter a course of destiny that has a long-term purpose." Silly, childish magic has no place in the life of a true magician.

When you first started this course you learned to *talk to* everything and to work with rocks, water, the wind, and fire. This progresses in the initiates training with learning to *listen to, converse with,* and *observe* the elements around you.

Learning first to understand the elements before you start directly to affect them and

work with them is a major key to this work. Understanding the elements is not about theoretical thinking, philosophising, or knowing what they look like under a microscope. It is about knowing if a rock wants moving or not, or if a storm is angry or just doing its own thing. It is about knowing what inner power fuels or dampens a fire, what the mood of a river is, what the needs of the springs are, and how to listen to the ocean.

The consciousness of a rock is much quieter and less powerful than the consciousness of a mountain, and some mountains are more powerful than others. How do we know? By listening to them, visiting them, and paying attention. How do they speak? By resonance, and sometimes through other beings who mediate their power.

Resonance is a magical dynamic that flows through virtually everything: as one thing vibrates at a certain frequency it can cause things around it to vibrate at the same frequency. Some objects, elements, and living beings are more sensitive and responsive to the shift in vibration than others. Humans have the innate ability to pick up on such shifts, but it is a *latent* ability that in most people has to be worked on and developed.

That work starts with first communicating, which creates a bridge for communication. You have already done this.

The next step is listening. You do not listen with your ears but with your inner senses: you look for subtle shifts in sensations, emotions, subtle bodily reactions, and so forth.

If a storm is aggressive you will feel it as fear—which is not the same as feeling afraid of the storm—or anger, or that something is 'off balance.' If a stone needs moving you will feel it as you walk past the stone. Sometimes, if you are lucky, a being or beings will be connected to an elemental expression and will mediate communication between you and the element.

This is recognisable when an element speaks directly to you: you hear it in your mind but you know it is not you. The being or beings translate the communication between the element and yourself. When they commu-

---

[6]Wind, storm, water, fire, and earth.

nicate this way it is usually for a very good reason, and they often need something from you or need you to do something.

In the earlier part of your training I talked about going out and talking to the storms. The next step is going out and *listening* to the storms, hearing that communication through your inner senses and your body.

When you visit rivers, mountains, springs, volcanoes, or fires, and during storms, stop what you are doing and sit quietly in their presence. Do not try to force a communication and do not try too hard to be still. Just shut up and sit down. How do you feel? Have your moods shifted? Do you feel 'lit up' or heavy? Do not try to interpret; just listen, feel, and respond.

When you connect strongly with an element in nature that is resonating harmony, your whole inner self lights up and shines. When you strongly connect with an element that is out of harmony, is hostile, in need, suffering, or is trying to warn you about something, you will feel unbalanced, *as if something were wrong*.

This subtle communication through resonance is a major skill and a gift to the magician if they can develop it. The strength of this communication grows to be the greatest tool the magician has, as it needs nothing but yourself to work.

It has saved my life more times than I can count, and has helped me tune deeper and deeper into the elements around me. Divinity talks through nature, and we answer back with our inner and outer voices. The more we practice listening and talking back to the elements, the more the skill of utterance to the elements develops.

A baby learns a single word, and from there begins to learn to the skill of the spoken word. It is the same with this skill: it starts simply with practising words and sounds, then when the inner beings around the elements pick up on the magician using utterance they begin to talk back, at first quietly, then eventually loudly and clear.

This skill can also be used to connect with your ancestral blood lines—even if you do not know who they are. Call out to them and then listen, and keep trying until you get a response. This is the next step on from opening the north gate and connecting with your ancestors and the ancestors of the land where you live.

5.11 *Task:* Uttering

You are going to start the process of magical bridging through Utterance by working with a small section of the *Trimorphic Protennoia*. This is the voice of a deep power of the Divine Breath that utters into the act of creation, and exclaims the Divinity within everything.

Exercise one

Prepare for this work by not speaking at all in the hours leading up to it: do not use your voice. If you have a life where you have to begin speaking from the start of the day,d[7] then do this in the middle of the night or very early in the morning. Before you start, ensure that you know the recitation below by heart so that you do not need to look at a page. You can only bridge this if the words are embedded in your mind and memory.

Set up your work space, light the lights, and open the gates. Sit before the central altar facing south and meditate into stillness.

When you are still, go into the Library, into the stone temple, and see yourself sitting in the centre of the temple while still being aware of being in your work room. When you have the two rooms fused together in your mind, stand up and open your eyes while keeping the sense of the stone temple.

Do the Anchor ritual to tune everything in.

When you have finished stand with your eyes open but your mind in vision standing in the stone temple. See the angel, the companion, come from the south and stand in the south to witness your recitation. Feel the powers of the Light Bearer behind your

---

[7]Children, job, etc.

left shoulder, and the darkness, the power of Restriction, behind your right shoulder.

Hold out your arms to the sides and be aware of the ancestors, the stone from the depths of the Underworld and the goddess power behind you.

Now utter:

"I am the Invisible One within the All. It is I who counsel those who are hidden, since I know the All that exists in it. I am numberless beyond everyone. I am immeasurable, ineffable, yet whenever I wish, I shall reveal myself of my own accord. I am the head of the All. I exist before the All, and I am the All, since I exist in everyone.

I am a Voice speaking softly. I exist from the first. I dwell within the Silence that surrounds every one of them. And it is the hidden Voice that dwells within me, within the incomprehensible, immeasurable Thought, within the immeasurable Silence."

Ensure as you utter that you are clear that you are not saying this from yourself; rather you give the words and your voice as a bridge for that deep power to express through you. You may hear many inner voices uttering with you as you recite.

When you have finished sit down and close your eyes. Be aware of yourself in the stone temple. Simply sit and be in that space in silence and stillness. When you are ready do not see yourself in vision leaving the stone temple; simply open your eyes. You are strengthening the process of the outer and inner temple beginning to fuse themselves together.

Exercise two

Find a couple of hours in a day when you can go out into nature, by a river, in a forest, on a hill, or in the desert, away from people and towns.

Spend some time just wandering about and connecting with everything around you. When you feel your frequency change from the city to the natural land, sit down and meditate for a while in stillness.

When you are ready take your shoes off so that your feet are in direct contact with the land. If a wind is blowing, turn so that it blows from behind you.

Now recite the same recitation, slowly, and hold the sense that you are allowing the power of creation to use your voice to speak through you. Speak it to the rocks and trees, to any creatures: direct the voice to everything around you rather than just speaking it out.

When you have finished kneel down and place your forehead to the ground: let your mind and the land be one. Feel yourself flow into the land through your mind. Feel a sense of spreading out into the land, and feel the land flowing into you through your mind. Stay like that until the feeling withdraws, then stand, take a deep breath, and breathe out to the wind. As you breathe out be aware of the air around you as a consciousness: breathe into it. As you inhale be aware of the air's consciousness flowing into you and exploring you.

When you have finished, just spend more time exploring the land, watching the birds, laying on a rock or the ground, communing with a tree, or sitting by a river/lake/stream. Just be there. This is a preparation for working with the deities within the land, something you will start to do as a defined regular contact, in the practical work of Module five.

This recitation can be worked with in different places, which will give you different responses. A strong power spot out in nature will respond in a particular way either straight away, within a few hours, or at the most after twenty-four hours. A nature spot with no particularly focused power behind it will just feel good when you have done it.

This is one way of identifying real power spots in nature. Because the recitation is of the voice of creation, it will not jar any power there or insult anything, and if there is any real focus of power in the spot it will trigger a response.

You can also experiment with fusing the action of your recitation in nature and the stone temple: see yourself in the stone temple while out in nature. This will possibly elicit a different type of response. Responses from nature can vary from a creature's sudden visit to a storm or strong wind answering you: just pay attention and watch that space!

5.12 *Task:* Mediating the breath

Set up your work room, light the lights, open the gates, and do the Anchor to tune everything. Sit down and meditate.

When you are ready close your eyes and see yourself[8] in the stone temple with the angelic powers around you. Be aware of the stone deep in the Underworld, of the stars above you, and of the goddess power behind you. Be aware of the black and white path going into the south and the sun and stars beyond.

Stand up. Take a deep breath, hold out your left hand before you, palm up, as if you were going to blow something off your hand, and slowly breathe over your hand as if sending it into the south. As you breathe out, see in your mind the power behind you breathing through you. As you breathe back in, sense a gathering of power behind you. As you breathe out again, feel that power flow through you and release through your breath.

Now sit down and close your eyes. In vision, see yourself stand up and repeat the same thing, but as if you are watching yourself in the breathing you have just done: you are observing an immediate past action being replayed. See what is behind you, and look at the breath as it flows through you and how the south reacts to the breath.

When you have finished open your eyes and stand up. Now go to the east, and breathe (left

---

[8]Rather than going there in vision.

hand guiding the breath) into the direction over the flame.

When your breath has finished, say:

"I greet you, winds of the east."

Repeat this for the other directions. When you have finished, if you are not planning to do anything else in your ritual space, close the directions down and open a window to let the air in. Again, this is preparation for work that you will move on to in module five. Greeting the four winds will slowly prepare you for working directly with them.

Practice this a few times in your ritual space as you move on with the course: it takes practice to learn how to connect with the powers and the four winds.

You can also do this out in nature, and it can be powerful once you have built it up. Experiment with it and bear in mind that all you are doing is opening the gateway within yourself for the breath to flow through; and also you are making friends with the four winds.

The stage of greeting the four winds is the second stage of the work you did in your apprentice training when you learned how to connect with the four winds. You are at the stage of polite greetings as well as your breath. Soon you will work to meet and work with the deities and beings that are the consciousness of the four winds.

A note about the breath

The breath holds many different powers besides keeping you alive and giving you a voice. It also carries a great deal of information about you: you flow through your breath. When making friends with animals, trees, rocks, the wind, and the water, breathing gently to them is nature's way of introductions. Experiment with it. Experiment with just using your breath and breathing with the power flowing through you.

5.13 *Task:* Documenting your work

Write up any notes you have from these exercises and experiments, and keep them in a computer file.

5.14 The Cosmology of Neith

THE STORY OF THE CREATION

Before the Creation: The Birth of Neit.

The Father of Fathers, the Mother of Mothers, the Divine Being who was before all beginnings, She was found within the womb of the First Waters, She came into existence out of Herself, appearing unchanging, She reared up while the Earth was non-existent, while all the earth was still in darkness. It had not yet appeared, there was no growth, no plants, no living thing:

Her First Metamorphosis:

She took the form of a Cow, this Divine Being who was still unknown, whose power was still unknown, She then took the form of the Lates-fish and made Her way through the waters:

The Light:

She opened Her eyes, and they were radiant, and the first light came into existence:

The Primeval Hill:

She spoke then:

"This place where I am shall become an earthen hill within the First Waters, it will be a support for all the powers":

And that place where Neit spoke became the Place within the First Waters, that place became Ta-Senet, the Land of the Waters, and also Sau. The Word of Neit took flight from that which had emerged and with that Per-Neter and Buto came into being also:

She spoke again:

"I spoke well on that which emerged":

In this way did Dep become, as well as all the Earth of Good Being in its name of Sau:

The Creation of Khemet:

All things that Her heart conceived of, were realised immediately. In this way She created Khemet in joy:

The Creation of the Thirty Gods:

She created the Thirty Gods by pronouncing their Names one by one, and joy was known after She had spoken:

The Gods spoke:

"Hail to You Mistress of the Divine Beings, Our Mother who brought us into existence, You made all our Names then, when we were not conscious. You have divided for us the white dawn from the night, You have made for us the ground on which our power rests. You have separated for us the night and the day. All this effectively came from Your heart O You the Unique One, who came into existence at the beginning. Eternity passes before Your face!":

The Gods settle on the Revealed Earth:

She spoke then to Her children:

"Reach up now, rise up upon this place, it is the ground upon which we lean, so that your weariness is chased away. We return through the waters to this place, Ta-Senet and Sau. This Earth in the Womb of the First Waters, this emergence of Good-being upon which we settle!":

And She revealed an earthen hill in the Womb of the First waters, to which She gave the name of 'High Earth':

The Gods become worried about the future:

They then spoke to the Great and Powerful:

"O You, whose children we are, O You from whom we issued, we dreamt that we are still not fully born and we are ignorant of those who will be born next":

She spoke again:

"I shall inform you all of your births and your natures, for my intentions are generous. I gave you form in the stuff that fills your stomachs, formulating the words that appear on your lips, of the kind you know, the same today":

They understood all that She had said in the space of an instant:

The Announcement of the Sun:

The Cow Ahet put Herself into meditation and the One She Nursed appeared:

She spoke again:

"A Sacred God is going to be born today. When He opens his eyes the light will be made, when He closes them darkness will be created. Humanity will be born from the tears of His eyes, and the Gods shall emerge from the saliva of His lips. My strength will be His strength, My effectiveness will be His effectiveness, My vigour shall be His also. His children will rebel against Him but he shall cut them all down in His Name, He shall strike in His Name, because He is My son who issues from My flesh. He will be king of these lands forever. My arms make protection and no evil power shall affect Me. I go to speak His Name, who is Khephera in the morning and Atum in the evening. He will be the Radiant God for all eternity, in this his Name of Ra, each day":

The Ogdoad:

Then these Gods spoke:

"We have agreed that You evoke here things of which we are ignorant":

Thus 'Khemnu' distinguished the Names of these Gods and also the name of their City:

The Birth of the Sun:

Then this God was born from the excretions of the Body of Neit. She placed Him within an egg which was created within the First Waters. This was the origin of the Rising of the Waters and was the Unique Place of the Seed Fall. The God then broke the shell which He found around Himself:

This Sacred God, this being Ra. His being was also concealed within the First Waters in this His name of Amun the Ancient, and who was formed before all the Neter by His rays, in this His Name of Khnum:

Mother and Son:

His Mother, the Cow Goddess, called in great shouts:

"Welcome, welcome, You whom I have created! Welcome, welcome, You whom I have brought into the world. Welcome. welcome, You to whom I have given Life. I am Your Mother, the Cow Ahet!":

Then this God came happily, His arms open for this Goddess, He threw them around Her neck and embraced Her, for this is a good way for a son to act when He sees His mother. And in this way, this day became 'The Beautiful Day of the Beginning of the Year":

Then His Mother went away from Him and He cried in the First Waters because He could no longer see His Mother the Cow Ahet any longer, and Humanity was born from the tears of His eye, and the Gods were born from the saliva of His lips:

The Ancestral Gods and the Sun:

The Ancestral Gods now rested in their shrines. They were spoken into being, this Goddess had their conception in Her mind and She created as She travelled. These Gods now protected Ra inside the Cabin of the Solar Barque, and they acclaimed this God saying:

"Welcome, welcome to You, Discharge of Neit, Work of Her Hands, Creation of Her Heart! You are the King of these lands for eternity, as was predicted by Your Mother!":

The Birth of Apep, the Mind of the Revolt:

Then the Ancestral Gods repelled some spittle from Her mouth which She had produced from Her Womb of the First Waters; it transformed itself into a serpent, one hundred and twenty cubits long, this being named Apep. His heart conceived the revolt against Ra along with his allies who issued from his eye:

The Birth of Tehuti:

Tehuti came forth from the Heart of Ra in a moment of bitterness. He spoke with His Father Ra, who sent Him against the rebels in His Name of Lord of the Word of God. And this was the origin of Tehuti, Lord of Khnemu and of the eight Gods of the First Ancestral Company:

The Departure for Ta-Senet-Sau:

Neit then said to Her Son:

"Come with me to Ta-Senet, that is to say Sau, this earthen hill placed within the Womb of the Primordial

Waters. I shall pronounce Your Name in Your City, and it shall never cease hearing it, day and night. We shall travel together, for Your strength is considerable and the fear of You increases, so that Your power will slaughter the one who hatches plots against You":

The Seven Utterances of Mehurt:

In this way did Seven Utterances come successively from Her mouth. They became seven Divine Beings. She has pronounced the Names of the Ancestral Gods and given them their specific aspects. She has given name to the Word of God and She has Named Sau. These Seven Utterances became the Gods of Mehurt:

The names of these Seven Wise Ones are Nefer-Hati, Aper-Perhui, Neb-Tesheru, Ka, Bak, Khekh and San. They took the form of seven falcons and flew upwards, they assure the protection of Mehurt in all the places where She journeys:

Then in Her form of the Cow Ahet, She placed Ra between her horns and carried Him as She swam. and the Gods said:

"Here is the Great Swimmer with her Son":

And this was the origin of the Name Mehurt:

The Journey of Mehurt:

She passed four months in the Cities of the Southland, called Khent-tu, the Foremost of the Lands, occupied in battling the enemies that arose suddenly with hatred of Her majesty. She became a brilliant flame in Upper and Lower Khemet:

Sau:

When She arrived at Sau on the evening of the Thirteenth of Epiphi,

a great and beautiful feast was made in Heaven, on Earth and in all Lands. She took the form of the Goddess Oureret, the Cow-mother of Ra. She took hold of Her bow in Her hand, Her arrows in Her fist and She settled in the mansion of Neit with Her Son Ra:

The Setting up of the Feast of the Thirteenth of Epiphi:

Ra then spoke. He said to the Gods who were with Him:

"Welcome Neit on this day, come and delight in Her intentions on this beautiful day, because She has brought me here safe and sound":

"Light the torches for Her! Make feast in Her presence until the dawn!":

Translated from French records by Stuart Littlejohn.

Lesson 6

Observing the Inner Desert

You have read a lot about both the inner power dynamics of creation and some of the beings who work in the process of creation. The next step is to look at the inner landscape of the Desert, which is the visionary interface for this, and how this inner place and the creative/destroying powers operate from a magical perspective.

This lesson is a step forward in your visionary work: it gives you a chance to observe these powers in action from a safe distance. Once you have experienced this observation, which changes you at a deep level, then in the next lesson you will externalise that resonance in ritual work.

In your apprentice training you started the basic understanding of creation and learned to cross the threshold into the nearest part of the Inner Desert, and also met the companion.[1] In this lesson you will look deeper into the Desert, watch some of the powers at work, and understand what you are looking at.

Before we get to the practical work I want to give you a bit more information about what is there, why it is there, and what it is doing. This way when you go there you will better understand what you are watching.

6.1 The Inner Desert

You have already learned some basics about the Inner Desert. Many people ask why it appears as a desert. This interface appears to us as a desert because *no life grows there*. It is pre-life, an inner condition from which everything comes, but in which nothing actually lives in the sense of physical manifestation.

Things that are going to manifest appear here, as well as things that are withdrawing from manifestation. It is like a highway of action and also a place of 'pending,' be that creation or destruction.

When you watch a power preparing to manifest into the physical world, how it appears largely depends on what is going to manifest. There is a constant low-level traffic in the Inner Desert of things going into life and things withdrawing from life. Often this is not noticed by the magician as it is a constant action that should not be interfered with, and as such it does not generally appear to the magician.

When something is manifesting or preparing to manifest that will change the world in a major way, then it tends to appear to the magician in the Desert. Observing it gives the magician a heads up that something is brewing and that they may need to take some form of action.

The more the magician tunes into the

---

[1] Sandalphon.

Desert, the more its resonance vibrates within them. When something is brewing that could be dangerous we feel the shift in the Desert's vibration, which is a prompt for us to take action. That action could be as simple as going and observing in the Inner Desert, or it could indicate that direct work is needed.

Sometimes when the magician picks up on such a shift they also get a strong feeling to stay away from the Inner Desert. This is often a sign that a destructive pulse is brewing in the Desert. Unless the magician has a direct role in that destruction it is best that they stay out of the way and not become energetically connected with it. At times I have been told by inner contacts, deities, and my inner senses to stay the hell away from the Inner Desert, often for a year at a time, while something massive brews and then outs itself.

By being there and observing or acting you automatically become part of the process: you begin to resonate at the same frequency. Sometimes that is necessary—for example if you will have a magical job to do once the destruction expresses itself. If this is the case then you will be strongly pulled to at least witness the power as it rumbles out into the world. By watching, you change things.

This is a strong inner dynamic in magic in the inner worlds: you change a power's expression by the nature of your observation, and the observation also changes you. It is always a two-way street. Once you step into that observation you become part of the pattern either as an observer bringing something to the table or by nature of your magical work.

Sometimes you bring a counterpoint to the dynamic: the magician may bring the counterbalance of creation to a pulse of destruction building up in the Inner Desert. Just always understand that each time you go to watch the dynamics of action in the Inner Desert you change things simply by watching, and any energy that you bring with you should not be a conscious decision: it just 'is' whatever it needs to be.

It is for this reason that the Inner Desert should only be entered for a reason, and not out of 'magical tourism.' You and the power of change become interlinked and while that might sound a bit alarming, it's not really. The same dynamic runs through all magic and all life. The energy, vibration, and resonance that is you is constantly interacting with your surroundings, and those interactions trigger change to everything, including you.

This is why at certain times in the living world an adept simply has to show up and be somewhere—and that's it. Just being in that space and being present within themselves will trigger change if it is needed: an adept is essentially a *catalyst*. This dynamic is heavily woven into fate patterns too, which lead a person to certain critical points in their life where the catalyst of change leaps into action.

6.2 Learning from observing

Besides triggering the change dynamic, observing in the Desert can teach you a great deal about the powers of angelic beings and deities, not only by watching what they do, but also by how they present in the Desert.

When you watch the presentation in the Desert you also need to know what that presentation means for us as humans. Sometimes this knowledge is already within us from previous study, and sometimes we have to go away and look at very ancient texts—usually the best source for imagery in the Inner Desert—until we spot what we saw.

Once, for example, I began seeing huge firestorms in the Inner Desert. At one point a vast humanoid being strode through the fire and seemed to gather its energy with him as he strode towards the threshold of the manifest world. His long red hair trailed behind him and lightning struck all around him. "Uh-oh," was my initial reaction, "this does not look good."

Shortly after seeing the fire build up in the Inner Desert and pass over the threshold, all hell broke loose in the Near and Middle East.[2]

---

[2]When you see something very powerful building up

The imagery associated with the giant red-haired being was clear enough for me to go away and look it up. At the same time other magical adepts from around the world were contacting me after having the same experience in the Inner Desert. At that point I realised something major was preparing to out itself, and I still could not figure out what it was.

After some digging and research I realised that I had been dumb and the explanation had been staring me in the face all along. The firestorm was a power that the ancient Egyptians called Set: the Egyptian god of storms, the desert, turmoil, and conflict.[3]

For a clear understanding of Set we have to look at Old Kingdom Egyptian texts. This deity went through various relationships with the Egyptians, and through various foreign interventions he was morphed into the evil 'devil' destroyer to be shunned. More and more negative connotations were heaped upon him as the Egyptians shifted and changed in their understanding, particularly through the influences of the Hyksos invaders (1650-1550 B.C.) and later the Greeks. Set became the epitome of destruction, chaos, and evil.

Peeling back those layers of progressive propaganda and fear, we come to a far more accurate picture of a natural power that can be observed in action in the inner worlds. The power of Set is one of fire, heat, storms, necessary destruction, illness, and rage.[4]

He is also a deity connected with the *Ladder*, an inner concept from the Old Kingdom Pyramid texts. And I know this is a bit of a diversion, but it is an important one. Here is a section of a funerary text from the Pyramid of Unis from the north wall of the antechamber:

210 RECITATION. A ladder has been tied together by the Sun in front of Osiris, a ladder has been tied together

by Horus in front of his father Osiris when he went to his akh, one of them on one side and one of them on the other. Now Unis is between them.

"Are you a god of clean places?" (they ask). He has come from a clean place.

"Stand up, Unis," says Horus; "sit down, Unis," says Seth; "receive his arm," says the Sun.

And on the south wall it says:

178 RECITATION.

…

Stand up, you two uprights, and descend, you crossbars, that Unis may go up on the ladder that his father the Sun has made for him.

Horus and Seth shall take the arm of Unis and take him away from the Duat.[5]

What the Egyptians describe as a Divine Ladder is a phenomenon mentioned in a few different ancient texts, and is something that can also be observed in vision and in dreams.

When I first saw it in my dreams I was not sure what I was seeing. It took a while for me to connect the dots. I saw it as a huge wheel that churned the earth, a wheel of light and fire,[6] and out of the churning appeared a stairway reaching into the stars. People were getting on the stairway and some were being picked off and would fall from it.

It is also mentioned in Plato's *Republic* in *The Vision of Ayr the Armenian*, and it is the same thing as *Jacob's Ladder*: an angelic passage from the earth to the stars. You have already looked at these things in the apprentice section, and the involvement of Set with the Ladder[7] tells us that Set is a power of *necessary destruction* such as death.

---

in the Inner Desert, you can often see what the build-up was about if you watch world news carefully.

[3]Interesting that the chaos in the Middle East is being caused by a group that the West has named 'Isis': look up the connection between the Black Isis and Set.

[4]He also fights the true protagonist of chaos, Apep.

[5]*The Ancient Egyptian Pyramid Texts*, James P. Allen, 2005.

[6]An angelic being.

[7]It is sometimes called the Ladder of Set in funerary texts.

Your apprentice work to do with destruction and death should have informed you that Set is a being who brings destruction by fire, storm, and disease; but that this is part of the order of creation and destruction—his power maintains balance (Ma'at) and is not a power of true chaos (Apep).

This in turn should inform you about the beings that will appear in the Desert. When you see a destroying or demonic type being in the Inner Desert, *there is a good reason why it is there.* This slowly teaches the magician not to fear such destruction, nor think of it as 'evil,' or as a glamorous power: it is simply part of the overall order that keeps the wheels of existence turning.

So let us get back to the Inner Desert.

When you observe something in the Inner Desert, think back to what you have learned about the various powers that operate in creation: the dynamics of the Light Bearer, Restriction, the Grindstone, the Unraveller, Pure Balance, and the Threshold Guardian, the threshold between the Inner Desert and the manifest world. Knowing what all these angelic powers do informs you about the powers constantly in motion and opposition as they work in this deep place. When you observe something in the Inner Desert these powers are in action, and so whatever you see is being created for a good reason.

You will, when you are ready, stand in the power of the Inner Desert with all these powers around you and revisit your path into this life. This is the best way to truly understand how these powers work. So let us get on to the practical work, which for the most part is visionary work for this lesson.

6.3 *Task:* **The vision of observance—the Inner Desert**

The Inner Desert is a truly powerful place and because of that you will get used to it in small steps. This way its power cannot unsettle or unduly affect you—it can really impact your body if you are not used to it. This approach also helps the beings of the Inner Desert get used to you so that you are not aggressively challenged or attacked by its guardians.

When I used to teach group sessions I would take people to this place, and because I carried them over the threshold the guardians did not react to the new people. However once I wrote the same vision down in text and people did it by themselves, I found that many of them were challenged aggressively by the host of guardians who act as gatekeepers between humanity and this inner place. It had not occurred to me that this would happen. After I was contacted by a few magicians who had been physically injured, I learned from bitter experience to step people slowly into this place. Not everyone gets attacked when they are a new face in the Desert, but still I would rather you did this properly and forge strong, lasting bonds with this place.

Once the Desert and its guardians are used to you, there will be no problem unless you stomp in with a stupid agenda, in which case they will attack you. You have already stepped into the threshold of the Inner Desert and met the Companion, the Sandalphon, who guides and advises humans when they work in this place. Now we will take it a step further in a vision that will adjust you and the Desert to each other.

Set up your work room, light the lights, open the gates, and go round the directions a couple of times to tune the room in.

When you are ready, sit down before the east altar and go into the Inner Library. Take your time with this as you are approaching a new, powerful place: you want to stretch out slowly to deepen the vision. You will go through the east threshold. This means that you will approach the Inner Desert through learning and temple structure.

Once you are in the Inner Library tell the librarian you are going to take your first steps into the Inner Desert in order to learn. The librarian may or may not hand you a coat, robe, or some sort of covering; it all depends on the energetic weather in the Desert. If they do, take note of it and what it could protect you from.[8]

The librarian then points to two huge bronze doors that you may not have noticed before: the main entrance to the Inner Library.

As you stand before the huge ceremonial doors you realise that one has a smaller, more manageable door you can open by yourself. Pull on it hard and it will open slowly. Step through the door and you will find yourself immediately bathed in strong sunlight and the scent of the Desert.

You find yourself standing atop a massive step pyramid. The flat and lifeless Desert is laid out around you for as far as you can see. As you look back and up, you will see that the Library is a square stone building sitting on top of the step pyramid, and a flat walkway goes all round the Library building. In front of the bronze doors is a vast flight of stone steps that leads down to the Desert floor.

Walk round the Library building first so that you can get a good look at the Desert from every angle. Start by going to the right of the doors.[9] At each platform/side of the square building, stop and look out.

On the first side, look to the right in the distance. If you look carefully you will see a vast crack in the earth like a massive narrow canyon: this is the Abyss. Beyond the canyon on the other side are mists or a sandstorm: it is obscured from your vision. That is the realm of Divinity.

Now look left. In the far distance you will see a haze of mists. Beyond the mists is a river, and beyond the river is a huge range of mountains: this is the realm of death. The river is the same river that emerges from the Underworld and the Underworld Forest. The mists obscure the Garden—the manifest world.

Walk to the next side of the building, keeping to your right, and you may get a better view of the Abyss. Now move on again, still keeping right. You will see various temples and ancient buildings half-buried in the sand. These are the inner temples, some of

which will be sleeping. Move on again until you are back in front of the bronze doors.

Position yourself to the right of the bronze doors and as close to the platform's edge as you dare, and sit down. Just look around you—and look carefully. You may see in the distance bumps in the sand or things sticking up out of it: these are beings held in restriction until the time comes for them to release. Just spend some time, however long you can hold the vision for, looking and watching what happens.

When you have finished watching, get up and climb down the stone steps to the desert floor. When you reach the bottom you will hear a sound, and when you look you will see a small child sat at the bottom of the stairs. Do not be fooled: this is no defenceless child. It is a root power—of what, you can work out for yourself. Greet the child and tell them who you are, what you are doing, and where you come from.

If the child puts their hand out to you with an open palm, put your hand in your pocket and give them whatever appears in your hand without question. If it is something you recognise from your life, you must let it go when you come out of vision, whatever it is: you are paying your dues for your life.

If the child takes your hand and guides you somewhere, let them take you wherever they want. Simply observe. If they do not, simply sit down and answer any questions they have. At this stage don't ask them any questions; just be in their presence.

When it is time for the encounter to finish you will feel a hand on your shoulder. As you turn you will see the Companion at your shoulder. They motion for you to climb back up the steps. They will walk with you and may hold your hand, your shoulder, or simply walk alongside you.

If they stop on a step, still yourself and feel into the step's energy. Memories may come into your mind of something in your past. The angel is pointing out to you the various stages of your life that have brought you to this point.

---

[8] Water, fire, sandstorms.
[9] Out the bronze doors, turn right.

Various points or events in your life prepared you to step on a particular step in this stairway.

When you reach the top turn to the Companion, bow, and say thank you. He will go no further, and you must go back through the bronze door. As you enter the Inner Library a librarian will be waiting for you. Before you can speak to them they push a book into you, something that will guide you and teach you about the Inner Desert. Thank them, bow, then go to the part of the Library that leads back to your work space.

When you are back in your work room be still and think about what happened before you open your eyes. When you are ready open your eyes and immediately note down what happened in your journal. Draw anything that stood out in your mind, be it a being, image, or symbol.

When you have finished get up and go round the directions. Thank the contacts on the thresholds, bow, and put out the lights. When you get time, type up your notes into a computer file.

Lesson 7

Ritual Dynamics

This lesson is all practical ritual work. It brings together what you have learned so far and exteriorises it in ritual form. This will show you how these vast powers work at a ground ritual level. You do not need reams of background information—you have just read your way through all that—so we will get straight to the work.

This lesson works with three different ritual techniques. They approach this subject matter from different angles and will teach you more about in-depth ritual power and action. You may recognise some ritual dynamics from other rituals both in this course and in ancient texts.

Bear in mind that for the last few hundred years ritual methods in the West have been very heavily influenced by Christianity. If you wish to see this lesson's ritual dynamics at work in Western texts, you will have to stretch further back in time. Also, if you look at certain ritual practices in various parts of the world and spot these dynamics, you will know they are working magically with these powers, even if they are clothed in a very different vocabulary.

7.1 *Task:* Weaving

This ritual works with a mixture of ritual movement and visionary work, both eyes open and eyes closed.

Set up your work room, put out the tools (putting water in the vessel), light the lights, and open the gates. Do the Anchor ritual.

When you have finished stand in the centre with the altar before you, facing south. Lay the sword on the left side of the central altar and the vessel on the right side. Have the stone shield on the north altar and put your cord round your right wrist.

Light frankincense and go round the directions refreshing the thresholds with the smoke, passing the smoke to either side and over the top of each altar. Also do the cross-quarters.

Place some frankincense oil on your forehead, on the soles of your feet,[1] on the palms of your hands, over your heart, and at the base of the back of your neck.

Now stand and still yourself. When you are still, remember that this work is not something you will have any control over: you are about to work in service in order to learn a technique, weaving something that needs to come into being and then releasing it. You will most likely not know what it is, and if you do figure it out do not focus on it—just do the work and don't let yourself get in the way.

Go round the directions and bow to the contacts on the thresholds, but do not speak. Do not use your physical voice at all. Stand in

---

[1]Have bare feet or just socks on—no shoes.

the presence of each directional contact. Hold the intention in your mind that you are going to learn the art of magical weaving by doing a simple act of weaving service for the inner worlds.

Pay attention to which types of contacts come forward: inner adepts? Angelic beings? Deities? Something else? Each of you will get different contacts: you will be doing work unique to you and your area, so whoever is needed will turn up. Be in their presence silently so you can begin to resonate at the frequency they work from. You will feel a shift between each contact, as they are likely to be very different contacts in each direction.

When you have gone round them all go back to the east and hold your left hand out, palm up.[2] As something is passed to you, you will feel its energy in your hand.

Now hold out your right hand while keeping your left hand out. Whatever is needed to counterbalance the energy in your left hand and give it a completion in time will now be placed in your right hand. When both hands are holding power or energy of some sort, turn and go to the central altar carrying the energy in your hands.

Place your left hand on the sword and your right hand on the vessel. Hold them there. Be aware of the power of the Light Bearer behind your left shoulder and the darkness of Restriction behind your right shoulder.

As soon as you gain that awareness you will become aware that you are also standing in the stone temple room in the Inner Library: you are in two places at once. With that awareness the power levels start slowly to rise: keep the inner vision of the stone temple room while you work.

Focus your awareness on the sword. The energy that was placed in your left hand flows into the sword and awakens it. Now focus your awareness on your left foot, and feel the power of the Grindstone beneath it. The left side of your body will become heavy with power, and you will feel the difference between your left and right sides.

Now focus your awareness on the vessel. Be aware of the energy from your right hand flowing into it. Feel the Threshing Floor under your right foot and be aware of its power. Feel the right side of your body filling with power. Feel the light and dark from behind come through your shoulders and into your hands. This has set the foundation for the weave.

Go back round the directions starting in the east. Putting your left hand out, palm up, ask silently, in vision, for a thread of power to weave with. Take the thread and place it in the air above the central flame. Do the same for each other direction until all four directions have a thread running into the air above the central flame.

Place both your hands[3] in the air above the flame. Begin to weave the threads together into a pattern. Do not try to influence what the pattern will look like: let your hands work instinctively, picking threads with each hand and moving them about so they become interconnected. Take as long as you need.

When you have finished, keeping your eyes open, 'see' with your inner vision a weave pattern hanging in the air over the central flame. Leave it hanging there and pick up the sword. Take it to the south and place it in a 'guard' position by the altar.[4] Now take the vessel and place it on the north altar. The sword guards the future passage; the vessel collects and stores the magic in the past when finished.

Position yourself again before the central altar with the south before you. Close your eyes and look at your hands. Look at the light in your left hand and the dark in your right. Put your hands together so that the light is in the darkness and the darkness is within the light: this creates a particular quality of light that shines.

Using your inner vision and physical movement, see this light build until it stretches past your hands. Once it grows, pull your

---

[2]"Please give me something" position)

[3]Left is filled with light and right is filled with dark.
[4]Handle up, point down, leaning against the altar.

hands apart with the intention of leaving the light in the air. The light will hang in the air between your hands. This is your lantern to light the way of your deeds.

Using your right hand, physically pick up the light like a lantern while still looking at it using inner vision and outer vision. Hold it close to the weave so that it lights the air around it.

As you hold up the light you will notice that it opens the path of the south right up. You will detect this with your inner vision: see the path of the south open brightly and wide, and see beings on the pathway waiting for the weave.

Be still for a moment and be aware of the light/dark in your body, of the lantern, and of the weave. Something will place a hand on each of your shoulders. When you feel this, however faintly, take a deep breath and physically blow into the weave to fill it with your breath. Then take a second one and blow it into the south.

Be aware in your mind of the beings on the path reaching out and taking the weave. With eyes closed, using inner vision, watch them as they take the weave and start to form it into something.

When the beings take up the pattern you will become aware of two streams of energy. One will go through your left side from behind you and flow into the south taking light and energy with it, and the other will come back out of the south, run through you, and flow into the north, a stream that is full of darkness. Two streams, going into the future and composting into the past.

Stand in that two-way stream of energy for however long is necessary until it comes to a stop. Once it stops, it means the pattern has gone into the future, has done what it needed to do, and has been composted in the past. The job is complete.

As far as the light hanging to your right is concerned, the light that is also dark, you have two choices as to what you do with it: you can work with it or dismantle it. It is a lantern that lights your way so that you can see your deeds[5] and also see what you have learned. It illuminates by nature of your acquired wisdom through experience—recognise the imagery of the tarot trump of the Hermit?

If you choose not to dismantle it, it will stay within your sphere. This will help you to not fool yourself and to see your actions, learning, and deeds in a clear light. It will not stay there forever, and how long it stays is very individual.

If you don't wish to have the lantern in your sphere, then physically and in vision place both hands in the light and reabsorb it back into your hands. Once you feel the separation in your hands of the two powers, pull your hands apart.

Before you close down the directions, take the vessel and pour the water from it onto the land outside, or pour it down the sink, to compost it. The vessel must be emptied before you close the directions down. Place the sword and vessel back in their directions,[6] then go round the directions, thank the contacts, bow, and close the gates.

Documenting your work

On computer write down answers to the following questions:

> Why is an equal balance of light and dark the lantern?
>
> Why are there no words in this ritual?

Once you have answered the questions, read up on the tarot trump of the Hermit. If you then, in reflection, wish to add to your answers, do so. Also write up a summary of your experience of doing this visionary ritual work.

7.2 *Task:* Containing

This exercise is visionary but includes ritual actions while maintaining the vision. It is a key action that triggers the process of understanding containment: before you

---

[5]Right/Harvest/Scales.
[6]This resets the default magical pattern of the room.

can truly contain magic and hold it before releasing it, you must understand the actual act of containment in creation—this involves learning about your body as a container for Divine life force. Once this understanding has embedded itself in your subconscious through this action, it will slowly unfold over time in your conscious mind.

We generally think of containment (and binding) in terms of our direct experience in everyday life: putting clothes in a cupboard, food in a dish, and so forth; but it goes much further than that. The true act of containment allows something to exist within defined boundaries, which in turn allows it to express a certain aspect of its true nature. Once this is fully understood you are a step closer to working with the vast powers of creation in magic. The best way to learn this dynamic is through yourself first.

This next piece of work is also the beginning of the road towards the final act of your adept training: standing in the face of destruction. Once the real nature of the vessel is understood, then a vessel can be created, filled or destroyed within causing disharmony in the forces of creation and destruction. And the understanding is not an intellectual or emotional one, it is a deep understanding that is triggered by resonance: it embeds deeply within you and slowly filters its way up into your conscious mind over time.

Set up your work room, light the lights, get out the tools and put them in their directions, put on the cord on your right wrist and then sit down before the central altar facing south.[7] Still yourself and then go into the stone temple of the Inner Library. Go via the long route[8] in order to build up the power.

Once you are in the stone temple, be aware of the light/lantern in your sphere to the right of you. Reach out to it and draw it into your body, into your heart area. See your heart shine with the light of your experiences.

As it shines the Companion steps out of the south and stands before you. Regardless of what clothing your body is wearing, in vision see yourself part your clothing like opening a coat or robe to show the angel the light in your heart. The angel will stand and 'read' the light that is held in your heart. This will show them what your life has been like, what your deeds, learning, and experiences have been up to this point in your life. Stand like this until the angel turns away and starts walking back to the south altar.

Once the angel turns away, physically stand up and open your eyes while maintaining the vision of the stone temple. Walk round the directions from the east in a circle and stop at the north altar. Touch the stone shield on your altar to acknowledge that this is where your body comes from. Now turn and look at the south altar while also holding the vision of the Companion standing in the south. Walk from north to south round the central altar and stand before the south altar.

The road ahead is covered in darkness and all you can see is the Companion. Reach back into your heart and pull out the light of the lantern. Hold it up in your right hand. Also do the action physically, as if collecting something from your heart; and hold up your right arm to hold the lantern. As you do this, in your inner vision, be aware that the light shines into the darkness and lights the way.

Before you is a track through a flat, sandy landscape. Beyond, in the distance, is a mountain with a path leading up into its heights. You may see some movement at the foot of the mountain, but it is obscured. Close your eyes[9] and focus on the lantern. What is held within that light that is knowledge you have acquired, that will allow you to focus. Don't think with your mind; think with your feelings and instincts.

The light begins to shine brighter and the scene before you becomes clearer. Physically and in vision hold the lamp higher in order to see. Take a deep breath, breathe out, and

---

[7]With the altar in front of you—that is the default centre working position.

[8]Don't just see yourself there, go through the Library.

[9]Go into full inner vision.

speak: *I wish to see*. As the light brightens the Companion points to someone walking up the side of the mountain on the path.

At first they have the shape of a human, but the higher they climb the less human-shaped they appear: their boundaries seem to fall away leaving a bright, shining light travelling up the mountain.

The Companion now points to the ground on the road before you. There lies a body, devoid of life: a shell. As you look more closely, you see that it is your body. The shell has been cast off and the brightness that is you is slowly climbing higher and higher to the top of the mountain. As you look back at your body you see that it is dark, lifeless, and already crumbling back into the earth. The light has released from the darkness of life and is returning whence it came.

The Companion motions for you to put the lantern light back into your heart. As you do so, you notice that your body is filled with a very pure light: the lantern's light is a different, duller light than the light of your spirit. The Companion reaches over the threshold and touches you on the forehead, then pushes you back, away from the path. He turns and vanishes into the south. The vista before you vanishes. Open your eyes.

Take a step back and walk round the directions to the east. Stand before the east gate and be still.

Feel the light of your spirit shining, but hidden in the vessel that is your body; and see the duller light of the lantern in your heart. Also see sparks of brightness round your body: the lights of the organ spirits within you. They are contained within your organs, and together they make a vessel that your spirit can be contained in. The lantern's light is the record of your life so far.

Breathe in, drawing air from the east gate. Breath out and say:

> "The breath of life triggers this vessel into life. Thank you for this breath that I breathe."

Bow, and in your mind be truly thankful for the air that you breathe.

Now go to the south and stand before the altar. Look at the flame on the altar and feel the flame within you. Feel the warmth of your body and say to the flame:

> "The fire of life that connects me to this body, thank you for your warmth and energy."

Bow and be thankful for the vital force that flows through you to give your body life.

Step back and go to the west altar. Stand in stillness. Feel the moisture in your mouth and the water that flows in your body. Look to the west gate and say:

> "You have given me water from the well of life, freely, and I thank you for it."

Bow and be aware that without water you would die very quickly.

Step back and go to the north. Place your hands on the stone shield. Be aware of the ancestors at the north gate. Be still. Be aware that the rock in your hands is an aspect of the planet that is your container and that gives you flesh, a home, food, and shelter. This is your mother: keep that awareness and say:

> "Mother, thank you for giving my spirit a home that I may experience this life. Thank you for birthing me, for nurturing me, and for weaving me my life path."

Bow, kneel, and place your forehead to the stone. The stone is the ultimate resting place of the vessel, and your body is your vessel: one day it will be as stone and you, as the bright being you are, will walk away from your vessel, from your body. Stay with this thought for a moment.

When you pull away from the stone you feel as if you have pulled away from a great darkness, a heavy burden that bound your light into substance.

Stand up and turn. Go back to your position before the central altar. Stand in the awareness of your body, of all the beings that make up your body, that house you and give you life in the manifest world.

Cross your arms over your chest, put your head down, and say thank you to your body for carrying you through this life. It is only through your body that you can fully experience the wonder of physical manifestation, and it is only through your physical body that you experience the greatness of the whole of creation around you.

Sit down and close your eyes. Meditate for a short while and think about how you treat your body and how you treat everything around you on a daily basis. Life is short and is full of beauty no matter how hard it is, and through being contained in your vessel, your body, your spirit works under the pressure of the Grindstone in order to be polished.

When you are ready close the directions down and put things away. Spend some time thinking about how precious life is and yet how hard it is to be contained, and what this containment means in terms of learning versus freedom. Every time you create a vessel magically, every time you limit and contain something, no matter what it is, it experiences at some level that same feeling of restriction and also expression. Remember that.

7.3 *Task:* **The Child of Light**

The ritual of the Child of Light works with a dynamic that has become very badly misunderstood in some strands of modern magic. The Child of Light is an inner power that appears as a child with a brightness of light that flows from them:[10] does that sound familiar?[11] It is a power that is a part of the creation process of humanity and is a power both of itself, and also is a part of every human being. Like DNA, this Child of Light is within all of us, and yet still exists apart from and

beyond us. It is not 'your inner child' and has nothing to do with you in personal terms, rather is a component of human creation: it is one of the ingredients of the pattern.

The Child of Light carries the power of human potential, and also human history: it is our origins, our past, our present and our future. It is the template of human potential for pro creation. It is not really a shiny child, but that vast power appears to us in that form so that we can begin to understand it. Don't forget, a lot of what you see in vision is *visual vocabulary* that allows us and other beings to interact and understand each other.

When we connect with this being in various ways, we connect with the source of humanity and also its future: through connection we also plug ourselves back into the consciousness of the stream of humanity *in its greatest potential*. And that is one of the keys to the imagery that this being presents. The power of creation, from the creation of worlds down to gnats, one of the main impulses is novelty, which is to say something new that triggers a response.

Finding something new, a new taste, a new job, a new species, triggers focused interest, releases energy, and also triggers curiosity, experimentation and the absorption of experience. This is the lowest octave of the creative principle: 'new' equals attention plus an energy release. The novelty value of this being triggers and attracts interest from the powers within the creation process which in turn leads to energetic output and release. That dynamic of energy release with something new is a vital part of the deep process of creation and the Child of Light is a pattern for human creation that triggers such energy interest and release.

Every species has a core 'child' or new pattern of potential that triggers an energy release in the creative process. In a sense it holds that new potential as a deep well that the patterns can draw upon as they pass into creation. But what does that mean for us as magicians?

The Child of Light is all of human potential, all of past human evolution and the present fulcrum for human balance: it is the still point

---

[10]Hence the name.

[11]Remember the child in the Desert.

within us, the child we were in the womb just before birth. When there is disorder in mind or body, we connect back in with that pattern of potential.

Sadly some magical streams of work have not understood this and have gone in the direction of seeing the Child of Light as a thought form to be created and manipulated: a sorry state of degeneracy indeed. So to work: this is a ritual that must not be overused.[12] It is something done rarely in one's life when a reset button is sorely needed and everything else has been done first, without success.

The ritual of the Child of Light

Set up your work room, light the lights, put out the tools, filling the vessel with water, open the gates, then do the Anchor to tune yourself and the room. Then go and sit in the central position and meditate for a short while.

Once you are still and ready, stand and go to the east altar. Pick up the sword and hold it, point down, in your left hand, with your arms outstretched to the sides. See the contacts on the thresholds and bow your head.

Recite:

> "The Whirlwind of the Divine, the Breath of Life, I am your vessel, I am your worker, with the Limiter to teach me, I breathe out and give you back the breath just as I accept the breath."

Inhale and exhale slowly. As you exhale see the flow of your breath passing over the east threshold. As you inhale, see the breath of life come from beyond the gates, pass over the threshold, and into the air around you.

Nothing else in the world exists, only this passage of breath from the Divine to you and back to the Divine. As you accept, you must give back in order to receive.

Step back, place the sword on the altar, bow, and go to the south. Pick up your cord and hold it between your hands. Bow your head to the contacts at the threshold and recite:

[12]Remember the energy of newness?

> "The Fire of Life that gives vital force to everything, the fire that burns within me, as all fires peak and then die, so shall my own inner fire. This cord is the measure of my vital force that burns within me and keeps me warm. I hold this fire of vital force within me and I protect it in every step I take."

Using inner vision, see the flame within you, and see the flame beyond the threshold: the two resonate together and one keeps the other strong. Your flame is the light within the darkness, the Divine within flesh. Nothing exists except the flame within and the flame of the Divine. As you hold the inner flame within, so the Divine flame on the threshold upholds you.

Step back, place the cord on the altar, bow, and go to the west. Pick up the vessel in your right hand, bow your head to the contacts, and recite:

> "As the water from the Well of Life refreshes the soul, flowing from the river of Divine being, so too will the water of my tears nourish the earth; so too am I water that nourishes everything around me. My body shall be your vessel, my deeds your water."

Hold out the vessel and see a river flowing over the threshold from beyond the gates. The river fills the vessel. Lift the vessel to your lips and take a sip.

Place the vessel on the altar and stand silently. Be aware that by living, the world changes by nature of your presence: everything you experience and all your actions flow into the river that fills the Well of Life. Just as the land gives you clean water, so you give the river the richness of your experiences.

Bow to the contacts on the threshold, step back, and go to the north altar.

Pick up the stone shield, hold it to your heart, and recite:

"The Stone which is the anchor of all things, the collector of the discarded shells of all life, the vessel that accepts and releases the light out of the darkness, my Mother, I thank you for my body, for my vessel of life. Just as you gave me form, so shall I use this form in your honour. You are the Garden I will tend, just as you tend to me."

Look beyond the gates using your inner vision and see the Garden that is nature. See all those of your blood who have gone before you, and see the rock at the centre of the Underworld, shining its light in the darkness. Understand that this is all you and yet is apart from you: Divine creation is within and all around you.

Place the stone back on the altar, bow, step back, and turn to the central altar. Stand for a moment in silence and be aware of all the vital elements around you and how they make up the pattern that allows you to live and breathe in your body, and to express as a timeless being within the vessel of the manifest world.

Now turn your focus to the central flame. Close your eyes and see all the threads of creation, of the elements, and of the directions flowing together over the central flame to form a pattern. As you watch, the pattern becomes more and more complex and filled with the light of life and vital force.

The pattern starts to take on a human form, a child, whose light shines more brightly then any of the individual threads of the pattern. The child, who has its back to you, steps out of the pattern and stands on the other side of the central altar, still with their back to you. They stand facing south with the central flame of the Void behind them.

Open your eyes and walk round the altar to stand in the same position as the Child of Light. Physically stand within that inner pattern of the Child of Light and close your eyes.

Be aware of your body: its skeleton, its organs, its nerves; and the water, earth, fire, and air that flows through your body. Be aware of your breathing and remember the power of the Divine Breath flowing into you and your breath returning to that Divine source.

Slowly become aware of the Child of Light forming within you and all around you: you are standing within the Child of Light and the Child of Light is standing within you. Feel your body reacting and adjusting to that power: the conscious presence of that power is resetting all your body's systems, gently reminding each cell of its potential, its power, and its centre of balance.

As your body adjusts, be aware of the path of the south opening up beyond the gates. The path stretches off into the distance as it flows through gardens, fields, trees, and mountains. As you stand in balance and harmony, so too the path reacts and opens itself.

Feel the Child of Light within you and feel the balance within you. Keeping your eyes closed, take one step forward with your left leg. As you move forward, the Child of Light moves forward with you. When you take a second step with your right leg the Child of Light will stay behind. Stepping into, moving forward with, then leaving behind this power enables you to walk your path alone, which is as it should be; yet your body and spirit have been reminded of their true source. As you take a third step with your left leg[13] utter:

"I will be that which I will be."

Feel the pattern of the Child of Light behind you, feel the road into the future before you, the Breath of Life to your left, and the Water of Life to your right. Feel the anchor of the stone behind you, and beyond the Child of Light. Feel the Underworld and the Stone deep below your feet, and the stars and air above you. Be aware of the light, the spark, the flame burning within you, and feel its light fill your body and beyond so that you shine as a light in the darkness.

---

[13]If you are in a small space, take very small steps, but ensure that you do take them.

Sit down and meditate in that state and space for as long or short a time as you need to, until you feel the ritual's power start to fade and settle down.

When you are ready get up and go round the directions, closing the gates, thanking the contacts, and putting the lights out. Put the tools away and go outside, even if you live in a busy city: these powers of creation and life are in everything, so go out and be among the powers of creation in action for a short while.

Afterwards write down any notes that you wish to, as you will forget, then go and rest.

Lesson 8

The Ritual of the Fulcrum

The ritual you have worked the most is the Anchor. Now it is time to progress beyond that. It can still be used for grounding and tuning if you wish, but what you need now is to step into a ritual that can be used repeatedly to tune yourself to a higher frequency than the Anchor, a ritual that will put you in the *middle layer of power*.

The Anchor ritual is about being human and recognising the powers around you from a human perspective. But the magician has slowly to expand beyond the default, simple human life and spread themselves further and deeper into the Mysteries. The repeated use of the ritual called *the Fulcrum* slowly moves the magician's consciousness beyond everyday humanity and places it within the streams of creation and destruction.

When you work in *vision* you are placed deep into an inner state that can filter slowly down into your body to effect change and maturation. When you work in *ritual* the effects slowly filter from your body and effect change in the spirit.

The repeated use of specific rituals builds up a pattern, slowly, within which the spirit can learn to operate. First the ritual must become second nature to the body. Then, once the mind is no longer needed to navigate it, the spirit can begin to immerse itself in the pattern. It's like learning to drive. Once you no longer have to think about the pedals and gear stick then you are free to place all your attention on the road ahead.

Read through the following ritual a few times so that you understand what it is and what it is doing. Then learn it by memory so that you do not need to carry papers around with you, though you can keep a prompt sheet in your work room should you need to fall back on it. When you are ready to perform this ritual take a ritual bath first, smudge the work room with frankincense, and make sure you will not be disturbed.

8.1 *Task:* **The Ritual of the Fulcrum**

Get your cloth shield/temple cloth and look at the pentagram that is you. Behind/below the left arm paint a circle of white, and below/behind the right arm paint a circle of black.[1] You will need a long candle or taper to light the Lights.

Part I

Set up your room, put out the four tools[2] on the central altar. Spread the cloth on the ground with the altar over the centre of the cloth. Do not light the Lights or open the gates. Place the

---

[1] The Light Bearer and Restriction.
[2] Sword, cord, vessel, and stone shield.

taper and lighter/matches on the central altar and put out the light.

Sit before the central altar facing south, in silence and darkness, and meditate into stillness. Once you are still, before you move to stand up, utter:

> "In the beginning was Darkness. And a voice uttered out from the Void saying, 'Let there be Light; that it may shine in the Darkness.'"

Stand up and light the taper. Hold the taper in your left hand and light the central candle. Now utter:

> "And the Light shone in the Darkness, and the Darkness understood it not."

Stand before the flame and be aware of forces gathering in the cross-quarters. Feel them even though you cannot see them. Now be aware of the lantern in your sphere. With your left hand reach out in the air above you to the right and 'lift' the lantern across to your left: hold up your left hand as if holding the lantern and see its light with your inner vision. Once you have a clear sense of it to your left, drop your arm and leave the light hanging there.
Utter:

> "The Bearer of Light heard the voice utter from the Void, and stepped forth to take up the burden of the Light."

Feel the Light build behind you: the power of the Light Bearer. Feel that power fill the left side of your body, filling your foot, your hand, your torso, and your head. Feel the power of the Light Bearer hold up your lantern. Stand in that feeling for a moment.
When you are ready, utter:

> "The Light sought solace in the Darkness, and the Darkness responded."

Feel the power of Restriction build up behind your right shoulder and fill the right side of your body, filling your foot, your hand, your torso, and your head.
Utter:

> "I greet you Light Bearer, said the Darkness, and I give you the Restriction of my Darkness, that you may find your way safely."

Feel the two powers of Light and Dark within you, and the flame in your centre. Hold out your hands before you,, palms up, parallel to your shoulders, with your elbows bent, and utter:

> "I, (say your name) greet the Light Bearer and I greet Restriction. I am the fulcrum through which all may pass. Here is my left hand that guides you into being; here is my right hand that gathers you when you withdraw. I am the voice crying in the wilderness; I am the voice that seeks passage through the Desert in search of the Garden. Together we shall walk upon the Path of Hercules."

Pick up the sword and hold it out in your left hand, point down. Stand with your feet a shoulder width apart. Hold up your right hand, palm in a 'stop' position.
Utter:

> "With the light of my lantern and the Light of the Light Bearer, the Light flows through the Limiter which shall guard all that is created and shall limit its years. With my foot upon the Grindstone I shall be polished by the Light of the Lantern."

Take the sword to the east altar and lay it across the altar. Return to the central altar and pick up the cord. Hold it out between your hands. Utter:

"In my left hand is my birth. In my right hand is my death. Between the two is the measure of my time. I am the Vessel though which the Breath may pass."

Wrap the cord round your right wrist. Now pick up the vessel in your right hand and hold out your left hand, palm flat, to receive or give. Utter:

"The Darkness has formed the Vessel which receives the Light. The Vessel is that which holds my Measure and will weigh my Harvest upon my death. May the lantern of my experiences light my way and fill the vessel of my deeds."

Take the vessel and place it on the west altar. Return back to the centre.

Pick up the stone in both hands and utter:

"The Stone receives the substance of the Vessel. May it collect the Darkness when the Light has flown. Stone, remember me and place my memory among the bones of my ancestors."

Place the stone on the north altar and return to the centre.

In the air to the left of you, where the lantern hangs, draw the sigil of the sword with your left hand. To the right of you where the lantern normally resides, draw the sigil of the vessel with your right hand. Hold your left hand in the air over the sword sigil and your right hand over the vessel sigil.

Take a deep breath and breathe out slowly. As you breathe out see the Light and Dark behind you flowing through you and following your breath: they breathe through you. At the end of the breath, draw in your hands and cross your arms over your chest. Utter:

"I will be what I will be

Before me is the path that I must walk

Behind me is the Light to form me and the Darkness to contain me

Beyond them is the Void from which I was Uttered

Above me are the stars of generations

Below me are the bones of generations

Within me is stillness

Within me is the Garden

I am the Fulcrum through which All may pass."

Part II

Pick up the taper and light it from the central flame. Walk to the east altar and stand before the candle. Be aware of the Light and Dark within you and the powers all around you.

Light the light on the altar and breathe gently over the top of the flame.[3] With your breath, the gates open and a great golden light shines out of the east. Its light becomes too bright, so pick up the sword and hold it[4] up to the Light in your left hand. Utter:

"I limit you that you may express in this world without destroying."

Put down the sword, bow, pick up the taper, light it from the east candle, and then go to the south.

Light the candle on the altar and breathe over the top of the flame gently. The south gates open and bright, strong sunlight shines out of the south gate, illuminating the path into the south. The path seems to go on forever. Hold up your right wrist and show your cord. Utter:

"My length is limited, but I shall walk each step with the strength of the Grindstone."

---

[3]Don't blow it out.
[4]Handle up, tip down.

Drop your right hand and place it upon your left shoulder.

Utter:

> I accept the limitations of the Grindstone and I accept the guidance of the Light Bearer. Path ahead, uphold my feet as I walk upon you.

Bow, pick up the taper, light it from the candle, and go to the west altar.

Light the west candle and breathe over the flame as before. As the gates open, a deep blue light shines out of the west gates. The vessel also begins to take on a blue glow. Pick up the vessel in your right hand and hold it out.

Utter:

> "Vessel, carry the Harvest of my deeds so that they may be measured upon the Threshing Floor. And when my Length comes to an end, carry my Light across your threshold. You are my body; you are my lantern. Walk with me upon the path of Hercules."

Bow, pick up the taper, light it from the candle, and go to the north.

Light the candle and breathe gently over the flame. The gates open. Beyond them is total darkness. Place your hands upon the stone.

Utter:

> "You are my Foundation, the Darkness that the Light shines out of. Guide me through your wisdom, shelter me in the storms ahead, and protect me from destruction that has no purpose with me. And when my Light is released upon the death of my body, collect my bones and hold them in your arms."

Bow, pick up the taper, and go to the central altar.

Stand before the central altar and close your eyes. Using inner vision, see the pattern of threads you have formed from your actions, words, and breath. See the pattern hanging in the air over the central flame.

Open your eyes but keep a sense of the pattern. See the pattern in your inner vision descend into the central flame. See the road ahead in the south beyond the south gates.

Take a deep breath and breathe out slowly, blowing across the candle flame without blowing it out and blowing the pattern into the south onto the road ahead.

Utter:

> "I will be what I will be."

Sit down and be still. Think about what you have just done and write up any notes in your journal before the thoughts fade from your mind. When you are ready close down the directions and put the tools away.

About the ritual

This ritual can be used in its entirety, or parts I and II can be used as appropriate to tune yourself and/or the directions.

The Anchor was all about you. The Fulcrum moves you a step further into being a part of everything. It establishes the powers that flow through and around you, and it also mirrors the pattern of creation and destruction in harmony. You are the fulcrum in the middle of all of that. The second part of the ritual also tunes the tools and directions in together again at a stronger frequency that you have worked with before.

Did you notice that there are no beings or contacts in the directions? In this ritual you work purely with the powers that flow through you,[5] and you establish the deep workings of the tools above and beyond ordinary magic.

The Anchor is magic of the land, the body, and the human in relation to everything else. The Fulcrum is magic of the inner flows of creation and destruction, with the tools to balance and assist. This is your tuning ritual for the initiate section. It is also the fulcrum

---

[5] And therefore through creation.

between the Anchor ritual and the ritual that you will learn in the adept section.

This ritual is your deeper balancing, and will also establish the flows of creative and destruction power through you in small increments. You will learn how to adapt and incorporate the powers within this pattern in your general magical work as we go along. This process started at the end of your apprentice training and will continue to spiral deeper and deeper through the initiate section.

8.2 *Task:* **Learning to feel out your pattern**

When you get the chance, go out into nature early in the morning somewhere you will not be disturbed.

Stand and be still. Feel the Light behind you to the left, the Dark behind you to the right, and feel them in your hands. Feel the rock beneath you and the power of the stone shield behind you. Feel the stars above you and the path ahead of you, and feel the stillness of the flame within you.

Close your eyes and cast your mind round this pattern. Is anything blocking any powers? Is any power weaker or stronger than the other? They should all be equal. Is there any sense of blockage on the path before you? If there is, feel into it: what direction does its power *come from?* (Not "what direction it is in?") If you feel into it, feel if it is air/words, fire/disease, water/emotions, earth/holding on to something.

Learn how to feel around your own pattern without tools, tarot, or anything else. Learn to feel the web of fate, and to feel weaknesses, blockages, interference,[6] and the powers of Restriction or the Light Bearer being out of balance. Learn to feel the power of connection to the stars and the earth, to your past and your future, just by feeling into the pattern.

Once you have a sense of this in a clear place you will be able to tap into it and do it wherever you are.

And learn to read the signs of the pattern. If there is heaviness, a fire, or fast movement to your left, then there is hard work and learning on the horizon or a job to be done. Ensure its speed, weight, and power is balanced according to all the other powers around you.

If something is lurking to your right, then something is weighing down your vessel. It may be an unfinished job or unresolved issues or events that need bringing to a conclusion.

If the weight is directly behind you, then land, substance, resources, or family are pulling you back and you need to clear things. If it is directly before you, something is blocking your path that should not.

Obstacles which slow your path usually come from your right or left if they are caused by your actions: too much or too little engagement of the Light Bearer or Restriction will disturb your path ahead, as will not keeping your substance[7] in check. These are problems for you to figure out and deal with. Forward impulse with limitation and learning from experience are things which open your path up.

But an obstacle directly before you with no imbalance to your right, left, or rear is usually a block that does not come from you. In such a case you have to figure out who has put it there. Deities can put obstacles in your path, usually to limit and protect you. Or it may be that the Fates have set you a new experience, one that does not come from your own previous actions, to challenge you. Or a magician may have put the obstacle there to bind you, attack you, or block you, if you have crossed an immature magician somewhere.

You will also have to work out what the obstacle *is* before you try to deal with it. And only you can deal with it: at this stage you have the skill and knowledge to deal with such a block—you just have to draw from what you already know and have learned. By dealing with it yourself you will learn a great deal and also build the skills necessary to stop it happening again. Magic teaches you about life, and life teaches you magic.

---

[6]Magic from others.

[7]Body, family, home, sustenance, health.

Learning to close your eyes and feel into the dynamics and powers around you embeds the powers of the tools and beings within you. You do not need readings, rituals, visions, or anything else to check the status of your body and spirit as you walk on your path. The Fulcrum ritual wakes this process up. Each time you do it, it will strengthen the pattern around you. Then you use your inner senses to feel into that pattern wherever you are: it becomes your own health check and radar.

If you have picked anything up in your task exercise, write it down and draw out a small map of where you felt the disturbance in relation to your body. Use the mapping method featured on the cloth shield: south is up, north is down, left is Limiter/Light Bearer, right is Vessel/Restriction, and the centre is your fulcrum point. You can refer back to this in the future and when you do feel such a thing, map it out and track its progress.

8.3   *Task:* Bedding in the Fulcrum ritual

Practice this ritual until you are clear and comfortable with it. Then do it every new moon for a while until you feel it is time to stop. Also use parts of it, or all of it, to prepare for magical work in your work space.

Initiate Module IV

Birth, Death and the Underworld Part II

Lesson 1

The Vision of Death

In Apprentice Module IV you looked at death in terms of myth, magical pattern, and text to give you a background understanding of the various facets and dynamics of death from a magical perspective. In this module you will look more actively at death from a magical perspective. Throughout the module you will work in vision and ritual, and there will also be further learning and research to give you a deeper layer of the understanding of death, the Underworld, and birth.

Previously you looked at mythologies of death from Egypt and various other cultures in order to gain an overview of how death was approached within the ancient Mysteries. In this lesson we will look at the *Death Vision*, what it shows, how it works, and how as a magician you operate within that Mystery.

Working with the magical Death Vision is a major stage for the initiate and part of the process of the magician's *death in life* stage. Rather than being a single initiatory ritual, the process of *death in life* for a magician works in octaves: it is something one goes through in different forms and layers depending on one's steps and stages.

Part of this process is visionary. The rest visits the individual magician at various stages on their path and can sometimes manifest as a very close shave with death. It can also manifest in the form of dreams, memories, and deep understandings.

Like all magic you never completely 'get it'; rather you move in spirals of ever-deepening awareness which bring up new and more profound facets of magic with every step you take. Just when you think you have got it, another layer of learning comes along to sweep you off your feet and tell you that in fact you know nothing. We are constant beginners, all of us, and the more we delve, the more we find. Magic is an endless, bottomless cauldron that we can spend a lifetime exploring and still only scratch its surface.

Doing the Death Vision as an initiate action triggers the process of really learning about death rather than just reading about it. As you progress you will find that the dynamics, powers, and actions within the Death Vision are also the same powers that you work with in ritual and magical vision: all magic tracks back to the vast powers of creation and destruction.

The vision you will work with in this lesson is a pattern that sits on top of the Ancient Egyptian Mysteries, but is not directly *of* those Mysteries: the Death Vision is something that grew out of that phase of development. It is something worked with by the Greeks, and you will see many references to aspects of the Death Vision in various Greek and Roman texts. Once you have read about and worked with the Death Vision a few times, you will also start to spot aspects of it in various other cultures: different vocabulary, same power and process.

The one thing to remember with the Death Vision is it is not a tourist site. You do not go there to simply gawk and satisfy your own curiosity. After you have worked with it in this lesson it is something you will keep in your visionary toolbox for future work. And you *will* be put to work with it at some point. It can be used in disasters when a lot of people are dying at once, or it can be used to work with people who are close to you, like friends and family who have just died. You can also do the vision in your mind while sitting beside someone who is dying. The resonant effect of the vision done in your own mind will also affect the dying person.

This vision uses a lot of energy, and quite a few things can go wrong if it is overused or misused, so use your common sense. Don't get evangelistic about it and run around 'saving everyone' in death. For the most part the processes and stages that people go through in death are their business and their own path of development. The magician intervenes only when it is truly necessary[1] or they are strongly pulled by inner contacts.[2]

In the past I have been called to work when a large group of people have suddenly been killed. Other times I have been told to mind my own business. I have assisted various members of my family, lovers, and friends through death; other times I was told to keep out of their way and let them get on with it. So it is very individual to the person who has died and also to the magician.

When in doubt, always default to common sense and feeling into the situation, a skill you began learning in the last module. Often all the distressed dead need is time to adjust. When they are in a total mess, then is the time for intervention, particularly if indicated by inner contacts.

As an adept this vision can also be used to bridge a living person into death to say their goodbyes to someone they have lost. This is done when the living are not healing naturally from the shock of their loss.

Before we get to the practical visionary work let us go through the stages of the Death Vision and look at its different aspects. Then when you do the vision you will have a good idea of what you are looking at. But remember, the visual presentations were created by generations of magicians and magical priests; it is a *vocabulary* that we can use to *interface* with. The dead experience it in their own unique way. In my book *Magical Knowledge II* there is a chapter dedicated to this subject, but if you do not have the book, then the information you need is here.

1.1 The Death Vision in detail

The River

The Death Vision begins with a long walk across a hot, flat desert landscape.[3] In the distance is a river which the dead person is drawn to. Other people are often walking too, and some can be found sitting by the river. The dead person will be very thirsty and they rush towards the river to drink of its water. As they drink it begins to affect their ability to remember their newly-lost life. The more they drink, the more they forget.

This is why initiates in the Mysteries were trained to control their thirst and their inner actions. It was drummed into them from the very beginning of their advanced training not to drink of the River of Death. This allows them, when they die, to cross through death and retain the memories of who they were. The training of self-discipline and valuing necessity over desire in the Mysteries is far more than discipline for its own sake: it is a vital aspect of navigating the inner realms.

The act of not drinking and thus remembering is one of the ways an adept becomes an *inner* adept: they remember, and as such can choose to carry that knowledge deep into the inner worlds or to return to life in gnosis to do

---

[1] Remember the power of necessity.

[2] You just end up there without meaning to.

[3] Familiar?

a job. The more initiates of the Mysteries were taught how to remember, the more *reincarnation with intent* became commonplace.

I do not think this is always healthy; some forgetting and letting go is important for the soul's development. The continuance from one life to the next in a conscious line of work can become corrupted very quickly.

The balance for an adept is to drink only a tiny bit from the river, which lets you keep enough memory to recall your hard-earned wisdom and knowledge. The tiny sips will, however, wipe away most memories of partners, loved ones, worldly power, etc. This will allow the soul to move forward and understand the deeper rules of attachment: one must not be attached to anything or anyone.

When you die, all the people you loved no longer exist for you. For your sake and theirs you must let go and move on. By letting go you eventually will be able to reconnect with these people under different circumstances and different forms of relationships, but only if it is appropriate.

At this stage of the vision a person sits at the side of the river and ponders their lost life: they begin the process of shedding and accepting. Often angelic beings will make themselves available to help people through this stage of the transition. These beings guard the Bridge and the River, allowing only those who should to cross.

These beings will often cross-dress so as not to frighten people. They often appear as their aunt Betty, or as Jesus, Buddha, or whichever Deity, saint, or family member the deceased person would reach out to. This is not to deceive them; this is only to help those who are so traumatized that they cannot move forward without real, practical help. And angels appearing in their own guise would frighten the socks off most people, so they dress up.

In some cultures a dead person is held *in vigil* and priests or priestesses recite a guide to them, telling them what to look out for, which beings do what, and what to avoid. The Tibetan culture has this sort of guidance in their death texts which are read to the dead person's body—don't forget, dead people can often still perceive communication to their bodies for a short while after death.

I encountered a good example of cross-dressing beings in some inner work I did for a family a few years ago. A young friend of my daughter had a snowboarding accident and ended up with severe injuries. He was in a deep coma and the hospital informed his parents that he would not recover. The planned to wait a week and then turn off the machines that were keeping him alive.

My daughter asked if we could sit in meditation when they turned off the machines and do the Death Vision for him. I said yes. The day before this was due to happen I was suddenly told by inner contacts to sit down with my daughter and do the Death Vision straight away—so we did.

I saw the boy standing by the river. He was in shock. He refused to move in any way. He would not believe he was dead and refused my efforts to get him to move forward to cross the Bridge: crossing the Bridge would enable him to move on to the next, deeper stage of death.

In desperation I asked one of the angelic beings for help. A few seconds later a beautiful young girl with rather large breasts strutted over the Bridge towards the boy. His eyes nearly popped out of his head. He forgot his fears and immediately agreed to take her arm and walk across the Bridge with her, so off he went. The angelic being had dressed as a beautiful young woman to assist this boy. We later found out that he died naturally just as we were doing the Death Vision, thus saving his family from the terrible trauma of having to turn him off.

Back to the side of the river. At this stage people are often confused, bewildered, and angry. They are angry that death was not what they expected: there was no choir of angels to herald them into heaven and no endless supply of ice cream, sunshine, and all the other trivial things that were promised to them…yes, people can be that dumb. So they sit at the side of the river and wait. At this stage some of them realize that their imagination can take them back to the people they left behind. Some become particularly skilled at this and refuse to move further into death, choosing instead to haunt their lost loved ones or their lost property.

The longer they stay in death, the more the living world becomes a sort of inner world to them; that is to say, where they are becomes their total reality and the living world is accessed through their imagination. For us it is the other way round.

It is at this stage where you also sometimes find people who are in deep comas. They have a foot in death and a foot in life. They hang between the two and while their body is still alive in the living world their spirit sometimes begins the death journey and they find themselves at the side of the River. They cannot go any further until their body is dead. So they hang out, confused and afraid.

They have to choose whether go back or let go of their body. If they cannot go back, if the body is too damaged, then they must learn to let go and allow their body to die.

The Sands

Some do not make it to the River; rather they become trapped in the Sands[4] where they will stay for however long it takes them to slowly unravel. This often happens when a person was completely shut down in life and clung on to everything, or if they were totally out of control in some way, or if their spirit is unable or too weak to make the journey through death. They are held in the sands of restriction until they begin to move towards balance within themselves.

However this process is not clear and straightforward: I have seen all sorts of beings and human spirits trapped in the Sands, and the reason is not clear at all. Usually when I get too close to them an angelic being tells me to go away and mind my own business.

I am naturally curious as I want to learn, but sometimes we need to know boundaries and not interfere. Sometimes actions taken through curiosity can have far-reaching effects, and in such cases you are usually steered away or a guardian will confront you. When that happens, know to leave well alone.

The Bridge

The Bridge is a crucial part of the Death Vision; if a dead person doesn't cross the Bridge in one way or another they cannot continue with the death process. These people appear to stay at the River and can access the living world, which means they are ghosts. They remain frozen in a half-life world somewhere between life and death.

Crossing the River by way of a bridge is our way of seeing a process whereby the spirit severs connections with life and commits to moving forward in their cycle of development. Most spirits cross when they are ready, but some sleep in the Sands[5] while others vanish without crossing.[6]

The Bridge can appear to us as being guarded by angelic beings. They stand on either side of the entrance and act as gatekeepers, keeping out those who for whatever reason must not cross.

As magicians we can cross the Bridge safely, though it is best not to return that way. Once we cross the Bridge, if we wish as living beings to come out of the vision, we have to exit either from the top of the Mountain or continue and complete the whole cycle of rebirth.

The reason we do not return over the Bridge is that there is always the risk of some being who does not belong in life hitching a ride on you unnoticed. To avoid such cases, which do indeed happen, be sure either to climb the Mountain or pass through an angelic being or a threshold protected by, and created of, angelic consciousness. You can do this by approaching one of the beings working in the Death Vision and asking them to let you pass through them

---

[4]Restriction.

[5]*Sleepers.*

[6]I have no idea where they go, I have never followed them.

to get home. The thresholds of the Mountain and the Abyss are protected thresholds which only allow those who should to pass.

The Bridge is portrayed in Egyptian texts as the Scales: the Bridge is a *fulcrum point* where the next stage of the spirit's journey is determined by their tread upon the Bridge. The Bridge itself is a being that *weighs* their footfall.

The Plains

As the spirit begins its journey towards the Mountains it enters into a phase of letting go at a much deeper level. The spirit's physical appearance, and all that was attached to that form, begins to dissolve as they walk across the Plains towards the high mountains. This often appears to us as things falling off the person as they walk. They may appear to drop baggage, clothing, heavy weights, even limbs as they draw closer and closer to the Mountain. This is described by the Egyptians as the phase of the *choppers*: beings who cut things from you as you pass by.

While the spirit is in this phase, anything not dealt with by the River will be forcibly cut away from them. Some will be very disorientated and will be drawn by instinct to the mountains before them. The Bridge and the walk to the mountains is like a filter for spirits: some are torn apart,[7] some are already clear of their last life and are ready to climb, some know what they are doing and can maintain some semblance of their last lives without being held back by it,[8] and some continue to transform.[9]

The Mountain

The Mountain is the final hurdle that the soul must encounter within the Death Vision. The Mountain is the deep spiritual programming and the spiritual evolution that has happened to a person during their lives. Any religion they have been raised with, any cultural baggage they may have, and any deep-seated ideals are challenged at this point. The more

spiritual evolution there has been in a person's life, the less steep of a climb the Mountain becomes.[10]

This manifests in a couple of ways: the more dogma is entrenched in a person, the higher the Mountain is and the harder it is to climb. Once a person begins to climb they will start to hear many voices, some reciting sacred text, some praying, some political voices, some cultural voices, and some of their own ponderings. The voices will be loud and annoying as they try to climb beyond the programming that happened during their lifetime.

When the person hears the voices they will begin to be aware of them as something *outside* of them: they are things they acquired during their lifetimes when they had a body, but they are not part of them. The awareness that such thoughts are not of the spirit but a product of humanity can be a shock to some people—and the harder the shock, the harder the climb.

Such a letting go is probably the hardest: it is releasing everything you have ever held deep in your consciousness as being real, as being right. It shows a person the falsehood of their society, their religion, and their reasoning. It is a frightening and exhausting experience that weighs heavily on the shoulders of a person who is struggling with such a difficult transition.

Some do not make the climb and fall off part way up; others are picked off by beings if they have tried to force their way through the stages of death by magic—remember the spells from the Egyptian *Book of the Dead*?

By the time the spirit reaches the top of the Mountain they are exhausted and ready for sleep. There are many beings who work in this section of the Death Vision. Their duty is to guard, nurture, and prepare the soul for the renewal of life, for service in the inner worlds, or for passage deeper into Divinity.

The top of the Mountain appears as a plateau with a grassy flat area where people lie down to rest. The beings wander in among the sleeping people, singing to them and

---

[7]Second Death.

[8]The goal of the magician.

[9]Those encountering the choppers.

[10]The Ladder.

stroking them as they sleep—weaving them into a pattern. The spirit lies down and the angelic beings arrange them so they can sleep comfortably. They are laid out in a ritual position of one arm outstretched and the opposite leg outstretched. The other leg and arm are bent into the body. This position can be seen on some traditional tarot decks as a man curled round the Wheel of Life. It is also mirrored in some decks in the Hanged Man.

Spirits who are not going to reincarnate, who are going to pass into the inner worlds in service as an inner contact or teacher or step deeper into Divinity, do not lie down. They are urged to a far, dark side of the plateau where the Mountain falls away down a bottomless crevice or Abyss. The spirit stands on the edge of the Abyss and makes the ultimate initiation move by stepping off the cliff. Each spirit pulled to this place will have practised this action many times during their life in visions. The spirit steps out into the Mystery of the Abyss and vanishes into the mist. They will emerge in the inner worlds, ready to work or teach and guide humanity in a spirit of service, or they will step off the cliff and fully cross the Abyss to join with Divinity.

This is also a get-off point for you as a visionary should you wish to exit the Death Vision with esoteric purpose. By going through the Death Vision to this point and then stepping off into the Abyss, you fully complete the death initiation of the ancients. But rather than cross the Abyss, you will emerge in the sanctuary of the Inner Library.

The Awakening into Rebirth

At some point all the angels face east as the sun rises and they begin to call out the names of those spirits whom they have guarded to awaken. The spirits awaken and are immediately pushed down the opposite side of the Mountain, which is a gentle, grassy slope.

The spirits roll round and round as they tumble down the hill towards an Abyss guarded by an archangel. The angel appears as a woman with hair that flows in all directions, and her long arms reach out to slow the

spirits as they roll down the hill. This angel is also a deity, and we know her as Ananke.

Once they come to a halt the spirits uncurl and walk to the edge of the Abyss. The angel holds a protective arm out to stop them falling as they explore the power of this place. As they look over the Abyss they slowly become aware of potential lives that could relate to them. There is no past or present, as such concepts have no place where there is no matter. But all the lives that are within their field appear on the other side of the Abyss, and they can watch them.

The spirit fixes on one life that seems to connect with them more than the others. It is not a conscious choice but an instinctive one. All the cultural and religious programming that would have affected such a choice has long gone: all that is left is deep spiritual reaction and instinct.

Once the life has been chosen the angel removes her arm and the spirit falls into a whirling mass of air that appears like a whirlwind. The soul falls down and down, swirling round the directions as it falls towards a couple who are making love.

Now that you have an idea of the vocabulary and stages of this Death Vision, it is time for you to do the vision yourself. Walking through death and stepping off the top of the Mountain is a major step for the initiate. Do this vision when you are not tired and when you will not be disturbed. And ensure that you have the basic map of the vision in your head so you can find your way there without forgetting: as with all visions in this course, learn the key stages by heart. To make it easier, as this can be a difficult vision, I will outline this vision in simple stages, as you have enough experience by now fill in the gaps.

1.2   The Death Vision

Set up your workspace, light the lights, open the gates, and do the Fulcrum ritual. When you are ready, sit down before the central altar and be still. Once you are still, start the vision.

Go to the Underworld Forest via the cave with the goddess in it. Walk alongside the waters until they form a river and flow out into the Desert over the Underworld threshold. Step over the threshold into the desert scene and watch people walking towards the River.

Go to the side of the River. Observe people waiting, and look for the Bridge. When you see the Bridge and its guardians, watch people crossing over the Bridge. Sit at the side of the River for a while and think about how it is necessary to let go of everything and everyone upon death. Think about your Scales: what you need to rebalance in your life and what you need to let go.

When you are ready, get up and go to the Bridge guardians. Ask them to let you over the Bridge while you are still in life. As you cross the Bridge, think about how you balance your life and any changes you still need to make: you are *walking the Scales*.

When you get to the other side, walk towards the Mountains and observe any people walking near you. When you reach the bottom of the Mountain, start climbing the path up the side of the slope. Pay close attention to what you see and hear, and how difficult or easy it is for you to climb.

When you reach the top, observe the people lying down and observe what the angels do around the people. Ask the angel if you can stand and watch people rolling down into life. If they allow it, when you are finished one of the angels will point into the distance to you, to the edge of the Mountain obscured by mists. Walk towards the mists. As you walk through the mists you will come to steep cliff edge. You will not be able to see what is around you at all: all of your vision will be obscured. You will have to step out and take the risk.

As you step out you will find yourself stepping over a threshold and into a sanctuary that is a part of the Inner Library. The sanctuary is like a cave church or temple, with many lanterns hanging from the ceiling and a stone altar that you have to walk round. The sanctuary has many men and women there who are of a priesthood. They may ignore you or greet you. Commune with them, and when you are ready walk through the doors at the far end of the sanctuary, which will take you into the main Inner Library. From there, make your way back to your work space.

The reason this vision is so cut down is not only to give you easy references without too much to remember, but also to let you have your own experiences. This is the first real step towards crossing the Abyss, which you will do later in the course: it is the first step in that process and trains your spirit for the bigger leap to come.

As soon as you come out of vision, write your notes in your journal and later write up a full summary on computer of what you experienced. If you are being mentored, this will be assessed. If not, it will still be a valuable record for you to look back on for your future work.

This is not a vision to do regularly, but it is something you need to maintain understanding and proficiency in, as you will be called to do it in service from time to time. Use it wisely and don't let yourself devolve into inner tourism or develop a 'saviour' mentality with it.

1.3 *Task:* Research

Look back over the various texts on death that you have read, and the images from ancient Egyptian and other sources around the theme of death. Take your time with this and look deeply. Once you have done the vision, the knowledge of its Mysteries will be embedded within you. Looking back over the texts will help you gain a deeper understanding of what happens during this process. Just remember that each culture has its own vocabulary, but if you look closely you will the same dynamics in action. Take your own notes and keep images so that you can keep going back to them, as the understanding of this death process will deepen within you over time.

Lesson 2

Breaking the Web

When a person comes to the end of their life measure there is something that can be observed from an inner magical perspective, and that is the breaking of their web and the release of their vital force: the point of death.

Remember your fate web? There is a similar pattern in the layers of your energetic body. When you delve deeply into the human body in vision, once you get past the inner expression of the human form, past the layers of organ spirits and the flow of the vital force, then you come to an intricate pattern: the *web of your body*. It is the pattern that anchors your spirit to your body and melds the two together. If this pattern breaks apart or becomes badly damaged, the body and soul can no longer join together.

It is very clear to see when approached in vision, which makes me wonder whether the sight of this web in dreams and visions is why the ancients called the creation goddesses 'weavers.' When there is magical or energetic damage to a body, it is at this level, the pattern, that the repairs are made: no amount of healing will help if the pattern is torn.

Slight tears and minor damage in the weave can be fixed. These often come from severe trauma, hot spots in the fate weave, and so forth. When there is a tear in the weave, it means that whatever harmed the person's body was strong enough to reach the person's body was strong enough to reach the weave, the deepest part of someone's physical existence and the most protected, most vital part of their being.

But when the measure of life comes to an end[1] then the web pattern starts to break up of its own accord: the threads are cut. No amount of inner work, healing, or weaving will keep someone alive once their measure comes to an end.

2.1 The pattern within the pattern within the pattern

Everything around you, including your body, is built of energetic web patterns which interweave and roll apart in a constant motion of union and separation. When you begin to look deeply in vision it becomes very difficult to comprehend this constant weaving, moving pattern that is the whole of creation. The narrower you make your focus the more you see—and the more complex the whole thing becomes.

Each strand of your own web is made up of many tiny interwoven patterns. Each of those patterns is made up of yet more weave, and each aspect of the weave has an energetic polarity that keeps it powered up.

When a person is coming to the end of their *thread*, regardless of their age, it can often be felt by some visionary magicians and psychics

---

[1]Morta.

98

who come into contact with them: the person feels powered down at a very deep level. The threads are beginning to self-destruct and the first thing that happens before they crumble and break is that their energy polarity ceases. There is no tension between the strands. No energy travels along each strand to keep it energised, and the thread finally collapses. Once this has happened the outer physical body no longer has a proper inner power source, which in turn leads to the outer organs beginning to fail.

Why do you need to know this? As a magician you will find yourself, over time, in all sorts of odd situations, and needing to work on various people to heal them, keep them alive, or release them into death. In such situations knowing how the web pattern within the vital body works and what to do with it will come in very useful.

Also, nature is very efficient: the whole of creation is made up of the same systems and patterns, so if you understand the energetic web of a human, you then also understand the energetic pattern of a tree, a mountain, a cat… There are only small variations in the energetic web of a cat and a human, or a tree and a human. If you can work on one, you can work on them all.

And once you have understood the concept and worked in vision on your own web and the webs of different things, you will begin to learn about energetic weaving in terms of magic and creation. Everything operates within these patterns, including magic. It adds another layer of understanding and skill to your magical toolbox.

2.2 Layers of the pattern

People working with visionary magic and spirituality in the nineteenth century wrote quite a lot about the different layers of the human body.[2] When I started delving into the body as a young visionary magician I did indeed find that it had many layers, but they were not neatly separated and labelled;

rather they seemed to form a complex set of interlocking patterns that were constantly shifting and communicating back and forth with each other.

As magicians we separate these layers out in our minds so we can work directly on a problem, but it is important not to fall into dogmatic thinking—seven neat and tidy layers—as this will limit your experience and understanding.

This dynamic of layers in a pattern is inherent in all patterns of creation and destruction. Learning to recognise the shifting, changing layers and to work with them in a focused way allows the magician to act as a catalyst for change in anything they are working on.

Once the dynamic of destruction is triggered in anything—a body, a magical pattern, a land area—the inherent web begins to break apart. This lets the power of destruction into the pattern to dismantle it. The same holds true for bodies. When a point of death draws near, the pattern itself starts to fall apart. This triggers a loss of vital force and the integrity of the overall substance of the body.

If this process is a slow decline, often the organ spirits will at first fall quiet and not communicate. Then they will slowly withdraw their consciousness from the organ pattern. This triggers a decline in the physical organ, and though medication can keep them going for a time it only stalls the inevitable for a short while.

This can be observed in people who have a terminal illness. Where the inner organ and organ spirit should be there is often a dark hole.[3]

For example, I had been working occasionally on a magical priestess who had recurring cancer. She was thought to be in remission, but when I worked on her I found that a large area of her body showed no pattern, no vital force, and no organ spirits: the destruction preparation for death had

---

[2]The seven layers, i.e. the astral, etc.

[3]The same applies to any similarly affected aspect of the body's structure: the area in question will not show any patterns, inner body aspects, or vital force.

begun. Even though she was thought to be in remission, she was dying. I sent her back to her doctor for tests, which showed that her cancer had indeed returned.

I managed to patch up the deepest part of the weave to give her a bit more time, and indeed she lasted another five years; but in those five years her system slowly started to shut down.

It is impossible to continually patch up the weave: not only can you not extend a life beyond its measure, but such work is also dangerous for the magician to attempt. It is a very strong drain on the magician's vital force, and if the magician has any debility or unseen illness it can trigger a destructive cascade within them. In the priestess's case, I simply helped her to last to the end of her measure.

2.3   Recognising the pattern

The deep weave or pattern of the human life expresses itself in many different ways on a physical level. Because of this, the health of the vital force and life pattern can be observed by outer signs. These can show if there is a potential problem at a deep level. Such a disturbance in the pattern does not necessarily mean that total destruction is on its way, but it can indicate an underlying tear or weakness that needs attending to.

The pattern of a person's life force is mirrored in their genes. If a person begins to show signs of an altered or failing circadian rhythm, a damaged internal clock, or persistent depression for no outer reason,[4] then it is possible that the issue is a deep, underlying failure or a problem with their very life pattern. Such a failure in the pattern and rhythm can be caused by a variety of things, some very treatable; others not.

When as a magician you are presented with a case like this, or suffer from such an imbalance yourself, then once the usual treatable reasons have been discounted it is time to look at the deep life pattern itself. Often it can be patched and worked with to

regenerate it, but if serious illness is also in the picture then often the break has gone too far.

Each case is very individual and knowing what can be fixed, what can be delayed, and what is inevitable comes only from experience. Because of this, in your practical work for this lesson you will learn how to check and work with your own pattern. It is advisable to check your pattern once a year to keep an eye on it.

Before we get to that, we need to look, from an inner magical perspective, at the point in time when the vital force's core is removed upon the point of death. This will help you understand the angelic and inner dynamics that often occur at the point of death.

Of course we are assuming that the person in question is dying from illness and not from an accident or being shot or stabbed and so forth. If the body is suddenly severely damaged then the inner process very different. The body cannot uphold life if its weave is destroyed, but equally the weave cannot sustain vital force within the body if the body is damaged beyond repair.

2.4   The angel and the orb

I call this process *the angel and the orb* because that is exactly how it appears. You will work with this in vision in your practical work as an observer, but first let me give you some background.

This was something I observed repeatedly as a young magician when I attended to people in my family and friends who were dying. I did not see it every time: other times I would see other layers of process in action. Often you see only what you need to see, either to help the person or for your own learning. You cannot see all the different dynamics and layers in action at the same time: we simply cannot process that amount of information in one go. This is why we are often presented with aspects of a dynamic, not the whole show.

Most frequently I managed to observe this dynamic in action when a person was slowly

---

[4]PTSD, stress, hormonal fluctuations, and so forth.

dying and in their final stages, and sacred recitation was being spoken in the room for the dying person. I have observed the same process with Catholic, Islamic, and Jewish recitation being spoken: whether the recitation triggered the angelic presence itself or simply triggered me to see it, I don't know.

Generally the recitation would still the room, then at some point during the process an angelic being of fire would appear or step into the room and stand over the person who was dying. As soon as they were beside the person I would see the broken web in the dying person's body, and just above the umbilicus what appeared to be an orb of light in the centre of the web—the well of the vital force. The angel would watch the orb of light as its brightness dimmed, and once it got to a certain level of dullness, the angel would reach into the person and detach the orb from the pattern. The web would fall apart immediately and the angel would take the orb and vanish.

Every time I witnessed this, the person drew their last breath within a few minutes. A couple of times the last breath timed in exactly with the taking out of the orb. The body would appear dull, with no inner light at all. Once I had seen this a few times it did occur to me that such a web could be worked on to reconnect broken threads and plug the web back into the orb, which was the reservoir of life force for the person. Sometimes it was fairly easy to reweave; other times the threads would not reattach and would simply fall apart in my hands.

Sometimes when I would begin the reweaving process on someone who was badly injured or very sick, an angelic being would appear, place their arms through mine, and help me to reweave the life pattern back into shape.

You can do a lot of work with the body's different layers if the lifespan's measure is not at an end. If the illness or damage is from a hot spot of destruction, but the lifespan is still good, the person can often be put back together with a lot of work and time. But if the lifespan

is as an end, nothing can be done. It is simply a matter of witnessing the taking of the orb and the cessation of life.

Often the type of angelic being that turns up to detach the orb one that is essentially the 'Bringer of Death.' They will not heal, help, or advise: their job is to remove the well of vital force, severing the connection between the person's inner and outer energies. This breaks the connection between the spirit and the body. The body will die and the spirit will release.

This process happens for everything that is a living being. It is also an octave of a principle that works in magical patterns. Once you learn the principles by working on your own body and also by observing the dynamic in action through vision, you can absorb what you have learned and apply the principles to working on fate, magical patterns, and other living beings.

2.5 *Task:* Vision to tidy up your pattern

The best way to learn about the pattern that holds the vital force is to work on your own. Do this in your work space so that contacts can flow over the threshold and work with you.

Light the lights in the directions and open the gates, but don't put out your tools. Greet the contacts on the thresholds and tell them what you are about to do. Then sit before the central altar facing south and still yourself.

Once you are still step out of your body and turn to look at it. Look in detail: see the light of the vital force throughout the body and take note if there are dull areas.

Look at the centre of your body, between your sternum and umbilicus, and focus on that area. When you are ready step into the centre of the body with the clear intention of working on the web pattern and the orb of vital force. Remember, intention opens up the layers for you to work with.

See with your inner vision the body as a web of energy, and check all the strands of the web.

Ensure that the strands round the orb of vital force are all connected into the orb. If any are broken or frayed, reconnect them. If you need tools, reach upwards for them with a clear idea in your mind of what you need. Think about what you would use to fix wires or threads: crochet needles, electrical tape, copper wires, sewing thread…use what you know about so the assisting beings will realise what they need to hand you.

You are unlikely to see the beings working with you. In such work all that tends to appear is a hand with a tool coming down from above.[5] Depending on how your imagination works, you could also work like a spider: see threads coming from your hands as you weave.

What triggers the right energy and form for you to work with is being clear with yourself about what you are doing. If you are clear, the beings and contacts that will help will also be clear about what you are trying to achieve.

Work your way through your body, checking all the channels of vital force that appear as these threads of power, and check that all threads eventually track back to the central orb of vital force. Once everything is fixed, the whole pattern should glow with vital force and the orb should be strong and bright.

If the orb is still dull once all the threads are connected, there is likely an issue with your vital force. To regenerate that, reach upwards with the intention of filling up your vital force and see an energy line[6] coming down from the stars. Plug it into the orb until it fills with light and shines brightly. Once it is full and the web is clear and bright, hand the tools back and step out of the body.

Look at the body again closely to ensure everything is more or less okay. Once you are sure all is well, step back into the body and meditate in stillness for a short while.

When you are ready get up, bow to the contacts in the directions, and close down the room. If you can, go and have a nap or lie down quietly for an hour or so. In all work of this type, never dash straight back into the family/life/work; always have a little time to decompress and *let the work embed itself in your body and mind.*

This is really important, as the process carries on for a while after you have finished: the body needs to process the energy and organise itself. If you rush straight back into work or onto the internet/phone you can short circuit the inner process from completing itself: it needs to 'cook.'

If you spotted problems with your web, then a number of things could have caused that: a prolonged bad diet with few fresh foods, an unhealthy living situation, inner impact, clingers, long-term parasites, ill health, and so forth. Just fixing the web without finding out the cause of any problems and remedying it will bring about a return of the damage.

It is up to you to find out the cause and take whatever action is possible. If it is from an old injury or illness that has now passed[7] then a web repair should be enough—but you will need to keep an eye on it by doing three-monthly checks. You can use divination to help pinpoint the cause, along with a good dose of reality checks and common sense.

Also, the web can degrade with age, which must also be taken into consideration. It can be fixed periodically if the cause is simply ageing, but it is also important to live as healthily as you can.

2.6 *Task:* Vision to observe an orb's removal

This vision puts you in a situation where a person is on the point of death and their orb of vital force is being removed. When the magician does this vision they will be sent to wherever there is someone at the point of death and recitation is being used. So each of you who works with this vision will be sent to different places and experience different scenarios. The time could be past, present, or

---

[5]Work for the future.
[6]I see a gasoline pump.

[7]A bad long-term infection, cancer, etc.

future: you will go wherever it is best for you to observe and learn.

This is also a step that takes you a bit further in the methods of visionary work: you are not all going to one set place that is well-trodden and known by other magicians; rather you are learning to hear a call and answer it. You have done this once before in a simple way; now you will take it a step further and expand your technique.

Set up your room, put out the tools, open the gates, greet the contacts, and then sit in the direction which most pulls you. Sit facing the altar and close your eyes.

Meditate into stillness and feel yourself in the Void, in the 'nothing.' As you sit quietly you will hear a call or a voice reciting something: it is a sacred recitation of some kind to which you are instinctively drawn. Fix all your attention on the recitation and follow it.

You will find yourself stepping out of the Void and into a room or space. There will be a person on the point of death, and someone in the room or nearby will be reciting a sacred text which you may or may not recognise.

Look at the dying person. See their web and look closely: observe what the damage is and look at the state of their orb: it may be dull, dark, or still bright. Whatever the orb's state, you were drawn there because this is a point of death.

As you listen to the recitation a wall of fire appears, and out of it steps an angelic being. Its presentation will largely depend on the type of recitation: they will dress for the religious pattern being used. If the angel sees you and acknowledges you, bow to them and keep at a safe distance where you can observe but not interfere.

Watch what the angel does, how it acts, whether or not it talks to the dying person, and whether it touches them or interacts in any way with their web pattern. At some point the angel will reach into the person and lift the orb out of their web: the web will break up and fall apart straight away.

The angel may leave at this point or stay and observe; or it may help the dead person. Watch closely. Once the web and orb have been broken up the body will breathe its last breath. This breath can be observed energetically, so watch closely. It is at that point that you may be able to see the actual eternal spirit of the person. They may stay in the dead body for a while, or they may lift themselves out: death is unique to each person, so you will have to simply watch and learn. But remember that each death is very different and each spirit handles it in their own way.

Now cast your attention to the person doing the reciting. Look at the words and how the recitation affects the space round the person, how it forms in the air and what it does.

You will notice that it changes the energy of the space around the living and the dead and creates its own energy pattern: this is to stop the dead person immediately clinging to the nearest living person. The space prevents such an action, and also creates a pathway that the dead person can begin to walk as they let go of life.

Sometimes the dead person will cling to their body for days[8] and sometimes they will leave immediately. Just watch and learn. When the recitation stops you must leave, as it is no longer safe for you to be there as an observer: the recitation offers you protection. Sometimes the recitation lasts only an hour and sometimes it can go on for days, depending on the culture.

When it is time for you to leave, remember the wall of fire that the angel stepped through. Go and stand before it. You will see straight away that it is a threshold: step through it and you will find yourself in the Inner Library. Either go back to your work space from here, or spend some time in the Library touching books connected with what you have just witnessed. Whatever happens in the Library will be connected to your learning on this subject, so take your time. When you are ready step back into your work space.

---

[8]In our time.

103

Before you get up to close the directions down, think about what you just witnessed and make sure you remember all the details. Once the room is closed down, write it in your journal and type up a summary on computer.

2.7 *Task:* Exteriorising the learning

All inner experience is exteriorised in the physical world.[9] Trying to understand the process of the web and the vital force can be difficult intellectually, so the best way to really embed the knowledge in you deeply is to work with a weaving action in the physical world.

You can do this very simply by drawing, weaving, braiding, knitting—or even working with electric circuit boards. Do some practical work on creating patterns that all come to a central point: as you work the pattern, think about what you now know and have seen, and create the pattern as if you were creating a circuit for vital force to flow through. You have worked with creating patterns before, and this exercise should take you a step further in your understanding.

By doing this simple outer action you will begin to understand weaknesses in patterns and what strengthens them, what is a good pattern and what is a weak pattern. How many connections to the orb should a pattern make: is more better than less, or is it the other way round?

When you do this task, don't let your conscious mind get in the way: just do it and ponder as you work. The act of a magician weaving or constructing a pattern/circuit will trigger the deeper understanding and brings the outer and inner skills together.

2.8 *Task:* Observing patterns in nature

Look at magnified images of crystal patterns, snowflakes, sand, sugar, salt; look at stem cells,

any type of cells, neurons; and look at a map of the central nervous system. What you will see is patterns, lots of patterns. Nature is very efficient in that she reuses the same idea over and over in different forms. Look at images of the solar system, of galaxies: look throughout nature at her patterns. The inner world and the outer world are not very different in many respects, and the same unique patterns of life force, energy, and structure appear in everything, both inner and outer.

Here is an example picture of endothelial cells under the microscope: look how similar it appears to the inner web. Everything is a mirror of everything else: once you learn to work with one type of living web, you can apply the same skill to everything else with a living web.

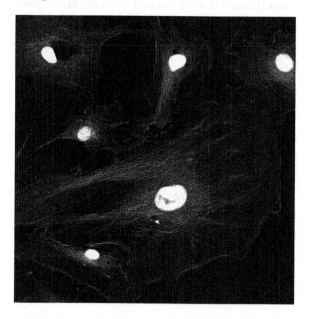

Figure 2.1: Endothelial cells under the microscope with fluro staining. (Public domain.)

2.9 *Task:* Construct a ritual pattern

This task teaches you to connect the patterns inherent in nature to ritual action. You are not going to construct a working ritual; rather you are going to construct a couple of *layers*.[10]

Look and find recitations that are used in death, regardless of the religion. And look at

---

[9]This is why magic has ritual—it externalises the power.

[10]Learning to walk before you can run.

more than one: find ones that have reference to powers, beings, or directions. The Tibetan and Egyptian texts are the richest sources for this, but also look at Hindu, other Buddhist, Catholic, Islamic, and Jewish ones: see what you can find, then settle on one.

Extract the pertinent information[11] and map out on paper what directions you think those powers would belong in. The central flame is the orb and the starting and finishing points of the ritual. Don't bother with any words at this point; you are simply focusing on the pattern itself.

Map ritual movement between the directions and cross-quarters, above and below. Figure out how the ritual would move around the space to connect or disconnect energies, and between encounters with different beings. The movements between the directions and quarters, and between the different beings, will create a pattern of movement: draw this pattern out on paper and map it.

Then simply walk the pattern around the work space without opening anything or calling in anything: see if it works as a mobile pattern that you can walk.

The pattern should have connections between various beings, the carrying of energy from one place to another, and connect to, or disconnect, the central orb. Now build in which light is lit when, what light is put out when, and which beings would be on which threshold. Remember that the purpose is the disconnection of the orb and the composting of the pattern of life.

Learning to do this without putting in any recitation is a good way to learn the underlying dynamics of power: too much emphasis is usually placed on words and tools in magic, often to the detriment of the actual pattern of energy involved. Of course a working ritual would have words and tools, but learning to work with the pattern first in this way teaches you what it is that upholds, works with, and powers up with the use of words and tools.

Write up the ritual steps and draw out the final pattern. Keep it on computer: it will be submitted to your mentor if you are being mentored.

2.10 Summary

The physical and energetic patterns in life are important layers to work with as magicians. You will also see, through your understanding of your fate web, that such patterns trigger events. In fate they appear as chance meetings, certain destinations, names, etc. These things can often appear on the surface as inconsequential or random.

The same happens with physical and energetic patterns: they trigger events in the physical or energetic life of a being, and also dictate how that substance or being will interact with other patterns. Each layer of nature's patterns of life, substance, and fate, are like locks and keys: they either fit or they don't. When they fit, they trigger something.

When the vital force is removed from a pattern, either a magical pattern, a vital force pattern, a fate pattern, etc., whatever that pattern is will fall apart and be destroyed/composted. This is a really important dynamic to understand in magic as it runs through everything, and this understanding can mean the difference between success and failure in magic.

---

[11]Powers, directions, Divinity, deities, spirits, demonic beings, landscapes, etc.

Lesson 3

Dynamics of Death and Destruction

Not all magicians properly grasp the magical dynamics of destruction and the death of something, and they can often, through misunderstandings, get themselves onto difficult fate paths that affect their own lives. Because of this I want to spend a lesson looking at this aspect of magic before you start dipping your hand in the cauldron of destruction in magical practice. If you understand the dynamics behind destruction and death, you are far less likely to get yourself in a mess with a magical act.

Once you start to work with power as a magician, what you do magically affects everything around you, including the local land and community. I do often wonder whether, in those areas in the world which are rife with violence, societal disruption, and instability, it is the very vicious, destructive magic that these areas so often have which is the culprit; or whether the effect of living in a violent society triggers people to perform such destructive magic acts.

After what I have seen of the various forms of magic around the world, my opinion is that the magic at least adds to the problem and in some places may actually cause the continued instability. But that is only my opinion: I have never stayed long enough in some of these countries to observe the long-term magical patterns and their effect on the local society.

But in some countries, destructive and vicious magic often go hand in hand with a violent society. What I have observed for myself after watching a place for a long time, is that magic I have done in the past that was destructive, even though I felt at the time it was for good reason, had an unexpected destructive reaction from the land which then affected the local society.

This is not to say that magic and destruction are off-limits; rather it is more about seeing the bigger picture and understanding the ripple effect of such magic on the land and people.

When I was younger I saw magic as being very isolated in its action: you do A to achieve B which is targeted at X; nothing else would be affected. I was wrong. When you do magic to achieve B, everything round it that is possibly connected in any way will also be affected: the threads of the pattern are all heavily interconnected.

This brought me to the understanding that nothing ever happens in isolation. Everything is truly connected in some way, and for magic to be balanced and successful it must flow in harmony with all the patterns of energy, fate, and existence that are connected to whatever you are trying to achieve.

When I understood this I changed how I worked. I found that often something needing magical destruction did not need a missile aimed directly at it: simply affecting the frequency of the right part of the web was enough to trigger a self-destruct. We become *catalysts* rather than missile launchers. This allows everything else connected to the target to shift, adjust, and maintain its inner and energetic integrity.

The key to becoming a truly outstanding magician is not making the same mistakes as the last generation, but learning from those mistakes and making new ones that will teach you if you pay attention.

3.1 Ritual and visionary dynamics

When magic is used in a targeted way to destroy or kill something it leaves a void that something else must fill. Whatever fills that void will be of the same ilk as what was destroyed. For example, if magic is used to kill something very destructive, what will replace it is something else of the same destructive power: the destructive influence, be it a mass murderer, a destructive being, an overgrowth of dangerously unhealthy plants/creatures/people, etc., will remain in that place's pattern.

People, creatures, beings and plants are inherently connected to a pattern on a land mass. Taking out the outer result of that pattern[1] will not destroy the pattern itself: someone else will express that pattern and fill the shoes of the mass murderer.

There are two reasons why this happens: (1) the pattern that is playing out on a land area or a genetic line, and (2) because magical destruction should actually be approached as magical *creation*: you create a pattern of destruction.

By using the flows of creation for the destruction you are reversing the flows of power: instead of triggering a creative impulse, sending it into the future, and weaving into it a completion time and composting/destruction mechanism, you do the opposite. The flow of destruction is used, with a time limit, and a creative impulse is added that moves forward

---

[1]The mass murderer, for example.

into the future. *You create the destruction; you do not destroy a creation.* In magical terms you are not removing a destructive element from a pattern, but adding a new catalyst to the pattern. This enables the deep fate process to continue along its pattern of time and expression, but it changes how that process expresses itself. It also bypasses the problem of leaving a void that something else will fill: the magician replaces the destruction with a new creation that will (hopefully) act within the pattern in a different way. Let's have a look at an example that shows how it expresses at a 'ground' level.

Harold is a magician. In his neighbourhood there is someone who is killing local children, but they have not yet been caught. If Harold works magic to pinpoint the murderer and destroy him, and does this without looking at the wider picture of the fate pattern operating on the land and which energetic web is in action in the area, he will potentially leave a void that another killer will fill.

However, if Harold first examines the pattern playing out in the area that has triggered this killer, he can identify it, look what it is doing, and see where it is taking the larger fate of the area. Though not always the case, *the killer is often a symptom, not a cause.*

Once Harold has identified what is happening, he can think about how best to change things for the long term in a way that will not draw in another killer.

An example of such a pattern playing out could look like this: the community is located over a land feature that is very destructive. Because people have built houses on it, it can affect people quite badly. In the past, local tribes knew about the destruction but needed to be there because of the water supply, so they channelled the destructive energy magically by using that spot to butcher animals for meat. They would leave an offering of a slaughtered animal for the land spirits, and take the rest away with them.

Harold realises, after looking magically using divination, vision, and research, that the neighbourhood is built right on top of this 'slaughter' spot. He also pinpoints the killer's residence as being one of the houses on that spot: the killer is manifesting the local destructive pulse.

The killer is a man called Jake. He has something wrong with his eye, has a dog called Blacky, and used to live in Florida—stay with me on this one. He has mental health problems and always used to imagine killing helpless people when he masturbated. This drew in parasites which in turn fuelled his urges. When he moved to this neighbourhood the urges overwhelmed him.

Jake was thin and weak, and therefore could not find helpless adults to dominate, so he turned to children. At first he was content simply to watch his potential victims, but when the parasites urged him on enough to tip him into action he would grab a child and enact his fantasy.

Harold the magician did not know these details. He knew only that the killer was local and expressing a deeper destructive pattern in the land. So Harold began to work in visionary ritual to remove the killer from the pattern and open the door for a better, healthier expression of the pattern. He worked with phases of the moon, with weave patterns, and with destroying deities. He worked with the reverse flows of time, energy, and impulse to ensure that he was creating a destruction that would then bring renewal.

Sure enough, six weeks later Jake was accidentally killed by stepping in front of a truck that he did not see. Harold was not aware that the dead person was the killer—which is an important point. Harold did not get personal, did not seek revenge, and was not connected energetically to the killer: he did *surgical removal and replacement magic*.

A couple of months later, a guy called Jack moved into the neighbourhood. He opened a butchers shop, as was his trade, and the locals started to get to know him. Harold went in to buy some meat and got talking to Jack. Jack worked in partnership with his cousin, Phil, who's last name was Black. Jack and Phil's dream was to work hard for a few years and make enough money to retire to Florida where they would spend their time fishing. Jack had a girlfriend and they played around a lot with bondage. He was a bit of a weakling: role playing with domination in sex felt good to him and both he and his girlfriend enjoyed it.

The local killings stopped. The pattern was not altered; rather it expressed through the new people in a less destructive way while still working from the same script.

These 'scripts' fascinate me. I have seen them in action countless times and still cannot figure out the deeper dynamics behind them. Often key aspects of a pattern appear silly or inconsequential to us, but nevertheless fate sometimes seems to follow these 'scripts' and they can appear as key points on a fate web when viewed in vision. We looked at this concept in mythic patterns in Apprentice Module V, Lesson 7.

A lesser expression of the fate web which follows the same script can replace a more unbalanced one. But most of the time we magicians do not spot these aspects of the script or do not recognise them, which is why it is better to work with the deeper pattern and allow fate's flows to do the rest. One step of working with the deeper pattern is not to destroy, but to create destruction and renewal, so that the expression of the script is replaced, not ultimately destroyed.

Before we move on, the other important aspect of this work for magicians to understand is the difference between necessity and want in this sort of situation. As we get older we can look back over our lives and see how very difficult times often gave us opportunities for strength and expansion. But when you are young difficult obstructions can seem insurmountable, and a magician would struggle to use magic to overcome these difficulties. Sometimes using magic is valid and works okay; sometimes it short circuits necessary development. We have looked at this a lot in the past.

With destructive magic this dynamic really comes into focus. If you use destructive magic to sidestep something ultimately workable, however difficult, you end up creating a pattern around you that is limited and self-defeating.

Using destructive magic should be a last resort in order to avoid unnecessary destruction or serious imbalance that affects a wider group of people. Less is better than more, also more effective. A good way to self-limit with such magic is to act as if you have a very limited bag of bombs: only use them when it is really a matter of life or death.

When a magician works in balance and with inner contacts, deities, and beings, most unnecessary destructive hotspots are diverted away from you and you only have to deal with the issues that will ultimately bring you to strength and growth—unless you do something really dumb, in which case all bets are off.

3.2 Destructive renewal

To avoid causing untold chaos through destructive magic that creates imbalance, magic can be worked around a pattern's periphery to bring regeneration through destruction. We have looked at this in the past in the course by way of 'gardening,' which nudges renewal through pruning, cutting, and brush clearing. If a garden has been magically linked with a larger pattern, i.e., the local community, then by working on a garden you will also work on the local land, its population, and the local beings and spirits.

The same magical principle applies through everything: when you consciously link one expression of a pattern to another, wider pattern, they start to harmonise to the same frequency. This then lets you work on one pattern to affect the other. This principle was well known in old folk magic and was used, often maliciously, to kill or disable someone. Knowing how patterns connect and interweave lets the magician understand some of the deeper aspects of cause and effect that can be used in these ways, and enables them to deal with this sort of malicious magic.

Take, for example, the use of poppets or mirroring to attack someone. In the case of poppets, the object is connected into the victim's pattern, usually by using something that belongs to or comes from them.[2] Then the poppet is attacked, which in turn affects the victim. Mirroring is where a magician starts to follow a victim and copy their every move, then at a key moment takes control of the pattern and enacts a movement that will damage the victim, such as stepping out onto a road when the victim's position would make them step in the path of a truck.

A skilled folk magician can be very successful at accomplishing such things; however, most of them do not realise that the pattern currently playing out does not change and the attacker can end up taking on some of the victim's fate pattern. In magic, a short-term outlook can end with a magician carrying a great deal of other people's baggage. Destroying the victim by interfering with their pattern does not destroy the pattern; it simply shifts it so that it can express itself another way.

A vessel's total destruction has a defined point in time with hotspots along the way. If the magician triggers destruction during a hotspot time, then the pattern will dissolve. Otherwise they will take on the pattern themselves and will have to carry it until its time of completion. It is vital you understand that the rhythm of destruction and regeneration has its own timetable, as at some point you will likely have to deal with such an incident and have to clean it up for the good of all involved.

If the total destruction of a vessel[3] is attempted magically and that vessel still has a length of time expression, the magic will either fail or its expression will transfer into something else. You will simply move the problem about; not solve it. And then you have the whole imbalance of the Scales to deal with.

If as a magician you are ever confronted with a dilemma where something needs to be destroyed to prevent widespread destruction,

---

[2]Hair, nails.
[3]Person.

don't get evangelistic and work from emotion or a sense of ego: simply step back and look at the pattern and what connects with it. Tread carefully, look round the edges, and see where the destruction could be used to shift an energy expression from destruction to regeneration or to a more compatible expression of destruction. The method for looking at a pattern is something you worked with when you looked at your fate web: the techniques and methods are very similar.

And when you look at a pattern you have to be very balanced and not look with emotion. Often what appears to be terribly destructive is necessary in the long term: we might not like it, but it is serving a purpose. When I have been faced with such a dilemma, I have found that I must trust the beings and contacts that work around me: if the job needs doing I will feel a gathering of the contacts around me who will guide my actions to an extent. But when it comes to either creation or destruction, the ultimate responsibility lies with your own choices.

As humans, we mirror the Divine capability for triggering creation or destruction. With this comes choice and responsibility. When you destroy/kill someone magically, you are committing murder. This will change you at a very deep level: be fully aware what you are doing, as there is no dodging the fallout from such an action—and hopefully none of you will ever be placed in that position.

Now let us look a bit deeper, as I think by now you should have a good idea of the surface dynamics. In the initiate module on the powers of creation you looked a bit deeper into the power dynamics that work with creation. The same powers work with destruction.

3.3   The deeper inner dynamics

Remember the Light Bringer and Restriction, with Perfect Balance in the middle? Those creative powers are also destructive powers. The Light Bringer not only forges a path for new life and creation, but it can also forge a path for destruction and death:

creation and destruction are inseparable. And where restriction can hold back something destructive, it can also hold back creation.

The only thing that never changes is the central fulcrum: Perfect Balance. Everything seeks balance but cannot actually achieve it in physical form, as physical expression is a dance between creation and destruction. The fulcrum serves as a *reference point* between creation and destruction.

When the fulcrum is suppressed there will be either too much creation or too much destruction, which is the major key to working with such vast powers: often when you encounter overcreation or overdestruction, the fulcrum of the pattern has been limited or magically and energetically bound either by humans or inner beings. Every pattern has these three elements within it. The key to working with destruction or creation is to ensure that all three powers reflected in the pattern are equal. Destruction is interwoven with creation and vice versa, and the fulcrum sits in the middle and keeps the balance.

When magic is involved in a situation, one of these elements has been magically suppressed which causes an overgrowth of the other dynamic while the fulcrum struggles to maintain balance. When magic is not involved, such imbalance is usually a natural process where something is *seeking rebalance*: the scales will swing back and forth until balance is restored. Occasionally a pattern can become heavily parasited. If the fulcrum is itself bound up with parasitical activity, balance cannot be restored until it has been magically cleaned.

Sometimes non-magical human actions can have the same effect as magic. In such cases nature will respond with an attempt to rebalance. Occasionally you get a perfect storm where a non-magical human act in a magically tuned place will have the same effect as a magical act.

The massacre at the mortuary temple of Hatshepsut that we discussed earlier in the course is a good example of this. The mortuary temple is a magically constructed place that was highly tuned. A human massacre done in such a tuned place will have the same effect as a magical massacre. The imbalanced power released into the pattern had to be restricted so that the pattern's future path could continue until its end date.

It is this understanding of the deeper dynamics that point the magician in the right direction of how to work, when to work, and when not to work. The mortuary temple needed a good clean, but it also needed the power of restriction to stop the cascade of destruction released into the pattern. The restriction was imposed magically on that destructive cascade of power by a magician. The clean-up will be for someone else to do, or the temple will gradually clean itself now that the balance of power has been restored.

3.4 Magic from the past still working

One dynamic nearly always overlooked by magicians faced with a destructive overbalance in a pattern is the effect of past magic. When we look at a pattern to see the source of the destructive power, if we look with the intent of finding current magic and see none we can falsely assume that magic is not the cause. How you approach the viewing is really important. Don't assume that an effect is from a current situation. Sometimes magic from the past can still be running and effecting a destructive imbalance in a pattern.

If a powerful and imbalanced magical act was performed a few centuries ago or more, it could still be affecting a pattern, fate, land mass, or community. How you approach viewing such a pattern will define what you will see. If you look only for current magic you will not see past magic. If your approach for such a viewing is "show me any magic affecting this pattern, regardless of when it was done," then any past magic still playing out will show up.

Past magic can act like ripples in water: it gets bigger and wider over time, and its effect can spread right out to affect everything around it.[4] Past magic is dealt with in the same way as present magic, but the rebalancing process may take more time if the situation has become heavily parasited. And the further back in time you go, at least in some cultures and land areas, the more powerful the magic gets.

If you do spot some very old magic still running effectively, it is also wise to look closely at what it is doing. Is it restricting a very dangerous power that flows out of the land? If so, were you to rebalance the pattern that dangerous power would release again. It might be fine and dandy for the land to express itself, but it may also destroy every human in its path. Which brings us back to something we looked at a lot in the apprentice section: *what is bad and what is good?*

At its heart, understanding death and destruction in magical terms is about understanding the construction, upholding, and dismantling of patterns; also understanding what those patterns are doing, whether it is a fate pattern, a creation pattern, or a magical pattern; and knowing when to intervene and when to stay your hand. It is also about understanding that absolute destruction is not for humans to initiate;[5] rather it is a matter of changing how a pattern expresses itself, ensuring that any creation also has death and destruction woven into it, and that any destruction has creation and regeneration also woven into it.

3.5 Withheld destruction

Before we move on to the practical work I want to look briefly at withheld destruction. This is a situation where destruction and regeneration should be happening, but something has stalled it[6] and this has attracted a parasitical element. This usually presents as a very unhealthy situation of violence,

---

[4]This is why you should always be careful what you do with magic.

[5]Unless you *want* a lifetime of unravelling your mistakes.

[6]Usually magical intervention, past or present.

disease, poverty, or degeneration in a group, household, community, or land area.

You see a mess in which the destructive pattern is there, and needs to express, but something is stopping its completion. But stopping such completion also withholds regeneration, which results in a picture of stagnation that is a rancid pool of semidestruction, which is to say everything around it degenerates but never quite *dies*, and therefore cannot renew itself.

This can be seen in areas where a lot of conditional folk/tribal magic gets used for short-term results.[7] Such magic is often very short-sighted and approached with a very narrow view which does not take into account the wider picture. When nature powers or land beings are trapped and used it gets *really* messy. We can see this in certain communities around the world that are steeped in such magic. They are also communities infested with drugs, violence, poverty, and despair.

To outsiders it often seems that the state of the community is what drives people to short-term results magic, which sometimes is the case. But in other cases it is the prolonged use of such magic that incorporates beings which ends up causing the festering mess. It is akin to a community only living off of candies and junk food, taking heavy drugs, and drinking fetid water when good food and clean water are available but shunned in preference to short-term tastes.

This sort of situation attracts parasites of all types. They have a vested interest in maintaining the status quo and will try to block any attempt to directly clear the situation. Such blocking can become vicious and dangerous: another reason to tiptoe round such a pattern and work round the edges to trigger change rather than confronting the situation head-on.

Often when such a situation has gone on for a long time, deeper and more powerful destructive beings come along. These either totally destroy the pattern to clear space for regeneration or, in the worst case scenario, contribute to the problem's continuation.

If a magician goes into such a situation as a hero out to fix it, they will likely get violently attacked or sucked into the pattern themselves. If a magician is willing to make himself insignificant and work on the periphery, he can often be successful at finding the weak link, breaking it, and thus allowing the destruction to complete its cycle and make way for creation. As I often say, "no one ever looks at the office cleaner..." It can be easy to be invisible if you don't allow your ego in.

3.6 About the practical work

The only way truly to grasp what happens with destruction and death in patterns, what is causing it, and whether or not it needs intervention, is to look at the patterns themselves form an inner perspective. The actual action of working on such a pattern is usually done in ritual, but before you conduct any ritual work you really need to know the larger picture you are working upon.

The best way to observe such a pattern is to look at a major destructive/death pattern form a safe vantage point, and take the time to look carefully at what is happening in regards to balance, the fulcrum, and so forth.

No matter how destructive a situation may seem to an observer caught in its midst, so long as the inner pattern has a balance of creation and destruction within it, its outer manifestation should not be interfered with magically.[8]

However, if it is obvious from inner viewing that the energies flowing in and out of the inner pattern are unbalanced, then it is likely that magical action would help. And by viewing the inner pattern this way, you may be able to see how seemingly small aspects of the picture are actually facilitating the major destruction.

To do this viewing, you will go in vision to observe the inner pattern of an outer

---

[7] Kill that person, limit that person, gain money and power.

[8] You would make a bad situation worse.

destruction. Where you spot unhealthy imbalance, you will then ritually work upon it. Getting close to such a pattern, even if you are in a safe viewing area, still puts you at some risk of getting sucked into it, so preparation is of the greatest importance.

Before you start, look around the world at places where a cycle of death and destruction is currently happening. Look for one that is powerful, has religion involved, and also where tribal or other types of magic may be at work, either in the present or the past, and which could be contributing to the issue. Write the name of the central city that is the focal point of the destruction—and write out its name both in English and in the script and language of its natives.

This working involves a vision and then a ritual straight after, so make sure you have time enough to work without being disturbed. You will also need a sheet of paper and a pen for this working's ritual aspect. Put it near or under the central altar until you are ready to work. Have water and fill your vessel. Do not wear shoes for this working. If it is cold you may wear socks, but no shoes.

3.7 *Task:* **Visionary observation**

Set up your working room, set out the tools, light the lights, and open the gates. Place your cord on your right hand and your cloth shield round your shoulders: use a safety pin so that it does not come off as you work. Put the paper with the city's name on the central altar. Greet the contacts in each direction, bow to each of them, then do the Fulcrum ritual.

Once you have finished, sit down and meditate into stillness. Once you are still, go in vision to the Inner Library and to the stone temple.[9] While in vision, and using your inner voice, call upon the Companion, the Sandalphon, at the south altar. When he appears, ask to be taken to the city you have chosen with the intention to view *the inner*

---

[9]Notice we are going for the higher frequency.

pattern that is behind the destruction and is the root of it.

The angel will walk into the south through the altar. You follow, walking beside the angel. You will find yourself walking on a path that leads through a landscape to a city boundary. The angel will stop at a safe distance and stand behind you: he will place his hands over your eyes so that you can observe the inner dynamics rather than just the outer, modern city.

Take your time, as it can be a bit of an adjustment to understand what you are looking at.

The pattern can appear as a weave, as interlocking patterns, or like a grid. Upon and within the pattern you will see beings moving back and forth. Some areas will be dark, grey, or colourless; others will be bright with some having strong colours.

First look for the Fulcrum. It can appear as a bright point of stillness where there is no action or beings. Everything will seem to flow to and from that point. It may be in the middle or not: it all depends on the dynamics of the energies at play.

If there are more dark, clumped, or congealed areas than coloured or light ones, then an imbalance is prolonging the destruction. Needful destruction may appear as fast, sparking, or strongly coloured energy or in any way that your mind can understand as indicating impulse and action. Destruction that shows as an energy clumping together, or which appears muddy, congealed, or lacking any vitality, is likely destruction that has stalled in its process.

That stall may be natural but need a bit of help to get it going, or it may be there because of human magical intervention or human intervention in a magical place. Don't assume anything and don't judge anything; just look.

Also, if the pattern is too bright or too light then too much creation may be flowing into the pattern which has triggered a manifestation of destruction in order to keep balance. Each pattern needs creation and destruction, not just one or the other. If you do not understand what you are seeing, ask the angel to help you recognise what is before you.

Once you have an overview of the pattern, look at the edges and sides. Look for beings blocking power flows and breaks and knots in the pattern;[10] and using your inner senses try to get a sense of where in the pattern would be a key area for a catalyst action that would not alert any hostile beings to your presence or to the changing of the pattern. If the pattern is unbalanced, all sorts of beings will be feeding on the situation, and they will defend their food source.

Stay as long as you can hold the vision and look in detail at every aspect of the pattern; but do not edge closer to it, and do not be tempted to take any action: simply observe. And while you observe stay balanced and still. Do not let any emotion, or any thought of action, creep in: it will make you visible. You are there to look and learn; all action that you will take will be done ritually, which is safer.

When you are ready follow the angel back to the stone temple. Stand in the centre of the space while the angel cleans you off. They may blow on you or dump water over you, or do something else to clean you up. When they have finished, bow to them and thank them, then sit down in the space. Go into stillness and be aware of your body in your work room and your mind in the stone temple. Fuse them together, then open your eyes. Now you go straight to the ritual while the pattern's resonance is still fresh in your mind and your inner senses.

3.8   *Task:* Ritual

Pick up the paper and pen. Map out the pattern as closely as you can remember, and mark any dark, clumped, or unhealthy-looking areas that you know are imbalanced. Also mark out the pattern's creative aspect.[11] Mark any overly bright areas[12] and also mark where the fulcrum is. Also mark down anything else

---

[10]Magic.
[11]Even if it was destruction that was being created.
[12]Too much creation.

to which your attention was drawn, anything on the pattern's periphery, or any gathering of beings that the angel showed you.

Write the city's name in English at the bottom along with the name used by its inhabitants in its own language—use the paper you have with the name written on it for reference. Place the map under the central light with the fulcrum under the light.

This is one of the rituals where if it will not distract you, playing one of the Tibetan chants listed early in your apprentice training[13] in the background will help you and protect you as you work.

If you did not observe imbalance in the pattern, still do this ritual but keep in mind that you are simply learning, and the ritual will contribute towards the current process without interfering with the pattern itself.

Pick up your sword and holding it in your right hand, blade up, stand before the east altar. Close your eyes and utter:

> "Powers of the east, powers of dawn,
> I ask for a thread to weave into the
> pattern which will restore the balance
> of creation and destruction upon this
> city of [*say the city's name in the inhab-
> itants' language*]."

Reach out with your left hand and using your inner vision see the thread placed into your hand by a contact from behind the threshold. Holding that thread, hold it up to the stars and utter:

> "Power of the Stars, power of the
> future, Father of all being, strengthen
> this thread with your power so that
> it may work in harmony with your
> will, with the powers of fate, for the
> future of this city of [*say the name*]."

Take the thread and, using your inner vision while your eyes are open, place it in the paper

---

[13]It is a specific one.

map. Now place the sword to the left of the map, touching it. Go round the directions to the west and pick up your vessel in your left hand.

Close your eyes and utter:

> "Powers of the west, powers of decline and death, I ask you for a thread of power to harmonise balanced destruction and creation to this city of [(name)], and trigger the destruction of any magic that is keeping this city out of balance."

Reach over the altar with your right hand and receive the thread. Hold it down to the floor and utter:

> "Powers of the Underworld, Mother who receives all, strengthen this thread with your power so that it may work in harmony with your will, with the powers of fate, for the past and future of this city."

Take the thread and place it in the paper map, then place the vessel to the right of the map. Remove the central candle and place it on the south altar.[14] Now stand before the altar, facing south, with the map and the two tools before you. Pick up the sword and at the same time see yourself in the stone temple before the central altar. See the pattern laid out on the stone altar and the map on your own central altar: fuse the two together in your mind. Feel the build-up of the Light behind your left shoulder and the Darkness behind your right shoulder: be aware of the Light Bearer and Restriction behind you and their power running through your arms.

Place both your hands on the sword's hilt, with its point down, and place the point over the part of the pattern you have been drawn to that needs work. Lightly hit that part of the pattern with the point of the sword and utter:

> "Any imbalanced destruction, I balance you with the power of the Limiter. Magic creating imbalance,

---

[14] Putting the fulcrum in the future.

I disperse you with the power of the Limiter. Stagnant energy that is creating imbalance, I disperse you with the power of the Limiter. Beings upholding imbalance, I limit you with this sword, that it may restrict you—leave this pattern or be bound into the desert."

Notice that you are only working on imbalance: if there is no imbalance in the pattern, nothing will happen.

Close your eyes and see the powers of Light and Dark behind you flow through your arms, into the sword, and into the pattern. Stay in that position until the flow finishes. When it has finished, place the sword, point down, against the left side of the altar and instruct it to guard the pattern from interference.

Now pick up the vessel. Instruct the vessel and water by uttering over the water. Hold it to your mouth so that your breath flows over the water. Utter:

> "Waters of the Underworld, vessel of completion and Harvest, gather up from this city of [name] all which needs composting, all which needs to descend to the Mother. Imbalanced destruction I harvest you; magic creating imbalance I harvest you; beings upholding imbalance I harvest you."

Close your eyes and see the powers of Light and Dark behind you flow through your arms, into the vessel, and also into the pattern. Take a deep breath and blow slowly over the water and also the map/pattern while the power is flowing through your arms. See the power flow back out of the pattern and into the vessel. Stay in that position until the flow finishes. When it is finished, put the vessel outside of the working area, by the door of the room—you will take it outside soon.

Go to the south and stand before the south altar. Place your hands over the central candle that is on the south altar and utter:

"Fulcrum of Light and Dark, absorb the power of the south, the power of the future, into yourself so that you may light the way forward."

Pick up the central light and place it back on top of the pattern. Stand in your central position before the altar facing south. Go to the north and get the stone shield. Place it before the central altar on the floor so you can put your foot on it. Stand before the central altar and place your left foot upon the stone.

Hold out your arms to your sides. Mark the sigil of the sword in the air to the left, with your left hand, and the sigil of the vessel in the air to the right, with your right hand.

Utter:

"Fulcrum of Light and Dark, centre of all things, may the power of the stars flow through you and uphold you; may the power of the Underworld support you; may the dawn rise to the east with a new flow of creation; may the sun be full in the south, lighting the way ahead for all beings, creatures, and powers that flow through this city of [name]; and may the sun set in the west, taking with it all the dead, all the decaying, and all the imbalanced. May all destruction be completed by virtue of your power and brought into your arms to rest. So then the new day will dawn once more."

Remove your foot from the stone and leave the room. Take the water with you and go pour it outside on the land, or if this is not possible then compost it by pouring into the toilet. Go back into the room and take with you a bowl or pan that you can put the map in to burn it safely. Go to the central altar, pick up the map, and put the pan/bowl on the altar. Light the map with the central flame and hold it over the pan until it is burned.

Close down the directions and put away the tools, but leave the central light going. Sit down before the central flame and be still. Meditate for a short while and 'feel' into the work you have just done. When you are ready, blow out the candle and dispose of the map's ashes.

3.9 *Task:* Divination reading

You are going to do *before* and *after* readings about the work you have just done. The first reading will look at the city before the work was done. This will give you a divination picture of the situation you viewed in vision. The second reading will look at the city/area's future dynamics as a result of the work that you did.

Bear in mind that the ritual work you did is more of a learning exercise than a job. Normally a group of magicians would work on such an issue, and they would approach it in a variety of different ways to trigger dynamic and lasting change. However, observing such a situation with an angelic being and then going straight onto ritual work will have some effect, however tiny. And sometimes, particularly when a situation has come to a head, it takes just the tiniest magical action to burst the boil.

It is important for you to learn this dynamic, as it will also teach you about how power works. When the build-up to something is in its early stages, it takes a great deal of magical power to shift the power's direction. But once it comes to a head and is ripe for completion, often a small catalyst of energy or a small shift in power can create a lasting change. Once something's peak has passed, magic will have little effect, as the process is preparing to compost anyhow.

You will learn a lot over your years as a magician by observing what works, what doesn't, what needs a lot of power, and what doesn't. Most important is learning to under-stand *why* magic is sometimes powerful and other times not. You will learn far more about power from your failures than your successes. One of the ways to track a failure or success, or at least a change, is by observing the outcomes and using divination.

The Quareia Magician's Deck layout

The following layout is a more detailed version of the Landscape layout. It is specifically designed for the *Quareia Magicians Deck*, but it will work with any deck. The important thing is to learn the meanings of each position and reading the position and card together.

If you choose to work with the Quareia deck you will instantly recognise many of the beings and contacts within it, as it is designed around beings and contacts that exist and appear in magic, and are outlined in this course.

The deck's accompanying book is available for free download on the Quareia website so you can look into the meanings of positions in more detail: many of the positions are also deeply connected to the cards themselves. The book will also be useful for some of your future ritual work.

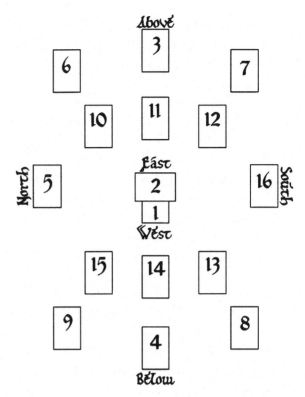

Figure 3.1: The Quareia Magician's Deck Layout

You will notice that the layout aligns with the ritual layout of your work room, and you will work with this layout in ritual in the near future, in order to work with and define contacts in the cross-quarters.

Learn this pattern and the meanings of the positions in terms of powers, places, and contacts, as you will work with this pattern in ritual in some future lessons. Once you know the meanings of the positions, spend some time looking at the layout in relation to your own magical workspace and the pattern we use for ritual space. Look at the positions in relation to each other and the magical directions. It will tell you a lot about the underlying dynamics of your magical ritual pattern/space.

Layout position meanings

1. **The Mother Earth** This is ground zero for the reading. It can mean the human body if the reading is about a person, or it can mean the land, a building, or the energetic body of a being. It is also a 'now' position: it tells you about ground

zero at the present time of the reading. The position tells of the energy, health, and state of the 'vessel' at the centre of the reading.

2. **The Lovers** This tells you about the relationships the subject matter is having that are important. If the reading is about a person, it tells you about the strongest interaction the person is having that is affecting them, for good or bad. It can indicate a person with whom they have a powerful relationship, it can show agreements or contracts with which they are heavily involved, or it can be a power or being they are interacting with. If the reading is about a place or community, it can show the overarching power that is influencing the situation.

3. **Star Father** is long-term future. It shows what is forming in a particular fate pattern and tells you the long-term pattern that will come to pass, if the road walked continues. This is a very important position for magicians to look at when they are using this layout. It corresponds

to the magical direction of future/up and shows the longer-range consequences, for good or bad, of the path currently being followed.

4. The Abyss is the position that shows what is deep in the Underworld, what has passed and will never return. It is the past, the magical direction of down. If the reading is about a place, it can show what is deeply buried beneath it. The card that falls in the position of the Abyss is deep in the past and cannot be revived.

5. The Gate Things that appear in this position are falling away from a person or situation. But a gate is always a two-way thing: whatever is indicated here can return, pause on that threshold, or continue its journey into the past, which will take it down into the Underworld.

6. Temple of Ancestors This position tells the reader what influence or contact is flowing from their deep ancestral line. This is the position in the layout where the ancestors speak to us, advise us, or let themselves be known. This position can also indicate inherited skills and gifts. It is the direct voice of an ancestor that you can work with.

7. Inner Temple The card that appears in this position shows us the deeper, more profound magical or inner aspects of a person or the subject. This is also the position of inner contacts, angelic beings, and deities. This is the threshold between the worlds, and what appears here should be read in that context.

8. Blood Ancestor Just as the Inner Temple is the deep threshold in the inner realms, the Blood Ancestor position tells of the deepest ancestral connection the subject has in the Underworld. The card that lands here tells you of a blood ancestor, what gifts they have passed directly to you, if they are willing to work with you, or if any ancestral line is particularly active or problematic, depending

on the question. It can also indicate magical work in the deep Underworld with the assistance of your own ancestors. This position is read in conjunction with position 6/Ancestral Temple. The Ancestral Temple is the externalization of the deep voice, and the Blood Ancestor is the source of the voice.

9. Foundation This position shows the deep anchor of a person or a subject. It is what has happened in the past that will deeply influence the future. Anything holding a person or situation back because of past events will show in this position. Similarly, anything that laid the foundation for a fate pattern within which the subject is now active will show here. It is the deep roots of the present that will determine how the future unfolds. Whatever appears in this position cannot be changed but must be incorporated into the future, whether the card that falls here is good or bad.

10. Weaver This position is one which tells of the fate pattern of the subject. This is the position of the short-term fate within which we are currently immersed. It can show if we are in harmony with our current fate pattern or not. Whatever card falls in this position is directly related to the card that falls in Foundation. What happened in the past defines how we engage with our current fate path, and both positions can be read together to get the most information possible.

11. Grindstone This position tells of what is limiting us that must be overcome. The limitations or difficulties grind us and polish us to make us stronger. This is a position of hard work that brings great success, of learning that may be difficult but which will be worth it in the end.

12. Magical Temple This position shows what is happening in our magical lives. It shows what powers are manifesting in our magical work, and can also show any interference or issues with our magical path or magical actions.

13. Home and Hearth This is the position of home and hearth. It is the family, the tribe, the local community, the family home…it all depends on your subject matter and question, but this position is always about the outer world around the subject. It is mundane, day-to-day living and the environment in which that day-to-day living is done.

14. The Unraveller This position tells of something that is being unraveled and prepared to pass into the past, through the Gate. Any situation that has reached its peak and is now unravelling will appear in this position. Whatever lands in this position is passing away from the subject and no longer has a place in the subect's life.

15. River of Dreams This is the place of sleep and dreams, of visions and night-times. Whatever is happening in the sleep/dreams/vision of a person will show here. If something powerful appears here, look to see what is in the Weaver, the Ancestral Temple, or the Inner Temple position. This will tell you where the power of the dream is coming from, which in turn will tell you what is potentially happening.

16. The Path of Hercules This is the path forward, the Path of Hercules. It tells of the short-term future and is aligned to the directions of east and south. Whereas south and up is a long-term formation, east and south tells of the future that is already on its way, has formed, and is unrolling itself into action. This also shows where the subject matter is going in terms of what happens next as a direct result of the action in the rest of the reading.

Translating the reading

The major key to successfully drawing information from this layout[15] lies in the interpretation. Over the course we will use this layout quite a bit. You will slowly learn how to work flexibly with it in very different circumstances. It is specifically designed for magical readings and you will have some idea already as to how it works, as the Landscape layout is embedded in it.

For the readings about the city you worked on, you would approach this reading with the understanding that it is about a city or area in conflict. Such a conflict can be balanced[16] or unbalanced, generally through layers of magical and usually religious intervention. Or the imbalance may rise out of the local land power, or it may be a combination of the two.

Position one tells you about the land power and city power themselves. If a destructive card lands here, either the land is disturbed or the conflict is deeply entwined within the land for some reason: prolonged conflict will express in the land powers, as it will have become embedded within the pattern of the land.

You can tease out what is actually going on with the land by doing Tree of Life readings and asking:

> "Show me the natural power of this land, and show me how the conflict is affecting this land."

Position two, which crosses the land, will show you the overarching power currently active in the conflict. Is it a leader who is out of control? Is it beings? Is it a fate power playing out? If you are using the Quareia deck it will be much easier to ascertain what type of influence is active, as many different types of beings are presented in the cards. If you are using your own deck, use what you know about that deck.

The key positions that tell you the deeper story of the conflict are positions six, seven, eight, and nine. These are cross-quarter

---

[15] And indeed any layout.
[16] Working towards a new beginning.

positions that tell you about the deep, under-lying powers at work, which are often unseen. You will notice a heavy emphasis on ancestral contacts, patterns, and bloodlines. These are major players in any current magical situation, as they are the foundation that everything sits upon.

Position six shows ancestral contacts, influences, or powers currently consciously active in the situation, along with any inner priesthood or tribal line still active from an inner point of view: it is all about inner contacts who are still working to affect the area for good or bad.

Position seven shows the deeper under-lying long-term influences in the area, such as deities, angelic beings, and so forth that are working for the very long term. It will also show the root power of any pattern playing out. The pattern of fate in its current expression will show in position ten.

Position eight will show blood lines, tribal grudges, direct blood lines, and any inherited behaviour that is currently active in the living. It will also show any inherited aspects in the living people that affect the conflict, such as racial memory, inherited aggression, or blood lust. It can also show underworld aspects flowing through the people: if there were past genocides of the local tribes, this influence would echo through this position.

Position nine will show the anchor of that city or place, what its deepest power is, what the culture was built on in terms of energy and power, and any reoccurring pattern of behaviour from past lives playing out in the present. This is more an issue for individuals, but cities too can be deeply influenced by the echoes of the past from the very first settle-ments upon the land. It can also be a position that indicates the deepest Underworld deities and land powers that still affect the present land.

The past defines the future in all aspects of life, magic, and culture; and paying close attention to what is in positions six, eight, and nine will tell you what deep past influences of people, beings, and land powers are bringing their power to bear in the present and future.

When you have done both readings, sit and compare them for a while. Pay particular attention to what each reading has in its third position—the distant future will tell you the long-term outcome of the work, and what it would have been without the work. It is hard to tell what sort of timespan you are looking at, but this is not important: it will unfold in its own time. All you need to know is what the long-term conclusion will be.

Also keep in mind when you do the reading what you are asking about: the city's buildings and its people are very different subjects.

If you are not clear in your own head, you will not get a clear answer. If you are concerned more about the land itself, then do the readings with that intention; but don't forget that a happy land might mean *no* humans: we are not particularly popular with a lot of land powers. If you focus on the people, it might mean the destruction of the city and a whole new way of living for them. So be very clear what you are reading for.

3.10 *Task:* Documenting and observing

Write down the readings, what fell in what position, and your findings/interpretations. Type it up on computer, and also keep an eye on the area for the next couple of years. Don't forget, magic is not like a Disney movie: the change will not be instant. Magic needs to work itself through the pattern, which takes time. Watch the area for a year through newscasts, then check in on it a couple of years later and finally five years later.

This sort of work can often take years to unfold. Saying that, sometimes if the timing is perfect and the work is just right, you can see quite a remarkable turnaround, and often not in the way you expected.

Lesson 4

Deeper into the Underworld

In your Apprentice training you learned to make contact with Underworld goddesses and to access the Underworld Forest and the River that flows out into death. In this lesson we will explore a deeper layer of the Underworld. By now you should have enough knowledge behind you to know what you will observe.

The first layer of the Underworld is very much about death and processing things that are composting[1] or which have fallen out of physical manifestation.[2] The next layer takes us deeper into the power of Restriction within substance. This layer holds ancient powers, spirits, deities, and other beings that have been withheld from manifestation in the physical world.

This layer of the Underworld is a mirror of the power of Restriction in the Desert: the Desert restricts powers until they are ready to express in the manifest world; the Underworld restricts powers that have expressed in the manifest world but no longer have a place there.

The inner aspect of any being or structure restricted in the Underworld is also bound out of the Desert: it cannot step back into the flow of creation for future expression. It is frozen in time, in substance, and will stay there for as long as substance exists.

From an inner visionary perspective, when a power is first bound out of the flow of creation it is held in the Sands of the Desert. If it is not going to express itself again it will sink into the Sands of the Desert, vanishing from that pattern of creation, and will eventually appear deep in the Underworld.

Remember the sleeping knights in your mythology studies? Though they are sleeping in caves, they can still express in the inner realm; hence the myths that they can be awoken in a time of need. Though we think of caves as being an aspect of the Underworld, they are in fact still part of the manifest world. Once those knights sink below the caves and into the rock, they will begin the descent into the Deep Underworld, and will ultimately be completely cut off from the manifest realm. You observed a little of this process in some of your earlier visionary work.

When something descends deep below the Underworld Realm of Death, it eventually passes a point of no return and then becomes totally sealed up. Below this layer is the realm of the Titans: vast powers that once were active on the surface of the land, but are now deep in the planet's substance. They still have consciousness, but it cannot express on the land's surface; instead it turns more deeply inwards, affecting the planet's substance. This can cause a ripple effect in the manifest world.

---

[1]Bodies.
[2]Temples.

When it comes to powers or beings that once expressed in the surface world, powers which have sunk deep into the Underworld, eventually the only way they can be accessed is via the Abyss. Many areas of the Underworld open out in the Abyss; but over vast lengths of time these Underworld access points close up, leaving only an expression in the Abyss, until at long last even that access point becomes sealed. We are talking about of huge lengths of time here.

When an adept ventures deep into the Abyss, they will come across the trapped forms of beings that roamed the surface world millions of years ago: this is true *Restriction within substance*.

In early Greek mythology, this deep place was known as Tartarus[3] and was the realm of the most ancient powers and deities.[4] Later in Greek mythology Tartarus was merged to some extent with Hades, and people began to see the two different locations as being the same place.[5]

In magical vision, we still see these two realms as very different places. Tartarus is a much deeper and more profound reflection of Hades—which is the Underworld forest. Tartarus, the Abyss, is the realm where in Egyptian mythology Apophis/Apep, the power of Chaos, is found.

There is another aspect of the Underworld that we have not yet touched much on: the layer of *ancestral consciousness*. We will work with this aspect in this lesson.

Just as beings and powers slowly descend down into Restriction, so too does the power of ancestral lines—of all beings, not just humans.

When we think of ancestors, we often think of conscious individuals with whom we can interact. Because of this, it is easy to become confused between interacting with ancestral consciousness in the land, and past blood family in the inner worlds or through ritual thresholds.

[3]Which you have already read about.
[4]Titans.
[5]And this was the precursor for the Christian idea of hell.

It is easy to forget that a human has two basic components that allow them to express in life: *bloodlines* and *spirit*. The bloodline is deeply connected to the body[6] and carries all the inherent knowledge of substance: genetics. The spirit is the eternal consciousness that resides in the body during a lifetime, which upon death flows back into the inner worlds. The shell of the body is left behind and slowly sinks into the land. So long as the body has not been cremated, the inherent ancestral knowledge that lies within the person's blood and bones sinks into the land, and while ever a fragment of it exists, it can be connected with.

Sometimes the spirit stays within the body at death rather than releasing. In such cases the spirit will stay in the land, slowly merging with the land's pattern to become a composite of human and land consciousness. Sometimes this happened by choice; other times ritual magic was employed to encase the spirit within the body. Those who stayed within the body sometimes express as what we call *sleepers*.

4.1 Magical significance of the two layers

Magicians find the ancestral layer very useful to work with as it shows us the behaviour patterns, skills, and land knowledge still held within the substance of ancestors. When we are in search of or need very old magic, first we "consult the bones." Which is to say we magically connect with the inherent knowledge still held in the bones of those who went before us.

At the same time the ancestor's consciousness is reached over an inner threshold, so that the wisdom of the ancestor's spirit and the knowledge of the ancestor's inherent substance can be brought together for learning.

We talked in the past about a magician or priest/priestess jettisoning their knowledge into the Inner Library upon death. The same mechanism also applies for tribal knowledge.

[6]Vessel.

The learning an ancestor acquired was released at their death and can still be accessed. If the spirit as a consciousness decided not to go deeper into death and renewal, it can stay close to the manifest world without becoming a ghost. In a sense, such consciousnesses become inner ancestors and can be connected with as you have done ritually.

The deep layer of the Underworld, beyond death and the Underworld temples, is a place where the adept can study and learn: here are kept all the powers which, if they expressed on the land's surface today, would wreak total destruction. By studying these areas carefully the magician can really begin to learn how the tides of creation and destruction operated in the distant past. They can also learn about how nature's deep 'immune system' works.

An adept will need to be able to work here in case they ever need to replace and restrict a deep power that has been magically released by stupid magical actions. To prepare for this as an initiate, first you have to go to this place and gain some direct experience of it.

What you experience in these deep layers expresses in visual vocabulary as *beings*: demonic-looking creatures, massive serpents, and other strange and terrifying beings. This is our way of understanding deep, ancient powers that were active before humanity—sometimes even mammals—came along. We are looking at the consciousness of the living planet from thousands and sometimes millions of years ago. We are also looking at the consciousness of the planet's very *substance*. It is no surprise that ancient mythologies tell of vast serpentine demons that can shake the earth[7] and spit fire from the land.[8]

As modern people we smile at such mythological fancies; yet such descriptions appear in ancient cultures all over the world, often with little variance. Does that mean that there are giant serpents in the Underworld that cause earthquakes? No, of course not.

---

[7]Earthquakes.

[8]Volcanoes.

What happens is that the profoundly ancient consciousness of the land expresses itself through imagery of beings that were manifest very long ago: the vocabulary is saying "yes there is this consciousness, yes it is very destructive, and yes it is very very old." Sometimes we can connect with such consciousnesses, and we perceive them as being Underworld deities or strange beings with whom we can connect and commune.

What was roaming about on the earth thousands and millions of years ago? Dinosaurs, giant serpents, feathered reptiles… As we go down deep into the Underworld we reach the layer of composting/restriction that dates from that time. As a result the land powers and consciousnesses express themselves through that imagery. I am sure that whatever type of living being predominates on the land in a few million years' time will perceive a layer of the Underworld as beings who have a human or mammalian presentation.

When you connect with these powers, or simply observe them, you are looking at the consciousness of the land and creatures from the very distant past. Think about those creatures, what we know of them, and how dangerous they would be today.

The same holds true, though in a much lesser way, when we come to ancestors. It is easy to think of ancient ancestral lines of consciousness as being protective and caring. But think back through human history: the further back you go, the more vicious humans were in their behaviour in their fight for survival and supremacy. Keep that strongly in your mind: it will serve you well when you deal with distant ancestors. Do not allow romanticism to creep into your work. The distant past was a harsh, cruel fight for survival, and this shaped the consciousness of its people and creatures.

The majority of this lesson will consist of visionary work and research, so we will get straight to it. This section of practical work will be about looking and learning. In your adept training, once you have a strong understanding of the different layers and how they interconnect with inner creation, you will roll your sleeves up and get to work, and by then you will be able to work sensibly and safely.

4.2 About the practical work

In the first layer of practical work we will work with ancestors in various ways. Then we will move straight on to the Underworld's deeper layers. If you understand your human roots in the Underworld, it will help you understand the deeper layers of this profound place.

Instead of writing out a long vision I want you to have as much of your own experience as possible, because you are now getting to the stage where you have to develop you own inner vision strongly in preparation for the deep visionary ritual work of the adept section.

It is also in the initiate phase where you will develop the visionary skills to find places and get into them yourself. We will do this in phases throughout the initiate section, which has a lot of visionary work: remember the ritual work is the *externalisation of inner powers*. To gain enough power in ritual, you will need strong visionary skills for the ritual to stand on, and to gain them takes lots of practice and exploration.

The first stage of the following vision takes you to a place I call the *Ancestral Temple*. I give it this name because it is a threshold place that is also a human construct, and it allows you to interface with distant ancestors. Remember these ancestors are not the same as recently dead relatives, who most likely will have gone back into the cycle of birth: these are deep ancestral lines of consciousness that remain in the land itself.

4.3 *Task:* Vision of the Ancestral Temple

Set up your work room, open the gates, put out the tools,[9] and still yourself. Put your vessel filled with water on the north altar and prick

_____
[9]For their influence.

your finger, squeezing a drop of blood into the water. Sit before the north altar and be still.

Close your eyes and *in vision* go round the directions to greet the contacts on the thresholds. Then return to the north altar. Hold the intention of going to the Ancestral Temple, the place where lines of deep ancestral contacts flow. Step through the altar, passing through the vessel and over the threshold, and find yourself walking down a long passageway that slopes downwards.

You are in an underground chamber with passageways leading off in various directions. A person or a group of people will come down the passageways to greet you. Tell them you are learning about ancestral contact. Talk with them, ask them any questions that you need to, and tell them you are learning about the Underworld. Take as long as you need.

One of them will take you down a passageway that leads to the Underworld Forest. When you are there, remember your vessel with the drop of your blood in the water and see it appear in your hands. Pour its contents into the Underworld River and watch what the river does.

Something will happen to the river. When you see that change, step into it and walk through the water with the ancestor. Pay attention to what happens, where you go, who you meet, and what you see.

At some point you will come to bones laid out in a burial. When you see them, pick up a bone and look at it with the intention of seeing the pattern of its deceased owner's life and blood line. Look at the pattern, the web of fate and blood, and see what connections you recognise.

Once you have finished looking, and have finished any communication with the ancestor who is walking with you, ask them to point you to the entrance of the Underworld Tunnels. They will not come with you, but they will show you where the entrance is.

Take careful note of where the entrance is in relation to the rest of the Underworld

Forest so that you can find it again for yourself in the future: they will only show it to you once, and the entrance will be specific for you: though there are many ways to get to where we are going, the entrance you use has to be compatible with you.

Go down the tunnel as far down as it goes. The tunnel will very likely get very narrow as it nears its end, and you may have to crawl through a small crack to access what is beyond.

Once you crawl through, explore that cave and who or what is in it, but do not touch anything or speak to anything: you are there simply to explore.

Go to the cave's opposite end and look at the wall. It may have a further entrance to another tunnel: do not go down it! It will lead to the Abyss, and you are not properly protected for that yet. Just look and take a mental note of what you see. Take your time, look around, and remember everything that you see, no matter how odd or weird it may seem to you.

When you are ready climb back through the crack and walk up the tunnel to the Underworld Forest. If the ancestor is still waiting there, they are likely to work with you again. If they are not, you may find someone willing to work with you the next time you do this vision.

If they are still there, ask them for a sigil that identifies them. Don't allow your conscious mind to shape it: if you have looked at lots of magical sigils, it is tempting to use that vocabulary. Let them trace a sign on the ground or on your skin so you can learn it. You can use this in ritual and in vision to connect with this ancestor to work with them in the future.

In return, tell them your name. It may come out as a sound, a shape, or a specific memory from your life: in vision what identifies us can express in various different forms.

Then bow to them and leave. Climb the stairs and stop off at the cave with the goddess in it who has animals sleeping around her. Spend some time in her presence, either in silence or in conversation with her. When you are ready climb back up to the surface

world and reappear by stepping through the threshold of the north.

When you are ready open your eyes. Immediately write down every detail you can remember—and do it straight away as it will fade quickly. You can type it up later in a computer file. If you are being mentored, make sure the file is ready for the mentor to see.

We have come to the point in the course where you will now choose how much you wish to explore something. More and more I will give you single views of a place, or a single go at a ritual in various aspects of magic. When you find something you really resonate with or have a deep interest in, expand on it yourself. Work with visions and rituals more if you feel pulled to, and experiment and expand out in order to learn more for yourself and in your own way. When you explore and expand on the work, keep records, notes, journal entries. If you are being mentored, let them know you are experimenting and expanding. If you wish to, offer to share your notes with your mentor so that they can observe your progress.

4.4 *Task:* Researching Apep and Jörmungandr

Read up on Apep, and also Jörmungandr. Think of these in magical terms, but also in terms of racial memory from a very distant past. Then in turn think of them in terms of a layer of consciousness from the land which has since sunk deep into the Underworld. These aspects are all interwoven and have deep truths attached to them.

4.5 *Task:* Researching Yama

Also research Yama.[10] Put aside the moralising and dogmatic threats and read beyond that to find the deeper pattern. Often these religious and mythological patterns, though they have become littered with dogma, contain ancient descriptions from past visionaries and

---

[10]The Asian version of the Underworld.

mystics from the early stages of the culture or religion. Look at the similarities to things you have already read about and experienced.

4.6 *Task:* Pondering the Stone, the Sisters, and the octaves of creation

Cast your mind back to the work you did in earlier lessons when you travelled deep into the land to a stone at the centre of all things. This was the place with the four directional winds are hidden deep in the Underworld, and the realm of the Sisters at the back of the North Wind. These Sisters are weavers of fate within substance and Underworld reflections of the Three Fates.

The Underworld forest, tunnels, caves, temples, and so forth are all a layer of the past. Once you get down to the Stone in the depths, you once more step out of time: in the planet's substance you find the same pattern of creation and destruction as in the inner worlds and the Desert. Everything in creation is mirrored and reflected, everything is in octaves, and everything is within everything else.

The stone at the centre of all things holds all the information of the planet's life, just as the bones did for the ancestor you worked with in vision.

With all this in mind, go back down in vision to this place, to the Stone at the centre of all things, and spend some time there. Place your hands on the Stone, and with what you now know, allow the pattern of the planet's life within the Stone to flow into you.

If one of the Sisters should come out of their tunnel to talk with you, converse with them and answer their questions. When you have finished, write everything down.

Remember that the Three Fates have a higher octave of female power/fate which was Ananke. The same higher octave is reflected in the Underworld. Just think about that, and about all the powers in creation you have

learned about: they too are all reflected in the Underworld.

Once you have thought about this and pondered on what it all means, look back over your notes from the visions in this lesson.

Lesson 5

The Steps of the Ladder

In a previous lesson you looked briefly at the Ladder, an inner construct that moves dead souls from one realm to another. It is not the image of a ladder that is important; rather it is the concept of overcoming certain obstacles while 'climbing up.'

This visionary dynamic has versions all over the world, from climbing a ladder, stairs, large hands,[1] or a mountain. It is an aspect of mystery religions and paths in virtually every culture, and appears as a person reaching upwards in ascent. We see it this way in dreams and visions because this is how it presents to us: *up* is future, rebirth, the Divine realm, the Garden, and so forth, whereas *down* is retirement from the cycle, sleep, and needful transformation.

The Ladder[2] is an angelic structure heavily involved in humanity's evolution, and probably that of other species. It appears not only in death, but also in life for a variety of reasons. And not only is it a structure, but it is also an energetic dynamic that can play out in the life of a mystic or magician.

It is important to recognise both the structure and the dynamic when they appear in your life: as a magician it gives you a sense of your own evolution and also signals that you are stepping deeper into mystical magical realms.

For clarity I will look at the two expressions of the Ladder separately. Then we will move on to examples and research to give you a good grasp of what is going on when this structure appears. This subject has its own lesson because of its importance to the magician not only for their own inner evolution but also for ritual and visionary work.

5.1 The Ladder of the inner worlds

This is something that sometimes appears spontaneously during certain visionary work, usually at the edge of the Abyss. The magician or visionary mystic is presented with a large angelic hand to step onto, a ladder, or a stairway; or they are transported upwards by angelic beings.

It cannot be forced or triggered by the magician; it is always presented while the magician is doing something else. It signals a time when the magician is presented with the opportunity to evolve at a deep level, and is an episode as potentially life-changing as crossing the Abyss.

It does not mean that the magician has become something that they were not before—you do not get a grade, a fancy hat, and a badge—rather it means the magician's deeper self is unfolding in spiritual evolution

---

[1] Angelic ones.
[2] I will use this term just for clarity and ease.

127

and the spontaneous vision seats it in the magician's consciousness. The unfolding effects of such a milestone do not often become apparent until years later: it signals the start of a new, tougher, and more demanding life path for the magician.

It indicates that the magician is slowly stepping out of the cycle of destruction in life, and begining to bridge into the cycle of *inner regeneration*. This does not mean an easier life; it means that a deeper profundity within the person's eternal spirit is finally finding a way to bridge itself into the magician's conscious life. Over the years from that point onwards the magician will be tested, challenged, and expected to walk a more careful and considered pathway through the Mysteries.

As the path narrows—"walking the sword edge"—so the life lessons come stronger, faster, and bring more insight. It gets harder to hide from yourself and your own deeds, and should you misstep the results will come hard and fast. You really begin to gain an understanding of what the Egyptians called "the Rule of Ma'at." The experience of the Inner Ladder in vision brings the powers of Ma'at into sharp focus.

No amount of rituals or visions can force this event: it flows naturally within the cycle of your own fate web and the evolution of your soul. That does not mean that a magician who does not have this spontaneous experience is not evolved: it has to time in with events in your life so you can build upon the experience in your daily life. If your fate path has a good intersection where you can build upon the inner experience in daily life, it will time in with that, however long that takes.

You can, however, observe the process as a bystander in some instances, which we will look at later in the initiate section. But first you need to understand the outer processes that lead up to it and also trigger it.

Inner life and outer life are never separate. If the two are not compatible, there is less chance of this dynamic triggering in your life.

For a magician, that means recognising the various life events, powers, and intersections that happen in your outer life that signal you are either walking towards the Ladder or climbing it.

Outer manifestations that signal interactions with the ladder have been deliberately woven into some magical graded systems, and some of the "initiation rituals" simply reflect on the process psychologically. The really dumb magical systems think that doing a grade ritual is all there is to it, which is just silly.

5.2 The Ladder in life

Ancient and old texts abound with references to the Ladder in terms of the steps of magical evolution and initiatory experiences. It is folly to think that these steps are simply mechanised levels of magical and mystical achievement; rather they are deep and lasting life experiences that affect how the inner spirit approaches and accesses the Inner Ladder that takes us to the threshold of Divinity: this is the dynamic of the *Merkaba*. In later lessons in the initiate section we will look more deeply into various aspects of the Ladder and the Merkaba, but for now let's concentrate on the foundation, which is life and how you operate within it.

When you step onto a magical or mystical path, your fate web changes, springs to life, and becomes more concentrated and more immediate. From then on, everything you do in life and everything that confronts you, for both good and bad, is not only directly connected to the Ladder, but it will also affect how the Ladder's steps of ascent will manifest in your inner and outer life. You step away from the mundane and step into the mystical union of man, nature, and the Divine. In this path you always have a choice: a choice to act or not, a choice to forge forward or give in, and a choice on how—or not—you balance your scales.

In a way it is a bit like growing up from being a self-centred toddler and moving towards adulthood.

For a toddler, life is about wants and needs. The child necessarily views the world from a very self-centred perspective: this is simply nature's survival programming.

As the child grows up, they have to learn the painful lessons of having to go to school when they don't want to, having to eat things they do not want to eat, and having to learn that the money mum or dad takes out of the ATM machine is not an endless source of wealth to be spent on toys, but hard-earned cash that provides for life's essentials.

When a magician steps onto the magical path, an octave of this evolving and maturing springs to life. Through living a magical life the magician learns the hard but beautiful realities of life, nature, Divinity, and the inner worlds; and how all these things directly influence your life and vice versa. You step out of being a mundane 'toddler' and step into the fast lane of mystical awareness.

How you approach these steps on the Ladder defines how you mature and progress as a magician: to hold and wield power needs a mature hand. No one hands the power of a multinational company to a fresh-faced sixteen-year-old. Nor do the inner worlds hand power to an immature, weak, power-hungry magician.

The steps on the Ladder that manifest in life forge and strengthen the Ladder's rungs for your inner visionary ascent: what you do in life can directly affect how accessible—or not—this structure of ascent becomes for you. Some make the mistake of thinking that simply living a pure and moral life will forge the rungs of the ascent; but as you will now know, life is not that cut and dried, and what is moral in one culture is not in another.

Cultural morality has no place in this structure; it is the direct, individual balance that is unique to you that forges each step for you to stand upon. You are never pitted against sections of humanity; rather you are constantly standing in front of a mirror so that your own personal successes and failures, your own creative and destructive actions, become your teachers.

It all comes back to *knowing oneself*, the maxim of the temple which one constantly strives for in the quiet of ones own spirit. Your own personal relationship with the outer world, with nature, with the inner powers, and with the Divine brings you to a better understanding of yourself and everything around you.

As each understanding dawns, a rung of the ladder forms. If you live by that understanding, the rung strengthens to carry your weight. The less imbalance you carry, the less inner weight you have to carry, and the lighter you become when it comes to treading upon this vehicle of ascent.

Everyone evolves in their own time and at their own speed. How you treat everything around you, and how you understand your deep connection to everything around you, defines to you, in your own way, how to forge your path through life. We learn just as much from our failures and mistakes as we do from our successes; and the more the ladder is forged in life, the more you begin to see the true interconnectedness of everything. This in turn challenges us to mature and to be mindful of how we as magicians affect everything around us, all the time.

You should know enough by now to understand what this means for you personally, and how to translate that into everyday living. But to what do we ascend upon this ladder?

5.3 An ascent to what?

The Mysteries of the Merkaba are old indeed and not specific to Jewish mysticism alone. Once you understand this aspect of the Mysteries you will spot versions of it in various cultures with mystical or magical aspects in their religious/spiritual practice. It is something inherent to humanity, and is the part of the magical or mystical path where the path itself starts to really narrow and become a path of Hercules.

In visionary terms the ascent can take a human through various layers of the inner powers of creation. There is a layer of the

Garden, the inner template for nature itself, where it is always balanced; there is the layer of the creative powers which are experienced as vast beings; and finally there is the layer of the Divine realm where the eternal spirit experiences the Divine presence, or as nearly as it is possible for a living human to experience it without dying. The Divine presence is not a man in a white robe and a long beard, but the pure, eternal, conscious power that is constantly seeking expression.

The experience of ascent is not to pull you away from your living humanity; it is to reconnect with the Divine within you—and all substance. Just as we reach down into the depths of the Underworld to reach the patterns of physical manifestation in the depths of the planetary vessel, so we can also reach up to reconnect with the powers of creation of which we are an expression.

To reach only one way is unbalanced; to reach both ways is to reconnect with Perfect Balance, with the Fulcrum. Then we come to an understanding that our human life is about being the fulcrum while in physical manifestation.

It is far easier for us to reach 'down,' as we are substance seeking the pattern of substance. To reach up, beyond and before substance, is to reach out of ourselves in our present form—which is what makes it so hard and difficult. And yet through that process we bring all the impulses of creation and destruction together: we *mend the shattered vessel*.

These various layers of the ladder change us deeply as magicians, and form the major impulse behind ceasing to 'do' magic and literally 'becoming' magic: everything a balanced adept does affects change around them simply by their presence or conscious projection. All very highbrow! But that process began for you when you started your magical training, and in the initiate phase of your training you will begin to forge and strengthen the rungs of the Ladder; or in different imagery *build your vehicle*.

As you study an aspect of magic it will externalise and present around you in everyday life for you to engage with and learn from. How you act and approach such presentations, how you stand up to the challenges, and what choices you make from gnosis, define how you develop as a magician.

5.4   About the practical work

Working with the Ladder in vision is very much an adept area of work, but to prepare for that, the best work you can do is research to give you an idea of how such things were documented by past mystics and magicians. The research will also help you should you spontaneously come across the Ladder in vision, which can happen at any point in a magical life.

When you do this research, look for and read the original texts, not someone's interpretation of them. A lot of these texts and the images that went with them were drawn from deep visionary and mystical experiences. Often when scholars, priests, and historians try to make sense of them, they devolve down into psychology, religious dogma, or, in more modern times, flights of fancy—aliens and the like.

Your job is not to interpret the following visions and writings, but merely to read and absorb them: let them do their own work in your consciousness. This will let you slowly make inner connections and allow the revelations of the text to speak to you directly over time. This will often come in the form of dreams, unexpected imagery in visionary work, and the 'ahha!' moment that comes to you out of the blue.

Some of this research consists of Christian religious texts[3] where the more ancient texts had been absorbed and then retranslated into moral codes. This is where it can get complicated. The mystical element of the Ladder in life does have a bearing on how you live your life, but not in a dogmatic, rule-laden way. It

---

[3]Such as John Climacus.

is really important to understand this in order to avoid getting stuck in the dead end of moral purity.

A lot of the Ladder's aspects in life are about how you live your life. But they are not about being a moral person; they are about being a *balanced* person so that you can delve deep into the inner, Divine aspects of humanity without tearing yourself or everything around you to pieces.

For example, in the Christian Mysteries of the Ladder, there is an aspect of the ladder called *subduing the stomach*. This is translated by Christian writers into "avoiding gluttony," or taking up fasting in order to purify the soul. This in turn teaches that it is "bad in Gods eyes" to enjoy something and 'good' to abstain. It is immediately turned into a battle of good and evil: gluttony is a Christian sin. This traps the mystic in the dead end of religious virtue as way to ascend the Ladder, which fails miserably.

Subduing of the stomach is more about teaching the mystic or magician how to eat to feed their body with what it needs to keep it strong—and therefore able to withstand the physical effects of deep visionary work. If you eat things that are bad or damaging for you, it weakens your body. This makes deep visionary work more likely to impact your health severely, which in turn will block you from deep inner communion. Subduing the stomach becomes discipline of giving the body what it needs and when it needs it, and not eating for the sake of it. Sometimes the stomach needs a rest, so we fast a little. This not only helps the digestion, at a deeper level it puts you back in the driving seat of your body, and not the other way around. But this is done from necessity, and is not about battling the body.

If you are heavily overweight from overeating, are diabetic from eating too much sugar, have heart disease because of a bad diet, drink too much alcohol, etc., your vessel is damaged. The damage will limit how deeply you can step into the inner mysteries; hence if you wish to reach as far as humanly possible into that inner experience, how you tend your body is very important. It is always about *finding and maintaining balance.*

Can you see how necessary actions become transformed into a good versys evil dogma when approached by someone who has not actually done the work themselves? Keep all this in mind as you read through the various texts you will find. Hence my warning not to read the commentaries, just to read the text. And where the text has been written from a place of ignorance, spot the mysteries hidden within the dogmatic text.

Remember, ascent is about reaching deep into the inner consciousness of creation and connecting with the deep, Divine roots of our existence. It is about working in vision to consciously reconnect with the powers of creation and destruction.

Often the people who read these texts and copied them or commentated on them were not adepts of the Mysteries, and the visionary aspects hidden within the texts was either not understood or overlooked entirely. Some of the Greek philosophers recognized this and commented on it, but in general, always remember: the Mysteries hide in plain sight. If you don't understand them, you do not see them. This is why you are given a lot of research and reading to do, so that in stages you will slowly learn to spot the keys—and later you will learn to work with them.

You may find yourself going back to earlier reading from your apprentice training as more layers unfold themselves to you: you will find yourself gaining a deeper layer of understanding as you progress in your development.

5.5 Task: Research

Ladder of Divine Ascent

Look up and read *Ladder of Divine Ascent* by John Climacus (seventh century). There are English translations available on the internet. Dodge the dogma!

Poetics of Ascent

Get and read *Poetics of Ascent* by Naomi Janowitz This book is the first English translation of *Maaseh Merkabah*, an aspect of early Jewish mystical texts known as *Hekhalot* or *Merkabah texts*.

Don't read the commentary and explanations, just read the actual translated texts. You are looking for the visionary aspects of the texts. Don't try to decipher them, just read them, and a particular part may jump out at you. Read that part to yourself a few times, then read them out loud, in nature if you can. Learn to absorb, do, and just be: let things cook within you rather than trying to make it an intellectual test.

Traversing stars in death and vision

Research what you can on traversing the stars in death and vision in different ancient religions. You may be drawn to a particular version or culture; just let your curiosity lead you. Stay away from modern interpretations, popular internet theories, and the like: stay with the images and the texts themselves. Let them speak to you.

Genesis 28

Read *Genesis 28* (again), the dream of Jacob. Note the connection between the Ladder and the earth, the sacredness of the land, and the stone pillow. Think about what you know of stones, focused land power areas, and of something that reaches from the land to the stars that enables the human to ascend and descend.[4]

The Persian Mysterires of Mithras

Look up the Persian Mysteries of Mithras, and the Ladder. It will be hard to find something that is not Masonic or reconstructionist, but look anyway, just in case.

The Four Rabbis

Look up *Pardes*. Read the story of the *Four Rabbis* (there are a few different versions).

Ezekiel 1–3

Read *Ezekiel 1–3*. Pay close attention to the mention of the *Chayot*.[5] Ponder on the presentation of ox/bull, raptor, lion, and man. Think about some of the deity presentations in ancient religions. In some cultures they are angels or guardians; in others they are deities. It doesn't matter, those are just titles we give beings. Think about how, why, and where these presentations appear in various texts.

The Apis Bull

Read up on the Apis Bull in ancient Egypt, looking for the early images and beliefs as opposed to the much later versions.

There are no writing tasks for this research. Just take your own notes so that you can refer back to them in the future. By reading, looking, thinking, dreaming, and then moving on, you will allow these various strands of the Mysteries to weave their way into your deeper self.

---

[4]And remember Plato's *Republic, The Vision of Ayr*.

[5]Look that word up if you do not understand it.

Lesson 6

Magical Application

In the wider picture creation and destruction are constantly happening. We see this all around us in everyday life in the births and deaths of things. Things are destroyed and composted to make way for new creative force to be expressed.

When it comes to magic, and living the life of a magician—and also living a modern everyday life—we become direct players in the dance of creation and destruction in small, and even major, ways.

This has particular relevance for magicians and how they work magic; yet it is rarely thought about, which can lead to all sorts of unwanted complications. It is all well and good for a magician to have a highbrow stance on creation and destruction, but if balance is not kept in their magical actions at ground level, the deeper the magic, the deeper the kickback that can happen.

When a magician works magic, regardless of its purpose, there needs to be an understanding of the flow of power. By now you will be starting to understand what that means.

The impulse of creation and destruction both come from the inner worlds, and the manifest world is where that creation and destruction express themselves. The Underworld is the storage facility that takes those expressions when they are spent and holds them in substance. Understanding that simple balancing act should have a direct influence on how the magician structures their magical rituals, actions, and visions; and how they release that magic and how it is dealt with when it is finished.

How the magician works with the magic and how they act/withhold actions in their daily life—these both add to the weave of magic and will define how it expresses—and whether it is successful or not.

The inner world and Underworld both lie on either side of the manifest world, with the living magician in the manifest world as the fulcrum: so long as the magician maintains an adequate amount of balance, as much as possible, the expressions that flow from the inner worlds and the expressions that flow into the Underworld will be more or less balanced: *power in equals power out.*

Successful magic in the long term depends on that balance. When that flow is interrupted in the magician's life, usually from magical interference, the action of rebalance should take the flow of creation and destruction into account and be part of the resolution.

So let us take some time to see how these deeper dynamics surface in regular magic, and how the magician can work with them successfully and without creating too much havoc. We will do this by looking at popular magic: money, home, safety, etc.

6.1 Short-term popular magic

When people are first drawn to magic, one of the reasons is a feeling of powerlessness and a wish to control their lives. Resources are usually at the forefront of their mind, so we will use money magic as an example.

When people first start trying to use magic to gain money, they usually do not need it, and are often working from a 'magical recipe book.' Largely this does not work, but when it does its effects are usually fleeting, and its fallout depends on the person's individual fate pattern. They either give up, or they develop and move forward in magic.

Remember, most magicians who claim to be successful at money magic usually gain the money in question from selling books and courses on money magic, not from the actual magic itself.

If a magician does develop into stronger forms of magic, usually that will involve beings, and then we are into a whole new ballgame. If they truly need the resources, and all other avenues of fate have been explored, and the money will enable them to continue with their work, then it is likely that the magic itself will work and work well. If they truly do not need the resources, then it will also work—but it will come with a large price tag attached. This is not about virtue or punishment; it is merely the dynamics of how magic works.

When a magician does not need the money, but uses powerful magic to get it, a few different strands of cause, effect, energy, and so forth come together. Usually a magician who uses power in such a way, without real need, is immature or weak. They do not want to take responsibility for themselves, they want an easy life, and often they feel *entitled* to it. The amount of 'magus' types who have told me they should not have to work because they are a magus is nauseating.

Let's have a look at some examples, so that you can see how the various dynamics play out. These are both real examples from people I have known.[1] I will not bother with the very silly examples, as it is a waste of time—you will be able to figure out the truly stupid people for yourself.

6.2 Example One: Frank

Frank is a ritual magician who has gained some status in a local magical group as a leader. He sees himself as a magus, and as a result feels the world and his students owe him. He charges his students, but it is not enough, his wife works two jobs to support him, and he spends his days playing video games and gazing out the window being 'thoughtful.'

He holds back with his students to avoid the possibility of his students surpassing him. He regularly has affairs with female students. He is overweight and unhealthy from sitting around so much and indulging his food whims, and now he is in his late thirties he is starting to get unwell from his poor lifestyle.

He is tired of his wife as she no longer looks like the pretty young girl he married—I am sure having to work two jobs to support this parasite hasn't helped her looks. Generally, he is an asshole.

He decides that the key to his happiness is money. If only he had money—lots of it—he could leave his wife and find someone else to look after him.

So he starts a round of magic to get a sizable sum of money. He works with spirits and makes bargains. He ritualizes the bargain by working with his magical tools, but the majority of the ritual is pleading, demanding, bargaining, and bartering.

At this point, we see a weak, immature, and self-indulgent person asking someone else—the being—to provide for him. His magic is all centered around that want and has no pattern to it. He has effectively transposed his neediness towards his wife onto the being.

This creates a very unhealthy pattern that will further draw on the magician's energies,

---

[1]Though I have given them different names for privacy.

which in turn will attract parasites. There was no balanced pattern of magic and no real need, so there is no real balance. Any money that does come to him will be taken from somewhere else within his own pattern of resources, which will create an energetic deficit.

He gets some money via a windfall, and he promptly leaves his wife and turns up at the door of a female magician. She opens the door to Frank and sees an overweight, unhealthy, immature, and very parasited person standing there, so she shuts the door again and turns him away.

Frank runs out of money very quickly and decides to work the magic again to get some more. More energy is taken from his future resources by the parasite to get the money to him, and Frank continues to wander around trying to get someone to take him in and provide for him.

When his future resources are exhausted, it starts to affect his present health in a bad way; but he has no health insurance as he does not work. He has no home, and his students tire of him when they realise he has been keeping them at beginner level indefinitely.

This might all sound very extreme, but it is a common picture in Western magic, one I have observed more than once with people I know—and have despaired of.

6.3 Example Two: Shirley

Shirley is a Western ritual magician, and she is also a cook at the local hospital. She enjoys her work as it does not draw too much of her energy and time, which allows her to work on her magic. She broke away from her magical lodge in order to walk a solitary magical path, but the head of the lodge, who wanted to have an affair with her, decided to magically bind her to the lodge to stop her leaving.

It didn't work, but the binding did start to cause her problems. Her energy started to get low, as it was working at a subtle level to hold the binds off.[2] At work the pressure was on as

there were cutbacks happening, but she could not energetically keep up with the longer hours and the harder work. Presently she was fired for not being able to keep up, and the place where she lived did not have unemployment benefits.

She had little savings and began to panic about where her next month's rent was going to come from. She applied for every job she could think of that she could do, and she also decided it was time to take some magical action.

She did readings to see what was happening to her health: the reading showed the magical binding that was draining her. She took magical action to remove the bindings, then opened the directions, got the flow of creation and destruction going, and stood in the centre of that power and asked for material help to get her back on her feet. She stated that she would do everything in her power to help herself, but she asked that the inner worlds also to help her.

Her call was heard over the thresholds: a being in one of the directions told her he would help her, on condition that she also help them. She asked what they needed, and they said it would be made apparent to her.

Three days later she received a letter from the tax people saying that she had overpaid on her taxes for a few years, and so here was the balance given back to her. It was enough for her living expenses for two months.

Shirley continued to job hunt and also kept her eyes open for how she could pay back the favour. After a couple of weeks she found a job working for a local landscaper. She had no experience, but the landscaper felt he would work well with her and could train her. He specialized in 'return to nature' gardens: planting herbs, wildflowers, and trees native to the area, and using fertilizers friendly to the land and the local creatures. Shirley's job was helping with the plants, doing his accounts, and dealing with the clients.

Two months into the job, she was worried that she was not keeping her end of the

---

[2]Her inner immune system.

bargain, so she opened the directions, called on the being, and apologized for being too stupid to see where she needed to help. The being told her she was already helping: the being had wanted her to tend the land, and help build tiny natural oases in the urban environment. It turned out to be a long-term job for her, and she became a business partner instead of employee. Her long-term material needs were covered, and she in turn created magically-tuned natural islands in a sea of houses.

The magic not only got her the short-term money she needed, it also took her out of a cycle of useless employment and put her somewhere she would be magically useful. In return, her needs were covered.

The magic worked because she stood in the flow of creative power drawn in, and destructive power directed into composting. This creates a pattern dynamic that is balanced and can therefore be sustained in the long term. She was willing to be useful and to work hard; and in return the inner beings ensured that her fate pattern was engaged to the full.

This sort of solution is never a happily-ever-after thing: the life's challenges and difficulties are what develop a person's maturity, wisdom, understanding, and compassion. It is how those challenges are met that makes the difference, and it is how the magic is patterned that decides the success or failure of a magical appeal for help.

If a magical appeal for help is done without a balanced exteriorized ritual framework, or is worked in vision without an exterior way to express itself, then it is less likely to work. If it is done purely from an exterior ritual without any inner connection, it is also less likely to work. If it is done without the balance of creation and destruction, it is less likely to be sustained or of any real use.

Shirley was in a situation of destruction[3] that was brought to a head by a magical binding. By drawing on and then standing

in the flow of creation and destruction, the flow took away any remaining fragments of the binding, and also flushed out of her the pattern of meaningless jobs that only provided the basics for her. The flow of destruction composted that short-term fate which in turn made room for the creative aspect to flow into her pattern.

The creative aspect of the flow of power triggered a latent fate thread in her pattern, one that would connect her with long-term service on the land. It also ensured that she had the necessary resources to accomplish this. While ever she did that job, the resources would flow to her. If and when she leaves that job—she is still there, years later—the magical deal will be done and she will then have to find a way to earn her living again that will not be so magically protected.

6.4 Divine names and letters

Divine names and letters can also be worked with magically when a specific thing, like resources, is needed. The key to working with Divine names is *necessity*: keep this in mind. It is also best to be working in a way harmonic with those Divine names and letters: if you are working in a stream or method of magic with the same dynamics as the religious or mystical system from which the letters come, they will resonate at the same frequency and switch on.

Such use tends to employ methods of *exposure* and sound rather than ritual or vision. Drawing out—exactly—or visualizing the letters or names, brings the frequency into the magician's sphere and triggers any latent fate threads that would lead to a needful conclusion. It does not create a new fate thread; it triggers what is already around you and brings it to life.

It also relies on how we act in our lives. If we are doing what we can to forge forward but something is blocking our way, and if divination shows that the block is unnecessary or there are alternative threads for power to flow down, then the use of names, letters, and sounds can open the way ahead.

---

[3]Dead end job that was slowly destroying her without her realizing.

If you sit on your ass and expect everything to come to you, and you use Divine names or letters to trigger wealth, then very likely nothing will happen. You as a magical being have to work in the manifest world to enable threads for that power to flow down. When you act you open up possibilities on your fate pattern. When your action alone is not enough, and you have tried everything in ordinary life to solve an issue, and you keep hitting a wall, then it is time to decide whether it is a wall you need to learn to overcome, or simply a block that can be moved—or is someone magically blocking you? Is it a problem with the birth of a new creative pulse in your life, or is it destruction? If it is destruction, is it needful, or has it been enforced upon you by something outside of you, and therefore creating an imbalance of power?

Working this way enables the magic to use the potential already there in your fate potential. This means it takes minimum effort, and is all still part of your own pattern. You are essentially solving the problem by working with your own fate pattern of creation and destruction to bring a better sense of balance.

Staying with the money theme, if the magician is working hard but is low on resources to accomplish their task, and every outer method has been tried, then sometimes working with the Divine names and letters can break up the blockage. However they are not to be used lightly, and can even be counterproductive at times.

And they only need using *once* when trying to address an issue. If you keep reusing or retriggering them, they can have the opposite effect—and you end up back where you started.

Before you work with such Divine powers of resonance, ensure you fully understand the inner and outer meaning of the names and/or letters, what carries creation and what carries destruction, how they combine together, how they sound, and how they are used in the recitation of texts. This will teach you a lot about the powers that flow through these letters—which are divine sigils—and why they flow through the letters. It will also give you deeper insight into the issue at hand.

The way they work is by changing the frequency around you by carefully inscribing the chosen name and placing it in the direction where it wants to go. Let the name find its own direction by carrying it around the house until it indicates where to place it. However, if it is strong in your fate path that you need to go through something, it will not work: the powers of creation and destruction[4] will not work against those same powers running through your life. Usually when that happens, when you look back a couple of years later, you can see how important it was at that time that you went through difficulties.

All magic, when it is working with the flow of creation and destruction, will work well. When it flows against it, or works outside of that flow of power, you get failure, weak results, or it creates a complex mess in your life.

6.5 Simply asking

If you work magically with inner contacts and thresholds, and also work in service when asked, then simply asking is the best way to get help when you really need it: this will keep it within the flow of creation/destruction and your own fate pattern.

The ritual way to do this is to open all the gates, connect with the contacts, then tell them what you need, why you need it, and ask if they can or are willing to help. If you really do need whatever you are asking for, then a contact will likely step forward and let you know that they will help.

But ritualizing it, rather than simply asking, can make it weaker rather than stronger. Don't ask why, as I have no clue; it is just what I have experienced over the years. I have also observed this with others. In times of major crisis, I found simply asking worked. Let me give you a couple of examples from my life of

---

[4]Of which the Divine names are a part.

when I went into meltdown from being under too much pressure from too many directions.

One time, when I was in my thirties, I felt like I was buckling under the pressure of work, children, and general hardship.[5] I went out in nature to walk and think, and I got myself in a very emotional state. In that state of meltdown I cried out in my mind for help. A stillness came around me, the wind dropped, and I heard a voice with my inner senses saying *"you have a healthy body, food in your stomach, a roof over your head, and healthy children. Why are you crying out for help? You asked for strength.[6] Well, this is your weight training, so get on with it."*

It was not my subconscious talking to me but a more profound voice:[7] it was what some magical people would call the Holy Guardian Angel. I was basically being slapped for being a whiny child.

I felt a bit angry at the response—I was still a kid—but I went home and continued to toil away. Over the following two years I went through a series of really tough trials, but that voice stuck with me, teaching me that strength comes from adversity...and boy did I get strong. It helped me deal with what at the time seemed unsurmountable difficulties, but looking back now, they were very necessary and put me in good stead for my later magical work that demanded real strength.

A few years later I really did hit my wall of endurance and could not take any more. I sat down and felt into the flows of creation and destruction in my own ritual pattern. One side of it was blocked, so no new creative pulse could flow into my pattern: I was backing up with an overflow of destruction. I had no idea what caused it or what to do about it.

Once more I called out using my inner voice, saying that I really could not take any more. Again the stillness surrounded me, the winds dropped, and I was enveloped in energy. I stated that I had tried my best but I no longer had any reserves to draw on within myself.

Once again the voice came and said: *"So now you know your limitations."* A hand appeared in my inner vision and I took that hand. My life changed dramatically four weeks later and I was moved out of the very difficult situation and set back on my fate path. I needed to learn what my own limitations were: what I could do for myself, and more importantly what I could not do for myself. The inner flow of my pattern was restored to a constant flow of creation and destruction, and I was once more stabilized in the centre as the fulcrum.

The income I needed came, the home I needed came, the work I needed came, and a whole new vista of learning opened up. I would not have been able to draw the knowledge and skill from that new path of magical learning if I didn't know my own limitations. I would have ended up killing myself.

When life or your own self is holding you back, the angel will walk the difficulty with you[8] but they will not lift that difficulty from you until you have learned everything you need to learn in order to progress another rung up the ladder.

However, when magic has been used to hold you back or destroy you it is a different ball game. If your fate path is strong enough to withstand the attack you can ride it out until it becomes irrelevant. If your fate path is not sufficiently creative, it will destroy you if you do not deal with it: creation balances destruction.

Simply asking will not work: what a human puts magically on someone must be magically removed or magically neutralized. If you are working as a Quareia initiate works, you can simply adjust the frequency around you. Most often that is enough. If it isn't, there are many different ways to deal with it, all of which you either have already learned or will be learning.

Staying with the theme of money as an example, here is another example from my crazy life. A magician from my past was

---

[5] I truly had no clue what hardship was at that point.
[6] I had, a year before.
[7] My inner senses were suddenly and unexpectedly on full alert.

[8] You must learn destruction before you can begin to put your hands into creation.

hellbent on revenge. One of the things he tried was to shut me down in all areas of my life. Some I overcame by simply making them irrelevant. One aspect that was critical, though, was income. I was being blocked at every step of the way from earning an income.

When I used divination to see what would happen if I just forged forward and ignored what he had done, the picture did not look pretty at all. So rather than get into complex magic I simply drew upon the Divine names.

I handmade a calligraphy of specific Divine letters that I had chosen carefully, and sat down to meditate. I meditated on necessity, balance, creation, and destruction. I accepted that I was willing to walk any path that was my own fate, no matter how hard it may be, and that I knew my limitations. In this way I accepted and reestablished my own flow of power.

Then I meditated on the magical work I had committed to do, and the magical block on my resources that had stopped me moving forward. I meditated without emotion on the fact that a person was using magic to block my flow of power and resources, and that this was not acceptable. I also meditated on the fact that I needed help to overcome this block, and that by putting up and reciting the letters I had triggered a magical act.

Finally I recited the sounds of the letters around the house, and ensured that the calligraphy was in the right prominent place.

It worked, and within a week all the resources I needed arrived. Note that I did not ask for the magic to be removed; I simply worked with the Divine power of creation and destruction in the form of letters to open my path forward, thus negating the magic used against me. I essentially triggered a stronger, higher frequency around me that drowned out the hostile magic and negated it. You do not need a nuclear bomb to crack a nut.

One of the major keys in magical actions is to be able to 'view' the power flow of creation and destruction that is constantly around you and to check that it is balanced. If it is, no matter what you are going through, it is taking you to a certain point in your fate pattern. However if it is not balanced and you are having problems, you know you have to act. In the practical work we will look at ways of checking that flow.

6.6 *Task:* Meditation and ritual on your flow of creation and destruction

The key to understanding how something is truly affecting you at a deep level is to learn how to sense when your flow of creation and destruction has been blocked, altered, or interfered with. Think of this flow like your arterial blood flow: it is critical to your survival and it is the energy that feeds and enlivens your fate pattern/web. If something is affecting your life badly, but your flow is still good, then the issue can be overcome through practical action or minor magical adjustments.

However if this critical flow is interrupted then you may be in for serious problems, which will then need magical or inner action. The way to view this flow is to embed the pattern within yourself, which you have slowly been doing through ritual patterns in your training. Now it is time to take matters a step further and embed this flow pattern deep within your consciousness, so that it is easier for you to be alerted when it goes wrong. This is done through ritual patterning and meditation.

In your workroom, light the lights, open the gates, put out the tools in the directions, and greet the contacts on the thresholds.

Go to the east altar. With your inner vision see the flow of creative energy come out of the east and flow through you to the central flame. Once you have a sense of this, turn and go to the central altar. See the flow going into the central flame, the fulcrum of the work space.

Using your inner vision, now see that flow go from the central flame to the south and vanish over the south threshold. While you are aware of this, also be aware that the flow from the east to the centre and from centre to south is a continuous flow that is always there.

Go and stand before the south altar. Be aware of the flow from the central flame: it flows through the left side of your body[9] and over the south threshold. See a flow come from the south directly to the west altar and pass over the west threshold.

Now go to the west altar. See the flow come back from the west and flow into the central flame. As you see this in your inner vision, walk to the central altar from the west and sense the flow from the west flowing through your right side.

Now go back to the centre, with the altar before you and the south before you. Sense the flow leaving the central flame and going through your centre and vanishing over the north threshold.

You have worked with this flow before; now you need to deepen it within you. Stand in the centre as the fulcrum of your fate pattern, and 'see' the whole flow in continuous action: east to centre, centre to south,[10] south to west to centre, and centre to north.[11]

Get a strong inner visual sense of the flow all around you. Be aware of the Light of the Light Bearer behind your left side and the Darkness of Restriction behind your right side. If any of the flow is weaker or slower, use your powers of imagination to move it along.

Now add in the sense of the stars above, the Underworld below, and the Divine spark, the flame of vital force, in your centre. Stand in that flow, and in that sense, until you feel ready to sit down.

This flow is the higher frequency of power that feeds into your fate web. You can also, if you can, visualise your fate pattern layered beneath the flow of the power.

Once you sit down, close your eyes and be still. Slowly let your inner sense of the flow around you strengthen as it moves around the directions. It is a constant motion of flow from creation to future, from future to breaking down/destruction, to composting and burial in the Underworld/past. Stay in this meditation until you are ready to stop.

When you have finished do not close the directions down, simply put out the lights and put the tools away.

Build up in your meditation an inner visual sense of this flow. Whenever you meditate, include this sense of the flow. When you have a moment to be silent at work or at home, with your eyes open, recover the sense of the flow around you in your imagination. If you do this regularly with eyes open, you will tune to it at a very deep level. If something disturbs it, you will feel it.

A few days ago, in the middle of writing this lesson, I felt a strong disturbance in my flow. When I tuned into the flow, I found something backing up the power in the south which was slowing it down. I could not sense what it was, so I did a reading.

The reading showed that something I am working on magically had become imbalanced at a deep level and was going to affect my future.[12] Through meditation and divination I realised that a magical action I had been working on had become imbalanced by one of my actions. I had extended the magical action to include the land, when the land didn't want or need it. It was irritating the land, and in turn beings that flow through this land were trying to block me from my own stupid interference.

When I realised what I had done I adjusted my work and the pressure came off immediately. My south flow was restored and the land got humbled apologies.

Sometimes the block can be that simple, yet it can have profound implications for your future. By working on the land magically when it didn't want it, I made myself a threat to the land. So the land beings blocked my future, which in turn backed up my flow, which would have manifested as serious long-term complications for me.

The act that I worked on was fairly simple and benign in my eyes—so never assume that something you consider simple will not have far-reaching effects on others. The reverse is

---

[9]You are standing in the flow.
[10]Creation and future.
[11]Destruction and composting.

[12]Hence the blockage in the south.

equally true: don't assume something that affects you powerfully will also have power elsewhere.

In terms of power and energy, I had ring-fenced something that didn't need or want it. That would have created a threat to the flow of power for that bit of land, and so the beings who defend it sprang into action. I inadvertently created an imbalance in the flow of the land itself.

You (and I) will always make silly mistakes, and you will never grow out of them, simply because we truly know so little, no matter how much we think we know. Just learn to identify your mistakes and always act to put things right. This way the flow is restored and no damage is done.

6.7 Readings

When you wish to see what could be blocking your flow of power, or whether magical action is needed, you can use the layouts you have already worked with. Choose your questions carefully.

You can also use an altered version of the four-directional layout you learned right at the beginning of your training.

To use the four directions in a reading with this pattern, though, you need to *reverse* the positions of the cards.

The east will be the first card you put down, and you will put it down to your left.[13] South will be at the top of the reading, west to your right, your Scales cross the central card, and finally north goes at the bottom. This way, the reading is lining up with your ritual patterns and power flow. When you shuffle, simply ask to see your current flow of creation and destruction, and the dynamics of that flow.

Look at the power coming into the east (the first card you put down), then your centre/fulcrum (the second card), then the south (third card), then the west (forth card). Then use the next card to cross the centre card (fifth card: what has been harvested and weighed on the scales). Finally put down the north card (what has been destroyed or placed in the past). Working this way will also add to your understanding of how the magical directions and the compass directions are two different things most of the time: magical south is always before you, regardless of where compass south is.

Map out the layout, draw out the layout, then work with it to look at your present flow. Don't overuse this reading on yourself by constantly checking your flow; use it only when it is really necessary to keep its efficiency.

If you over-read on the same subject[14] you will narrow down what you see and will not get a clear overview. Do it once for this lesson to see your current flow, and after that use it only when your flow is disturbed, or when you wish to check your observations with the flow of someone or something else.

If you use the LXXXI Quareia Magicians deck, the cards will also indicate what beings are transporting/involved in that power flow. This will give you more ideas as to what is forming and why. It will also warn you if someone is interfering in your flow, and indicate who they are.

---

[13]Before you is magical south.

[14]In any reading work.

Lesson 7

Birth and Rebirth

Birth is a very magical thing: all the powers of creation and destruction come together in equal measures to create a porthole for a new life to breathe its first breath. Before modern medicine and simple things like the midwife or attendant doctor washing their hands, destruction was often a close bedfellow of birth.

Birth is a good example of inner dynamics coming together in the expression of nature: if anything is not balanced, death will quickly follow birth. Though the birth process may not seem relevant to magicians, it really is: all the inner dynamics and powers that a magician works with are immediate and apparent in the birth of a new life. It is nature's expression of the inner powers manifest, and looking at birth from both an inner and outer aspect will teach you a great deal about how magic works for humans.

It also brings into sharp focus the wider weave and pattern of fate: how and when a new life chooses to manifest is vitally important for that new life if it is to fulfil its chosen path.

In this lesson we will look at the various inner and outer stages of conception and birth that are relevant to magicians. We will start with the various different aspects of preconception and conception through to birth and survival. Remember, though we will look at the birth of a human child, which is relevant in itself, all the dynamics and actions of birth also play out in the birth of new magic, new cultures, and new lands: nature is very efficient in that she reuses the same pathways and patterns for all creation. What you learn in this lesson is also relevant to your own deeper magical practice and actions.

7.1 The pull from the Abyss

In the lesson on death you looked at the mountain/ladder that the dead soul climbs as it casts off its memories and baggage from life. When the soul reaches the top, it rests until called if it is going back into life.[1]

At some point a call goes out[2] which wakes the soul from its rest, and it begins to seek expression in life. When observed by magicians we see this as the soul tumbling down the other side of the mountain or falling off the ladder back to earth.

When magicians do the Death Vision in life and climb the mountain, they can also go through the whole process rather than stepping into the inner temples/library. What I will describe here is what we see as living magicians working with the Death Vision. Some cultures see different details, but the actual dynamics and ingredients are the

---

[1] At least that is how we perceive it in vision as living humans.

[2] Vibration/sound.

same—something you will spot once you have done it for yourself and experienced it.

As the soul tumbles down the mountain it is slowed down by a vast female angelic being who stands on the edge of the Abyss.[3] The soul lands at her feet, on the other side of the Abyss. And this is the part that will pretzel your mind, or at least confuse you a bit: the part of the Abyss where the soul lands is 'above.'

When we go into the Inner Desert in vision, we are visiting the Inner Desert in 'our time', our lifetime. When we reach the edge of the Abyss, with the Divine realm beyond, that ledge is our *now*. The Desert is like a layer cake: above is another layer of the Desert that will express in the potential future; below is another layer of the Desert that is the past of our world.

When a soul tumbles down the mountain and lands on the edge of the Abyss on the Divine side, and looks over the Abyss to the Desert, they are in all times at once. The angelic being[4] has hair that flows in all directions, and her hair, along with her arms, stop the soul from tumbling down the Abyss in an uncontrolled way.

The soul stands on the edge of the Abyss and looks across the Desert. There they see lots of different lives all playing out at once. These are all different expressions in life for this soul that are within their fate pattern: they are in fact looking at their complete pattern of expression in creation.

They can express in any one of those lives, but they must choose one. It is not a conscious choice; rather it is a deep pull from the soul. As soon as the soul recognises where it needs to go, the angel withdraws her arms and the soul tumbles down into the Abyss. They fall into what we perceive as a *whirlwind* that guides them to their point of conception: they are falling into time and place.

7.2 The stars

Another layer of the conception process is the stars. The planets and stars each have their own sound. When all the sounds come together in a specific harmony, it creates a threshold for the soul to cross on its way into manifestation: it falls from the stars into birth. The dynamic at the Abyss and the dynamic at the stars are two sides of the same coin, and the expression in the stars is where the soul is falling into its fate in human life.

On the Divine side of the Abyss is the deeper phase of the expression where the soul mirrors the first impulse of Divinity to express itself in manifestation. Once the soul crosses or falls from that realm, it falls into the stars and into mortal life.

The sounds of the stars coming into harmony is an ancient bit of knowledge. If you look carefully at some paintings from past visionaries, you will see aspects of it. You will also come across it in religious and mystical texts, and it is something you too will work with many times in your magical life. I think we have talked about some of this before in the course.

The harmonics of the stars are also the astrology of the conception: everything needs to be in the right place for the pattern of life expression to lock in place. This then allows the soul to fall into the mother's body.

The harmonising of the stars happens when the sperm penetrates the egg. Some women pick up on this moment, particularly if they are sensitive: you know immediately that you conceived. I know I did, and I know many other women who can trace back to the moment in time when they conceived: somewhere, your deeper self 'hears' that harmonic. The same feeling occurs when a lot of powerful strands of magic come together and move into completion in the future: you feel it. Everything has its precise moment when all the powers come together in creation or destruction.

I assumed for the longest time that the call to wake up to life, the falling through

---

[3]On the Divine side, not the Desert side.

[4]Ananke, the weaver of fate and time.

the whirlwind, through the stars, and into a mother all happened at the same time: that once the soul tipped into the whirlwind it would immediately express in the mother's body. But then I started to pick up on 'children' hanging around women before they got pregnant.

The first time I felt this was with my own grandson: he was apparent and hanging around my daughter for nearly a year before he was conceived. But the timing of his conception was very specific, and lots of different fateful events came together to make sure he was conceived in a particular place, with a particular bloodline, and at the perfect time.

This made me curious. And once I had experienced it with him, I became aware of it with other women: I slowly started coming across some women who had a child in their orbit but who were not yet pregnant. Sometimes it was a few months before their conception. I did not pick this up with every woman I knew who then became pregnant; only with a few very strong souls who were very clear that they were waiting for just the right time to lock in the conception with their fate pattern. Then I thought back to when my children were conceived—and yes, I knew I was pregnant straight away. It is fascinating.

7.3 Timing is everything

Timing, along with sound/vibration, is everything in the birth of anything new. We as humans have known this in magic for a very long time, to the point where many magicians will purposely wait until certain star alignments or moon phases are in place before they will act.

For the most part I have found this level of control counterproductive: if you use deeper instinct and just go with the flow, then often when you look back at a major magical working you will discover that the magic chose its own time. Often there was a more powerful coming-together of events than could have been anticipated. Birth is the same.

If a powerful bit of magic, or a soul, is left to choose its point of creation by drawing on its deep instincts, then the timing is often powerful and perfect. If the magician tries to control that point of creation, then it often lacks that final push of power. Remember that. When the time is right, all the power rushes in and all the forces come together: the magician will feel that coming-together as an overwhelming urge to act. The magician *gives birth*.

And when a woman goes into labour, unless it has been chemically forced or the woman has had an impact that triggered it, usually it is the child itself that triggers the labour, not the woman's body.

When a child's lungs have fully developed, a protein called *SP-A* is released from the child's lungs, which triggers labour. The child is essentially saying "I can breathe now and I am ready to come out."[5] This can go wrong if the mother has a bacterial infection, as the bacteria can bind to the receptors that the SP-A should bind to, which triggers her labour earlier.

Think about this for a minute in terms of magic and magical practice if you are birthing something new and powerful. Destructive elements[6] can latch onto the magical 'receptors' and trigger an early release or interfere with the magic. This is why when working with powerful magic, all the thresholds and the temple[7] must be strong, healthy, and clear.

7.4 Crossing the threshold: life and death

The birth process is naturally very dangerous for mother and child. This is part of the *rungs of the Ladder* in nature: the child and the mother must survive a tremendous ordeal. Before modern medicine, birth was one of the major killers of women and babies. It was the

---

[5]SP-A is a surfactant which allows the child to breathe.

[6]Like the bacterial infection in the mother at birth.

[7]Womb.

balance of creation and destruction, and many times destruction won. Disease, giving birth when too young or too old, weak bodies, badly put-together bodies... the things that could go wrong were[8] many.

The dance of creation and destruction are part of the evolutionary process, and nature's way of making sure that no single species overgrows too much. This process comes to sharp focus during childbirth. With the marvels of modern medicine, good resources, etc., more children and women now survive birth. The result of overcoming that destruction, though, can bring different, sometimes more vicious, elements of destruction into play for humanity, something we have to grasp ethically and intelligently and deal with as modern humans.

Again, the same dynamics apply in magic: if you block every possible avenue of destruction in a magical act, it will find other and often more vicious ways to express itself. Deflection and balance are the keys.

But as humans we are hardwired to survive, and we will do anything to achieve that. We may not realise it, but we live in a 'Golden Age' of resources for humanity.[9] A child born at this time in history has a far better chance of survival into adulthood. We have food, medicine, heat, light, and societies geared to protect those things. Should a soul need to express in life into adulthood and achieve certain things, now is the time to be born.

It will not always be that way, and already in the West those who watch carefully will see the beginning of the sharp decline.

Again, timing is everything. If I had birthed my children in any other age but this one, my first child would not have survived and nor would I. Which brings me to the next aspect of birth: the beings involved in the process.

7.5 The beings that work with birth

There are many beings that sometimes work around the birth of a child. Their job is to ensure that the fate pattern of both mother and child are upheld. They also bridge the threshold between the child being connected physically to the mother, and break the union so the child becomes an independent being in its own right.

When a woman becomes pregnant, the child's soul or spirit fills the vessel of the mother: the two are held in the same space. As the baby's body develops, the soul slowly begins to shrink down into the foetus, but right up to the moment of birth it is upheld and deeply connected to the mother via the umbilical cord and the placenta. The vital force of mother and child flow back and forth through the umbilical cord until that cord is cut.

I had never thought about this until I gave birth for myself, and so many magical things happened during that process.

With my first child I haemorrhaged, and there was a race to get the baby out. I could not have a caesarian section, as there were problems with the hospital's surgical theatre, and there was no time to get me to another hospital.

But fate works in wondrous ways. A midwife from Nigeria was on the ward, and she took control of the situation: she was used to midwifing births in very difficult circumstances and was the perfect person to have there. I was fading out, and in that state I became aware of many different beings around me, doing various things.

The midwife got the baby out, then started punching and massaging my abdomen to make it contract and so stem the bleeding. As she leaned over to cut the cord, I became aware of a being standing by her: this being leaned over and cut the inner cord at the same time. I felt the break between myself and the baby.

---

[8]And still are, to some extent.

[9]Depending on where you live, sadly.

At that point a feeling deep within me gave me the choice simply to drift into the stillness and stay there—impending death. The midwife was having none of it. She moved round the bed and grabbed my right leg— it took me years to figure out what happened and the significance of that action. Then she proceeded to shout at me in words I did not understand.

Something snapped me back. The noise, pain, and chaos returned, and I woke up.

As a strange aside, my baby daughter was also in danger: she was premature, weak, and struggling to survive. In the intensive care unit for babies was a mother who had also prematurely given birth while on holiday in the UK: she too was from Nigeria. I was too weak to breastfeed my daughter, so she volunteered her milk until I was strong enough.

I never learned this woman's name, but her milk was thick and rich and gave my daughter the strength to survive and then thrive. During the fortnight I spent in hospital I was constantly aware of beings flowing back and forth, but I was too young to understand what they were and what they were doing: I was twenty-one and clueless. But thanks to two strong women from Nigeria, we both survived.

Over the years since, I have been in situations where I could observe these beings in action, and later I began to work with them. When I first started observing them, I noticed that they upheld some babies and others not. For some births none of them turned up except for the cord cutter. They were working on the fate weave of the mother and baby, upholding them sometimes, reweaving at other times. Sometimes they simply watched but did nothing.

For a long while I could not understand why they did not help and uphold each baby equally. It was not until I had matured that I understood the deeper balance of nature. My mother's instinct was to save all things all the time, which is of course unbalanced, however unpalatable that may seem.

And why should you learn about this?

Because the birth of a child and the birth of a new pattern of magic *work the same way,* with the same beings involved. Which types of beings attend what creation does not depend on the outcome[10] but on the powers at work: creation, stasis, destruction.

When you are working with a preexisting pattern, the beings that work with you are ones that uphold the pattern. When you create a new pattern, the beings and powers of creation work with you. When you totally destroy a pattern, the powers of destruction work with you.

Creating a whole new pattern of magical manifestation is an octave of the act of creation itself. This involves many different powers and beings. It involves complex pattern-making and weaving, and it also involves the need to oversee and take responsibility for that pattern.

Just as a parent's responsibilities do not end when their child comes of age, you will always be parent and upholder to what you create throughout its lives in one way or another.

And this brings us to the flip side of this dynamic, which is a really tough one for a mother to come to terms with: *the child is not yours.* You are the guardian of that child, their guide, their giver of resources, their protector, but they are not *your* child; they are the child of the Goddess.

This might sound very New Age, which would be to misunderstand the statement. Rather than referring to a particular deity, the term *Goddess* refers to the Divine *receiving* power, the vessel which is also an expression of our planet.

Remember back to your work with the forces of creation: we perceive the outputting power of Divinity as male and the power that receives that output as female. This has nothing to do with actual gender and everything to do with how the power works. That power is mediated through deities which enables us to connect and interact with it. In terms of a baby, it is the child of the female power. We translate this to a female deity who embodies and mediates

---

[10] A child, a city, a tree, a war.

146

that power, hence the Eastern Catholic title of Mary: *Mother of God*.

When a child is born into a magical family it is understood that it is a child of the Mother. The birth parents are responsible for the child's day-to-day upkeep, but the soul itself is under the Mother's cloak.

When the birth mother births the child, that soul is externalised in the physical realm, so we attend to its physical needs throughout its life. But deep inner protection comes from the Mother. When a magical child is born, it is presented to the Mother for the safekeeping of its soul.

The physical act of standing before the female deity, presenting the child to the Mother, and stating that you are simply its guardian, guide, and the upkeeper of its physical life, becomes a deeply magical act that triggers the protection of that deity from passive to active. You open the gates, present the child, and relinquish total control and ownership over them. This puts it within the protective sphere of the Mother. This is an ancient action, and I suspect is the root of the idea of baptism in Christianity.

The same is true when a magician creates a whole new magical pattern: once it is completed and set in motion it is handed over to the gods and powers with the understanding that although we created that pattern, it needs inner governance to nurture and unfold it. By doing this, the fate path of the magic is governed, protected, and guided by the deities. This is a reversal of roles: here we are the creators and the inner contacts/deities are the day-to-day guardians.

7.6 Dangers and magical amulets

As birth was one of the most dangerous times in the life of a woman and child, a lot of magic to do with pregnancy and birth developed in various cultures. Again, what we discover from that old magic also applies to the creation of magical patterns.

Various things need protecting during birth. Besides the obvious life and death scenarios, there is also the matter of the well-being of the child's fate pattern and their pots of resources. A new pattern is always vulnerable until it is fully filled with power, and the resources within the fate pattern are also vulnerable until the new life or pattern is fully established.

The fate pattern of the child and mother[11] are heavily entwined at birth, which affords the child a certain level of protection: it can ride on the strength of the mother's fate pattern until the full flow of power is released into its new life/pattern.

When a child is involved, I have found in practical terms that the power seems to complete and fill the child's pattern when it reaches about seven years old. I have never found any ancient reference to this; it is just what I have found by magically observing the children born into my own family and circle of friends.

There is the Jesuit quote "give me a child until it is seven and I will give you back the man," but I am presuming this quote has its roots in the developmental process of a child's brain and body as opposed to anything esoteric. But as magicians we do know that outer mirrors inner and vice versa.

With my own children, working magically and also by magical instinct, I did find that I was urged less and less to protect them magically once they hit the age of about seven. The urge would then wake up again when they hit puberty.

With a small child the protection is very much about strengthening the creative process within them and dampening the destructive flow of power. It is also about keeping at bay the beings who could potentially take advantage of the child's weak nature in its early years and the predatory beings who would 'sweep up' the life of a vulnerable child. Again, everything here also translates into magic and new patterns, so read all this in both contexts.

---

[11]Or magician and created pattern.

In your apprentice training we looked briefly at destructive powers that sweep across the land and bring death to anything weak, whose fate pattern is either close to the end of its life thread or at the beginning of its life thread and therefore vulnerable.

The destructive being Lilith was an example we looked at. The *Lilitu*, the Mesopotamian storm demons, who are often represented by the screech owl, are destructive powers of the wind.[12] They are powers that 'weed' life in nature. Their job is to pick off the most vulnerable and leave the strongest,[13] and the job of the parent is to protect the vulnerable child from their power.

In the early days of a baby's life, the entwining with the mothers fate offers a modicum of protection. But magical amulets were also designed to deflect, redirect, or reject these powers—and they are still used. You cannot stop the wind in its tracks, but you can deflect or redirect it, which is precisely what midwifing magic does. Any new pulse of creation attracts a reflected pulse of destruction, and protecting one while deflecting the other is one of the most basic forms of magic.

Redirection is the most commonly used methods of magical protection of a new life or a new created pattern: something is magically created along the same lines as the baby in the hope that the predatory power will focus on the distraction-object and not the child. This object can take various forms: a model of a baby with some of the baby's hair twined round it, or a baby creature[14] which lives in the baby's bedroom.[15]

Other forms of passive magic used are mirrors round the baby's cot, a line of salt round the cot and across the thresholds of doors and windows, and pouches of salt sewn into the baby's clothing or swaddling. Another very old method is mixing a few grains of magically consecrated salt with the child's saliva, then dabbing it in their ears, nostrils, and lips. Note the use of consecrated salt to act as a barrier. This method can be applied to the creation of a new magical pattern by giving the pattern an exteriorisation[16] which is then protected by a ring of consecrated salt.

Some cultures use recitation. Verses from sacred text would be inscribed on vellum or parchment, rolled into a tiny package, then placed in a small pouch round the child's neck. Another method of protection is the *Vigil of the Flame*: a flame[17] is kept going near the child day and night, and the baby would not be left alone at all. This was a method I used: for their first year my babies did not leave my side, day or night.

You have worked with this principle in a very small way in your ritual work: you leave the candles burning when you leave the room and let the magic 'cook.' The flames keep vigil over the magic and protect it until it locks in place and is completed.

The other major method of protection for babies is images. These are usually deities, often of goddesses who are also mothers, which are enlivened and placed close to the child's cot. Every night the deity is asked to watch over the child during the dark hours.

Elements of ancestral work can also be used, where ancestors take turns to watch over the child. This is also something I worked with, and I returned the favour by working in vision to watch over newborn babies brought into my family. I would do the vision, which then triggered my deeper spirit, and my energy would then flow to the child at night to protect it. I would wake up battered and exhausted, but it was worth it for the times when those babies were ill, weak, or otherwise at risk.

Most of these methods are passive magic that anyone can do; more complex methods require a magician. I used to work with stuffed toys and porcelain creatures, bridging guardians into them and telling them to guard the child. The guardians would then wake me in the night if the child was in any inner

---

[12]One of the destructive four winds.
[13]Evolution!
[14]Usually a baby chicken.
[15]The chickens always get the short end of the stick.

[16]A map, a sigil, a construction model, a tool, etc.
[17]Candle.

or outer danger, which worked very well. But what protects children more than anything is their parent's vital force and fate pattern.

Although mother and child are cut apart into separate beings when the cord is cut, you still have overlaps in vital force and fate. When one of my babies was seriously ill at barely two months old, it was my sheer force of will, vital force, and bloodymindedness that kept her alive. Any mother is a fierce adversary against anything that threatens her child, and that includes inner threats. And any mother who has a fierce warrior goddesses behind her is too much trouble for any destroying being to want to tackle: these powers seek out weakness, not strength.

7.7   Paying the Ferryman

At the birth of a child there is an old custom, one you can find versions of throughout the world, of putting a coin, usually silver, into the baby's right hand. This is a 'good luck' tradition which wishes the child a life of plenty, but which also ensures that at the end of their life they have enough to "pay the ferryman." As some cultures have become squeamish about death, that part of the tradition has got skipped over, yet older communities understood that birth and death are both part of life, and birth is the beginning of the march towards death.

Giving the child a coin to pay the ferryman would give them a resourceful life and a safe passage into death…hopefully in old age. In some Celtic areas of Europe, particularly ones with faery traditions, it was said that if a child had their coin of safe passage, the faeries would not take them: they would be fearful of depriving the ferryman of his fee, which would enrage him and bring death to everything.

At death the coin would be placed in the deceased's teeth or right hand to guarantee them a safe and helpful passage through the Underworld. Forms of this tradition can be seen in China (Zhau Zhou), Armenia (Agra Hadig), and elsewhere around the world.

In the Celtic areas of the UK[18] this is still widely practised and is known as 'silvering' the child, or 'crossing the hand with silver'. In the UK when there is a royal birth, the Royal Mint distributes silver coins to a number of children born on the same day, so that they can share the good fortune of the new royal baby.

Some of these folk traditions are very old and strong. The ones best to work with are those with versions practised worldwide, where different communities have figured out the same thing and are working with it because they see it being successful.

As magicians this type of old passive magic can be incorporated into our magical practice when working with magical streams that run along similar lines. They add a small layer to the pattern which helps protect it as it develops. When I have had to build new magical patterns from scratch, I would sometimes bury a silver coin[19] as a gift to the powers that will compost and settle the pattern once it has done its job.

Never think of magic as an isolated thing: it is intricately woven into life, and everything is a version or mirror of something else. The birth of a magical pattern is the same as the birth of a child; the death and composting of magic is the same as the death of a human.

When you need guidance for an aspect of a magical act and you draw a blank, look at folk magic that runs parallel to what you are doing: often the answer can be buried in old folk practice. If you analyse what that folk magic is doing passively and can recognise the dynamics behind it, you will be able to spot how to use that method in an active, stronger way.

Magic is not a series of unique systems around the world: it is inherent around us in nature. The various systems are just ways that different people have learned or created to tap into that natural dynamic and actively engage with it. There is no such thing as a magical

---

[18]Scotland, Ireland, Wales, north of England, and the islands off the coast of Scotland.

[19]Sending it into the Underworld.

system that is supreme, or one that is wrong, any more than one language is supreme and the others are wrong; though some systems of magic are more efficient than others, some are haphazard, and some have evolved while others haven't. They are all just methods of interacting directly with that natural force and working with it.

Over time you will learn to spot valuable magical methods in different systems and you will recognise what is behind them. By approaching your studies this way, you will expand your knowledge outwards away from dogma and towards a more pragmatic understanding and evolution. The problems start when the religious mindset creeps into magic and things become based on dogma, faith, belief, and ritual habit. Don't let that happen.

Look at everything around you. Look at the powers of creation and destruction playing out in big and small arenas in life: that is where you will find fragments of magic hiding in plain sight. Putting a coin in a baby's right hand is a powerful magical act, yet it is done every day around the world as part of tradition. Everyone ignores it, yet it is these little gems that tell us a great deal about how ordinary people learned to live in the face of these powers and draw on their imaginations and instincts in order to protect and survive. These everyday things should draw the attention of the magician, so that they can look closely to see what lies behind them.

7.8   On the Practical work

For this practical work you will look at what happens at a birth from an inner point of view. This will give you an idea of the different forces, beings, and dynamics that come into play when a child is born.

Not all births are equal: at some you will find very little happening, and at others you will find all sorts happening. It all depends on the fate of the child. If the fate pattern of the child is very much about their own personal path, then often not much happens around the birth. But if the child has a strong fate that will affect the fate patterns of others or the land, then more likely a lot will happen to protect them during such a dangerous time.

It does not necessarily mean that a strong-fated child will do great things: sometimes their life affects others in major ways but through simple situations that act as a catalyst for change. If a human life is fated strongly then lots of protection will be placed around them, as a strong fate often also attracts strong opposition to that life: it is the fight of balance. So bear that in mind.

7.9   *Task:* **Attending a birth in vision**

Look on a map for a maternity hospital in your area. When you find a place, write down its name on paper and place the paper on the central altar or somewhere in your work room.

Timing is everything with this work: when you place the paper on the altar or in your work room somewhere,[20] do it with the intention that you will visit that place at a time when you can observe a birth. Even though the room is closed down at this point, talk to the room and tell it that you wish to know when the time is right. Even though the gates are not open, by now you will have done enough work in the space for a resonance of the inner thresholds to be there all the time.

You will feel when the time is right to do the work: it will pop into your head and you will have time to do it. If it is not the right time, you may think about it but you won't quite have the time, energy, or inclination to do it. Although a lot of magic works out of time, because you are dealing with the direct physical manifestation of something[21] on the land you are living on, it is best to work within the flow of time.

When you are ready open the gates, light the lights, and have a small silver coin in your pocket. Using the method you learned in your apprentice training to go out of your house and travel to the hospital in vision: you may find yourself able to cover quite a distance as you

---

[20]South is best.

[21]The birth of a child.

don't have to walk every step in vision, unlike walking when using your body.

When you get to the hospital follow your instincts. You may find that a being begins to walk alongside you who will guide you to where the baby is about to be born. Go to the baby/mother you are drawn to and stand in the room to observe. Keep out of the way of the beings that are working so that you do not interfere: just watch, listen, and pay attention.

Once the child comes out, as soon as the outer and inner cord has been cut, reach into your pocket in vision,[22] take the coin out, and place it in the child's right hand as a gift.

When you have finished, come back out of the labour room and go home. Once you come out of vision, go and bury the coin somewhere in the land. As you bury it remember the baby and tell the land that this is the silver for the child's passage: you are paying their ferry fare. Write up your experiences in your journal, then type it up on computer.

7.10 *Task:* Working with the Death Vision

Do the Death Vision again. This time, instead of stepping into the mists, lie down at the top of the mountain. When you hear the call, you will get up and tumble down the mountain. Work out how to set up the room to do this vision, and go into the vision knowing that once you tumble from the mountain you will have to follow your own vision and go with what presents itself.

When you have finished immediately write up what you saw in your journal, then type it up for the mentor.

7.11 *Task:* Tarot/Quareia Deck Readings

If you have the Quareia magicians deck, use that. If not, use your usual tarot deck. Write these readings down so that you can go back to them.

Landscape layout

Using the Inner Landscape layout, ask:

> "Show me what was happening from an inner perspective at the birth of that child."

Card number one will be the baby itself. Look at the dynamics around the child, any beings that present, and what beings are in the child's long-term future.

Quareia Deck layout

Using the full Quareia Deck layout, ask to see the fate pattern of that child. If you don't have a Quareia deck, the book is available for free download on our website. The layout can be found at the end of the book.

Tree of Life layout

Using the Tree of Life layout, ask what effect the coin you gave the land will have on the death of that life, whenever that happens. What will their passage into death be like?

Four-directional layout

Using the Four-directional layout, ask:

> "What are the powers that will dominantly express through the life of that child?"

These are powers that flow into the child's life over its lifetime. They may express in different ways throughout the child's life, but there will be at least one overall quality of power that repeatedly expresses itself over the child's lifetime.

Write up your results and think about them in terms of a lifetime: what do they tell you about the life of that child?

---

[22]Also put your hand on it physically with your left hand.

Lesson 8

Ritual Patterns

In this lesson we will bring together everything you have learned in this module and look step-by-step how these dynamics are used in the construction of a ritual.

To construct a ritual from scratch is not to create magic from scratch: these are very different things.

A ritual externalises a magical pattern into the manifest world and sets it off in the flow of time. Constructing a magical pattern from scratch is something very different. A newly constructed ritual engages a magical pattern into completion. If an adept was to create a magical pattern from scratch, it would then need a new ritual constructed to act as its vehicle and guidance system.

In cultures linked to the Abrahamic faiths, many of the rituals call on aspects of those religions which are embedded within the ritual pattern. This can take the form of god names, angelic names, and so forth. If you use these god names, the ritual is immediately bound into the pattern of that religious system, and will bring into the pattern any of that system's inherent benefits and imbalances.

We see this a lot in Western magic: all the embedded misogyny, collective dogma, and degeneration that has built up over time in Christianity and Judaism expresses and externalises itself when the ritual is performed. It always expresses first through the magician, then into the actual magical pattern itself.

A lot of Western magical rituals have patterns that have been essentially copied from Christian or Jewish rituals and prayers. When a magician has been raised in a Christian society, the religion's habits, rituals, and belief system become deeply embedded within their psyche and they can unconsciously carry that embedded system across into their magic if they are not careful.

Their system of understanding the universe and themselves, and their relation to Divinity, can be coloured by this embedded pattern. This is fine if the magician is Christian and operates their magic within that religion's way of thinking, but if they do not then it starts to get messy.

As soon as a magician starts performing declarations to deities with unfamiliar words and enacting patterns without understanding where they came from, they stop doing pure magic and start doing dogmatic regurgitation. As well as weakening the magic it can shake up any imbalance within the magician—but not in a way that brings resolution; rather it *strengthens* the imbalance.

The powers of Divinity, and how they express as forces of creation, destruction, and so on, are very valid and indeed needed for many levels of magic; but how we perceive, interact with, and relate to those Divine forces, and in what context, has a strong bearing on how the magic will work and how it will affect the magician's development.

A lot of English magic shows a mixture of deep understanding of magical dynamics trapped within dogmatic Christian patterns. Some is heavily connected to mythic patterns, and while some of this has deep roots in the land of Britain, not all of it has. Some draws on Jewish Kabbala without fully understanding the deeper spiritual dynamics behind the religious structure, and all these unthinking approaches can have a direct bearing on how the magician matures and evolves.

As developing magicians, it is a major skill to be able to look at rituals and see what is at play, what powers are being brought in, why, and how. And by looking at ritual in such a way you develop your critical thinking. This in turn is important if you are to understand what magical patterns underlie a ritual's power and what drives it. From that understanding, the magician develops skills in constructing new magical patterns.

Too often magicians birth new magical patterns simply by copying bits of the previous generation's work without truly understanding with what they are working. When you create a new magical pattern, you must be able to understand fully, and from an *inner power* perspective, what is actually being woven into that pattern.

It is also important to understand magical evolution: we stand on the shoulders of those who went before us, and all shoulders have weaknesses! The magicians who went before us had failures as well as successes.

Critical thinking is of major importance to magical development: never take something at face value simply because it has been that way for a long time. As evolving magicians, we grow just as much from the mistakes of the past as its successes. I hope that future magical generations will do the same for Quareian magical work; that they will spot its weaknesses. That is the only way magic can evolve.

So you can start learning this process of analysis, we will look at two well-known and heavily used magical rituals in Western magic: the *Qabbalistic Cross* and the *Lesser Banishing Ritual of the Pentagram*. We are not looking at these rituals to tear them apart or criticise them; it is more a matter of learning to look and see what is behind something, where it comes from, what it is doing, and why. I will point out the origins of the rituals' aspects, and also what dynamics are being used; then in the practical work you will look at them deeply for yourself.

The major questions we need to ask are:

"What is it doing?"

"Why is it working?"

"Within what pattern does it function?"

"How does that blend with the magician?"

8.1 Extract from *Liber O*

This first extract is from the *Qabbalistic Cross*.

Touching the forehead, say Ateh (Unto Thee).

"Ateh" is *Atah* (*ATH* in Hebrew: אתה), which means "you." It can also mean "coming" or "becoming" and in *Daniel* 7:13 it is used as "Ateh" in the context of "was coming":

כְּבַר אֱנָשׁ אָתֵה הֲוָה וְעַד־.

We see the use of *Atah/Ateh* in the beginning of Hebrew prayers:

"Baruch atah Adonai elohaynu Melech ha'olam"

Blessed are you, Lord our God, King of the universe.

So in this ritual the first words are: "You are."

Touching the breast, say Malkuth (The Kingdom).

Malkuth is the Hebrew word for kingdom, rank, authority, and sovereignty. It is the last Sefirot on the Tree of Life: the expression of life as the kingdom of God.

Placing Malkuth in the heart (breast) is to say: your heart is a realm over which the sovereign exercises his authority.[1] This is interesting when you think in terms of the heart spirit[2] that you learned about in the apprentice section. However, it could also be about the Gnostic understanding of the Kingdom of God as being *within*, which is found in the New Testament synoptic gospels.

But in Kabbalistic terms, placing Malkuth in your breast is to potentially deny the path beneath your feet, that carries you through *olam*: through the distance. It also cuts off the lower Sefirot powers that drive you along your path. Was this intentional for a good reason?

Touching the right shoulder, say ve-Geburah (and the Power).

This is where the ritual dips deeper into Kabbalah. *Geburah* ("Gevurah") means "strength of judgement," not muscular strength or "power." In Hebrew texts it tends to refer to the power of God's judgement and the strength of withholding/restriction. Magically this is correct, as the right arm is the arm of the scales and the right shoulder is the magical power of restriction.

However when given an English understanding it loses a lot in translation: it becomes the "powerful right arm," but such power comes from judgement and restriction,[3] not from being strong. It is often referred to in Hebrew as *middas hadin*, the expression of law, and there is a saying in Hebrew text:

"Who is a strong person? He who sublimates his own passions."

—*Ethics of the Fathers* 4:1

So you can see straight away how magical misunderstandings can easily happen and why it is important to know the root of something, particularly where magic and Hebrew are concerned.

This part of the ritual shows a deep understanding of the magical Mysteries that can be drawn from Jewish Kabbalah; but I wonder how many people who copy the ritual from the net and then enact it without deeper training actually know what it means and what it does.

Touching the left shoulder, say ve-Gedulah (and the Glory).

Opposing *Gevurah* (Restriction) is *Chesed* (Mercy), which is sometimes replaced with *Gedulah* ("greatness"). The deeper mystical aspect of this power is the Light Bearer: one who shines a light into the darkness to show the way ahead. It is the merciful giving into life that is boundless, and thus must be restricted by Gevurah to keep it balanced. Judgement and Mercy mean very different things to "power and glory," and as we will see in a moment, the root of *Gevurah* and *Gedulah* used in this ritual come from a Jewish and Christian prayer to *describe God, not humankind*. These two Sefirot are higher dynamics of creation and restriction: they are Divine expressions. Which then takes us into the modern mess of understanding Divinity within humanity: Divinity is within us and everything around us. But when some coked-up magician declares they are a living god, something has gone badly wrong in the program: the *ego trap*. That trap is a strong one in this ritual, and I suspect that it was done deliberately to confront the magician with themselves. Clever. This aspect of the ritual declares the powers of Divinity and acknowledges those powers as being an inherent part of our existence.

---

[1] Or it could be taken as you are the sovereign of yourself.

[2] The king in the heart.

[3] Withholding from life and returning to source.

Clasping the hands upon the breast, say le-Olahm, Amen (To the Ages, Amen).

Le-olam or *ad-olam* is often mistakenly translated into English as meaning forever or eternity, which it doesn't.

So where did the Golden Dawn get this from? Let's have a look:

> ...And lead us not into temptation,
> but deliver us from evil:
> **For thine is the kingdom,**
> **and the power, and the glory,**
> **forever and ever.**
> **Amen.**

The Lord's Prayer is the oldest known Christian prayer of which we are aware, and it would have been spoken in Aramaic. By the time it had gone through translations into Greek, then Latin, and finally English, it had lost a lot of the subtleties of its wordplay, puns, and sense. Even so it is still a powerful declaration.

When I was writing this lesson I assumed, wrongly, that the GD ritual went back to the Lords prayer, as it is an obvious copy. But once the lesson was written, it niggled me that I was missing something—and I was. After digging deeper, I got back to the original source of this text, which can be found in the Tanakh (*1 Chronicles* 29:11). This was a good lesson for me to not take things at face value myself, and to listen to my own advice: keep digging until you are sure you have reached a true source! Here it is:

1 Chronicles 29:11

> *l'khä y'hwäh haG'duLäh w'haG'vûräh w'haTif'eret w'haNëtzach w'hahôd Kiy-khol BaSHämayim ûvääretz l'khä y'hwäh haMam'läkhäh w'haMit'naSë l'khol l'rosh.*

Thine, O Yahwe' יֲהֶוֶ, *is* the greatness, and the power, and the glory, and the victory, and the majesty: for all *that is* in the heaven

and in the earth *is thine*; thine *is* the kingdom, O Yahwe' יֲהֶוֶ, and thou art exalted as head above all.

I noticed in this that two words used; 'aretz' (*erets*—the earth/land), and 'Mamlakhah' (*realm*) and not Malkuth (*rule/dominion as ruled over*)

If you continue reading *1 Chronicles* 29:25, the transliteration is:

> *way'gaDël y'hwäh et-sh'lomoh l'ma'läh l'ëynëy Käl-yis'räël waYiTën äläyw hôd mal'khût ásher lo-häyäh al-Käl-melekh' l'fänäyw al-yis'räël*

29:25 And the LORD magnified Solomon exceedingly in the sight of all Israel, and bestowed upon him such royal majesty as had not been on any king before him in Israel.

Note the use of Malkuth (mal'khut) in this context.

Now think back to the ritual and the use of Malkuth in the centre. I am not the best person to talk about the twists and turns of usage in the Hebrew language, but in magical terms, this brings up an interesting point to ponder. Think about it for yourselves and what it means magically, as opposed to religiously.

When we think back to the people who first structured the LBRP in the Golden Dawn, the group's members came from Christian families and had a Christian education. Though many of them had wide and varied interests, their roots were strong, as they were for everyone in Victorian England. You draw from what you know and what is deeply embedded within you. We all do, whether we are conscious of it or not. The early GD members and founders would have read their bible in depth as children, and then as adults some of them learned Hebrew and Kabbalah.

This is a good example of the weave of religion and magic brought together, as opposed to non-religious spirituality and magic, i.e. a connection with Divinity that does not operate through a prescribed religion. Both are valid and the success of one or the other largely depends on the individual magician and how they operate their daily lives in balance to their Divine connection.

This ritual puts the magician within the Abrahamic pattern but does not compensate for the long historic changes that occurred within that pattern: it went from an understanding of male/female and creation/destruction, to having one male god i.e. Divinity. Divinity is not a deity, yet the Abrahamic pattern, particularly Christianity, treats Divinity like one, which can cause all sorts of complex inner magical and spiritual issues.

The magicians who developed this ritual did not lift themselves completely out of a religious pattern and into a spiritual/mystical one; rather they embedded a weave of Victorian Christianity with Jewish mysticism without stepping out of their more dogmatic mindset at a deep level.

This is not a criticism, as I think taking such a step at that time in history, in that group, would have been near on impossible: I think they did the best they could at the time, which is all any of us can do.

So what should this teach us about the construction of ritual and the powers of creation, destruction, and the Underworld? How does it balance within it the dynamics of the flows of power, and what does it do? Is it magic, or is it magical religion?

8.2 The dynamics in action

Using the Kabbalistic pattern, the *Qabbalistic Cross* part of the *Lesser Banishing Ritual of the Pentagram* ritual creates a V-shaped pattern on the Tree of Life. The two opposing forces of *Gevurah* (restriction) and *Gedalah* (expansion) are balanced in the centre by *Malkuth* (dominion). But the balance on the Tree of Life between these two powers is *Tiferet*: the Fulcrum between the two. *Malkuth* is the *end product* of the tree, not its centre; it is the world that you live in, that you affect by your own actions, and the path that you walk.

However, placing Tiferet in the centre of such a magical pattern for beginners would be begging for trouble: the LBRP was initially designed as a training exercise for the early students. To place Tiferet in the dominion of the heart would pump up the ego to the extreme in a hapless beginner. There are powerful dynamics woven into this ritual to do with *waking up* at a deep level. It is a catalyst that can trigger the dawning of awareness, or it will shut someone down; one or the other.

When psychology is brought into the pattern, as many modern Golden Dawn groups do, the ritual becomes all about the self: all the Divine names and powers are seen simply as aspects of the self. This will limit and reduce the ritual's power right down to self-analysis and feel-good factors: that is not magic, that is using magical patterns in psychological self-therapy.

From a magical Kabbalistic perspective, replacing Tiferet with Malkuth bypasses three key powers of the Sefirot: *Netzach* (the Grindstone), *Hod* (the Unraveller) and *Yesod* (the threshold of creation into generation: the inner foundation of the outer world). These three *Lower Sefirot* are known as the *action powers* or the "drivers of man." The *Higher Sefirot* of Gevurah and Gedalah (Chesed) are the dynamics of creation/restriction itself. They are not rooted in man, but in the Divine impulse of creation and destruction that flows through everything.

If you plug a device into your computer but you do not have the drivers for it, it will not work. In this metaphor, man is the device, the lower action Sefirot are the drivers, and the higher Sefirot are the software and then the computer itself.

In Jewish Kabbalah, these lower three Sefirot are the actions/dynamics by which we achieve things: Netzach and Hod are the two 'feet' that carry you on your path through life, and are the 'action' balance between the two dynamics in your life: they are expressions of your free will. Yesod is the vehicle of the imagination/creativity/generation that keeps the two in balance.

Most people look at the map of the Tree of Life and see Netzach to the right: that would be to *mirror* the Tree. But you do not mirror the Tree, you *are* the Tree. Netzach is your left foot which carries you forward with the impulse of Chesed/the Light Bearer at your shoulder and behind you. Without having these two feet to carry you forward, then working within this system, and using the two opposing higher Sefirot without feet to carry you on the path, would be cutting yourself off magically at the knees.

And if people then throw in the odd dolphin, cherub, and the occasional fish,[4] then it can *really* get messy.

8.3 Prayer, declare, or ritual?

There is a major problem in Western ritual that people do not often see, as it is so engrained within our culture's psyche. The problem is differentiating between what is a magical ritual, what is religious ritual, what is a declaration, and what is a prayer.

Religious rituals often have magical aspects, but they are not magical rituals: there is a major difference. Religious rituals are there for the *deity's benefit*, and to *deepen the relationship between deity and human.*

Magical ritual is an active 'doing' pattern that is created, enacted, and empowered to *achieve something magically regardless of whether a deity is involved or not.*

A declaration is where a person either recites or declares their allegiance or devotion to a specific deity and belief system, and/or invites that deity's power into a space. This is used in both magic and religion, and places the magician/priest in a particular 'club'—the egregore of the religion.

A prayer is where the deity is asked for something, usually within a religious pattern, and is flattered in return.

A magical utterance is where the magician externalises a magical pattern using speech/sound in order to trigger its outer expression through the use of magical utterance. It is like pressing the 'go' button for a magical pattern.

As you can see, all these things are very different: they have different effects, different audiences, and different functions. Knowing which is which, and why, is vital to successful magic: if you don't know what you are doing, how on earth do you expect it to work?

It is an important stage of magical development to be able to look at a ritual and identify what it is actually doing and what it *is*.[5] From there you can ascertain whether it will work for the job in hand.

Always understand that often the lines between magic and religion are blurred in ritual: stronger magic flows through Divine channels of power, and religious ritual often has many elements of magic embedded within it. But each type will have an overall specific impulse that takes it one way or the other.

The *Qabbalistic Cross* is a religious ritual being used magically. It is not a magical ritual. Think about the dynamics and outcomes of such a usage. There is also another element in such a magical-religious ritual that has a distinct influence on its outcome and success: its emotive content.

8.4 Emotion versus impersonal

Because of the influence that religion has on a lot of Western magic, emotive content is often overused in Western magical work. This can seriously undermine its effectiveness. Think back to the three principles of Creation, Fulcrum and Restriction. None of those dynamics have any connection with emotion or emotive thought: you are working with power/energy, not human feelings.

In many religions there is a strong tendency to seek a parent substitute, which colours

---

[4]I shit you not.

[5]Religious, magical, etc.

everything that happens in that religion. We want God to protect us, feed us, nurture us, smite our enemies, and love us unconditionally—like a parent. As a result we give God a human gender, usually male, sometimes female. This parent-seeking is reflected in the religion's prayers and rituals:

> "…Give us this day our daily bread,
> And forgive us our trespasses…"

In magic this has no place: it is as absurd as entreating and praying to the electricity that flows into the your house to feed you and keep you warm. The Divine powers of creation and destruction have no human emotions; as a magician you are working with Divine *power*, which is driven by necessity.

Understanding this can be very painful for some people, who will rebel against such a statement. The need for parental love is hardwired into us for survival. Yet it is important to overcome such hardwiring if you are to become an adept magician.

You can love God/Divinity with all your heart, but is wise also to accept that such an emotion flows from human to divine power. What flows from Divinity to humanity is *necessity*, not emotional love. It is powerful, it is beautiful in its manifest form, but it is not woven with human emotion: it is Divine expression in its pure form. We can interact emotionally with deity powers that are closer to us, but the deeper, underlying Divine powers flow through the *needs of the pattern*, not an emotional relationship.

This is better understood in polytheistic religions and mystical patterns than monotheistic ones. If you take out the beings, deities, and so forth that are closer to humanity and focus only on the One, then the human is left emotionally bereft. Then comes the cry: "why did God allow this plane crash/tsunami/death?" Humanising Divinity is folly in general, and in magic it can be dangerous.

The deeper powers of creation and destruction are beyond human structure, and they have no desire to make you feel better. Nor do the lesser powers closer to humanity[6] have surface human emotion: that is a product of your hormone system. However they are receptive to deeper communion/union/relationships that engender a deeper level of emotive energy, and will connect with that and sometimes mirror it. But even then it is still tied in with necessity if you look closely enough and pay attention.

This can confuse many magicians who make contact with beings that will protect them, help them with resources, and so forth. The beings do this not because they emotively 'care' about you, but because you need those things to achieve some necessary end in the larger picture of your life path. It is a *means to an end*.

Just to make things more confusing, when a magician connects with deeper Divine powers, we often experience a deep inner emotion in response to that connection. When we experience union with that Divine power, our bodies translate it as deep emotion. Yet it is more about 'communion' and 'union' than physical emotion. The emotion we feel is *our physical endocrine system reacting to that power*.

Learning to separate out hormonal emotion from deeper spiritual connection and response is an important step in your magical development. This starts with learning stillness, then learning to distinguish between energy/emotions driven by your body's physical structure and the deeper response to Divine recognition from our spirit.

Learning that distinction comes from taking steps to move away from seeing the Divine as an attending parent[7] and moving towards seeing the Divine as a creative and destructive power that is everything manifest. The beings that mediate between Divinity and humanity are ones we can communicate emotively with, but their impulse is driven by overarching necessity, not human emotion.

---

[6]Which express through beings that interact with us.

[7]We have Christianity to thank for that conditioning—treating Divinity as a deity.

When we receive that impulse of necessity, our minds/bodies translate it into an emotion so that we will bond, interact, and respond appropriately.

In magic it boils down to this: you do what you are supposed to be doing to grow and evolve, and the inner beings that mediate between Divinity and humanity will ensure that the necessities are dealt with. Respect and the necessary response from the magician to deity and Divinity goes a great deal further than flattery and entreaties. Divine love is ensuring the balance of creation.

This also takes out the ego trap. If you work from a place of "I am Divine" and do magic with a mix of command (control), entreaty (begging), and flattery, then you will trigger a whole bunch of your own emotive responses. This in turn colours how you see the magic and also how you emotionally processes your success or failure. The number of times I have heard comments from magicians like "it worked because I am the Divine commander of my own destiny,"[8] or "it failed because God doesn't love me."[9] The staggering lack of magical understanding in those two statements is depressing, and very telling about how the magician perceives the Divine and themselves.

What I am trying to take you to, which is deeply important in magic, and as an initiate it is something you would do well to ponder over, is the meaning of emotion and what it means to you. Separating out what is driven by survival instinct, what is driven by hormones, what is driven by blood connections, and what is driven by the deeper self, is a difficult and lifelong task that magic will bring into sharp focus for you. There are no right or wrong answers, as this is deeply dependent on the individual. It is a matter of learning to listen to the deeper self and to be true to yourself and to the flow of Divinity of which you are part.

All this has a direct bearing on your magic: if you truly know and understand yourself, you are a major step closer to understanding the Divine in everything, and thus also in magic.

To this end, it is interesting to look at various magical rituals[10] in terms of religious content, magical content, and also "it's all about you" psychology. The removal of personal emotion from magic, and understanding the deeper, more enduring connection that can translate through emotion, is a key to magic.

8.5 Purpose: banish and invoke?

So now that we have gotten emotion, religion, and parents out of the picture, let's go back to the Qabbalistic Cross and Lesser Banishing Ritual of the Pentagram, whose purpose was a training exercise that could be used for banishing and invoking. Let us take a look at the second part of the ritual, and we will look in depth in terms of what we have just covered. We will ask, "why does it banish?"

This part of the ritual works with the four directions.

> Turning to the East, make a pentagram with the proper weapon. Say "IHVH." (Yahd Hey Vau Hey)

The first step, making a pentagram before you, expresses the manifest power of humanity away from the body. It is assumed that it represents earth and will act as a shield. Think about that for a moment.

The words are the *Tetragrammaton*, the four letters which together form completion of Divinity manifest in the world. It is not a word/name to be spoken or which even can be spoken; it is a deep mystery of breath/utterance, combined with inner knowledge of the power that flows through the letters both individually and when combined. It is the *HaShem*, the *Name* which draws upon the Gematria of the letters and an understanding of the powers of the 'four winds'; and it is a *declaration* of the Divine manifest. Uttered properly with deep

---

[8]Yawn.

[9]Blink...

[10]There are tons on the internet.

knowledge, and within its own religious pattern, it is a powerful trigger.

> Turning to the South, the same, but say "ADNI" (Adonai).

Again the pentacle is externalized. This word means 'Lord.'

> Turning to the West, the same, but say "AHIH" (Eheieh).

The letters AHIH are אהיה which means "I will be." It comes from a name of God in Exodus that is אהיה אשר אהיה, *Ehyeh asher ehyeh*: "I will be that which I will be." It is a *creative* name of power referring to that Divine impulse that seeks constant creation.

> Turning to the North, the same, but say "AGLA" (Agla).

Agla *is an acronym for* Attar gibbor le'olam Adonai, which are the first four words of *Gevurot*, the second blessing from the *Ha Amidar*, the standing prayer said facing the *Aron Kodesh*, the ark that holds the Torah. These first four words mean: "You are mighty in the world, O Lord." The second four words of that blessing are: *Mechaiyeh metim attar*, which mean: "restorer of the dead you are."

The rest of the ritual is a version of a breast-plate, calling upon angelic beings to be around the magician. It places the pentagram around the human (externalizing it) and the hexagram in the central axis.

> Extending the arms in the form of a cross say:
>
> "Before me Raphael;
>
> Behind me Gabriel;
>
> On my right hand Michael;
>
> On my left hand Auriel;
>
> About me flames the Pentagram,
>
> And in the Column stands the six-rayed Star.

So what magical elements are at play in this ritual? There are declarations (*God is*), there are the creative aspects of the Divine in the form of names, and the protective element of Divine power (the use of AGLA). There is a fulcrum: the hexagram in the centre of the column.

So we have a creation/birth impulse and we have a fulcrum, but we have no corresponding restriction or destruction other than Gevurah at the right shoulder: there is a lot of creative impulse, not a lot of restriction, and no destruction at all. The flow of directional power is *into* the space and around the human, but there is no *outlet*.[11] And think about the angels called in that section of the ritual: you have looked into one or two of these angels in your training so far. How relevant or appropriate to the task in hand are these names?

The magical pattern of humanity (pentagram) is exteriorised outside the body and linked with fire (to protect). There is no magical verbal direction (asking) in the ritual to protect, to banish, or to invoke/draw in. This works on the presumption that the utterance of *HaShem* is enough to protect. If you are *living* within the stream of consciousness, flow, and substance of which this pattern is part,[12] then connecting with aspects of Divinity around the directions will work well: being immersed in the stream of Divine power is all that is needed. This does not mean having to be a devout Jew or Christian; that is something different again.

God is not Jewish: Kabbalah is the vocabulary and operating system that Jews use. As a magician, if you are operating at the same frequency as this particular flow, it will work; if you are not, it will not. It's that simple. If the blue wire is plugged into the blue inlet, power will flow. If you try to plug the blue wire into your nostrils, it will not.

---

[11] Though bear in mind this was a beginner ritual, and a full flow is not always appropriate for someone just starting out.

[12] Living a religious, spiritually aware, or mystical life; which system does not matter so long as it is compatible with the power.

If you are working mystically as a magician, with all that entails, then it will work. If you are Frater Gadoodoo in a polyester robe and holding a very expensive wand, who hates all religion, hates concepts of Divinity, sees themselves as an all-powerful godhuman/superwitch/insert-stupid-ego-here, and wants protecting from all the nasty things in life they are trying to avoid by hiding in the basement of their lives, then it likely won't work.

To take another step forward in your critical thinking, we will look at the magical dynamics of what 'tips the on switch' of a magical ritual. Then you can go back and look this at this ritual again.

Editor's Note

Hello, it's the editor here. I have always assumed—I don't know how correctly—that the archangel breastplate section of the LBRP was a version of a Jewish prayer I knew as a child, with the archangels assigned to different quarters and the Shekinah replaced by the Hexagram.

The prayer is called the Bedtime Shema, or the B'sheim Hashem after the prayer's first two words.

בְּשֵׁם הַשֵׁם אֱלֹהֵי יִשְׂרָאֵל
מִימִינִי מִיכָאֵל
וּמִשְׂמֹאלִי גַּבְרִיאֵל
וּמִלְּפָנַי אוּרִיאֵל
וּמֵאֲחוֹרַי רְפָאֵל
וְעַל רֹאשִׁי שְׁכִינַת אֵ-ל

B'sheim Hashem elohei yisrael,
Mimini Michael
Umismoli Gavriel,
Umilfanai Uriel
Umeachorai Rafael,
V'al roshi shechinat el.

In the name of the Lord, the God of Israel,

At my right hand Michael,
At my left hand Gabriel,
Before me Uriel,
Behind me Raphael,
And above my head the Shekinah.

It had never occurred to me to look at this prayer's directional attributes, but when I did after editing this lesson I was very pleasantly surprised.

Once you know that magical south is whatever direction your nose is pointing, it is easy to work out where this prayer stations each angel:

S
URIEL

E   C   W
GABRIEL   SHEKINAH   MICHAEL

N
RAPHAEL

If you look up what these angels do in the Bible and in the Book of Enoch, and what their names mean in Hebrew, then you will discover that each of them has been given a very specific job here: guarding, communicating, showing, or healing/binding something.

When I showed this prayer to Josephine, she pointed out that the Shekinah, or Brigh as she's known round here, is in an unusual position: normally she would be underneath and around the speaker. As a result this venerable suit of armour has developed a hole in its bottom—though possibly Raphael is keeping an eye on it.

8.6 Elements of power

What is its purpose? Is it is direct action or indirect action?

A ritual or magical pattern or act has a reason for its existence. Achieving an end result in magic can be done directly or indirectly, and conditionally or unconditionally. Often magical patterns are multilayered and have both direct and indirect actions.

A direct action would be using magic for protection by asking for it, or using a protective tool, or changing something by mediating the power of change into it.

An indirect action would not be so obvious. The Lesser Banishing Ritual of the Pentagram is an indirect action. By the use of Divine names, declarations, and sigils (pentagrams) it seeks to change a place's frequency. The ritual does not explicitly ask for protection, balance, or anything else: the ritual's protective aspect (banishing or invoking) comes from declaring Divine sovereignty and triggering aspects of the Divine through the use of the Sefirot.

It is a perfect ritual for a magical beginner: command and control are taken out of their hands and they surrender the space to Divine impulse. However the fact it was a beginner exercise seems to have gotten lost in the mists of time. Nowadays it is used a cure-all by every Tom, Soror, and Asmodeus.

When you do a ritual your first question should be:

> "What is its true purpose, and does it achieve that directly or indirectly?"

What will power it?

What powers a ritual is an important thing to think about. What power levels does it need to achieve its purpose? The frequency of the magic dictates the power levels, and it does not matter if you call upon "Zork the giant crusher of planets" to do your bidding: if the frequency is not right, the power will not flow properly.

The LBRP, just like the early rituals you did in your apprentice work, draws on the Divine flow of power. The LBRP draws strongly on the Abrahamic interface of that Divine flow, which adds a layer to the filter. This could be good or not depending on who is doing the ritual and what opinion they have.

Other things that can power rituals are angelic beings,[13] deities, land powers that have an interface with humans, under-world beings, ancestors, faery beings,[14] or drawing on the Divine within the human as it reexpresses itself back out to the Divine.

This last is known as the *adept mirror reflection*, which is badly misunderstood and the biggest bear trap for immature magicians. Essentially, the adept mirror reflection happens when the adept gets to a level where all tools, patterns, beings, and so forth are no longer used and the Divine within the human consciously looks back at the Divine in creation: the ultimate magic. This process begins at the very start of training by placing the human in the fulcrum. The Golden Dawn's version of that was the LBRP.

What are the creative and restrictive impulses in a ritual?

Often magicians mistake the *power* source for a ritual or magical pattern for its *creative* impulse. Power is just power: what sort of power is used and how/why is a different important ingredient for the ritual. As you know, a magical pattern needs a creative and a restrictive or destructive impulse for it to be balanced. Too much creative impulse in a ritual can unbalance the magician, just as too much restriction can bind the magician out of action.

The creative impulse can be the Divine creative impulse, such as the creative Sefirot (Chesed) in the LBRP. If the use of Divine names and Sefirot are used, they must either match up, or counterbalance one another.

If a deity is used, their creative aspect must be balanced with their destructive or restrictive aspect.[15] If the natural elements are used, then again one must balance the another.[16]

Often when deities are used the religious mentality creeps in: then only one deity is used, and usually a subdivided one, which will cause imbalance in the power flow. If you use a creative deity, their restrictive or destructive counterpart must also be present, unless you

---

[13]Mediators, thresholds, etc.

[14]Tricksy.

[15]I.e. the two sides of a divided deity.

[16]Fire and water, or fire and earth.

are dealing with a complete, undivided deity that fully expresses both powers.

And this is where a lot of magicians also fall down: when a deity is described who is a divided deity, often the attributes of one are also explained in the other, and the magician becomes confused.

If a destructive/restrictive deity is given positive attributes, and those positive attributes have another deity expression then that other deity expression needs to be present as it is the other half of the subdivision. So for example if you look at Sekhmet, who is a destroying power, but she also has a creative side, which is Hathor, then you are working with a subdivided deity and both versions, Sekhmet and Hathor, need to be equally present.

What composts the magic?

If the pattern or ritual is magical in its purpose and has an intention, then it needs to have a *composting element*, something that opens a path up into which the depleted magic can flow. This is where serious problems can occur, particularly if religious elements are used haphazardly and the purpose is magical, not religious.

If creative Divine power is called on in its guise as anything below Kether on the Tree of Life (if Kabbalah is used), then you are in fact working with a *subdivision* of pure Divine power. And whenever you work with subdivision, you must balance it out. The same is true of deities, angelic beings, and so forth.

The magic has to have somewhere to drain off to when it is finished, and usually this is the Underworld.

If there is no path to composting, the remnants and straggles of the depleted magic have nowhere to go, so they will stay around the magician and the magical temple/space. This slowly builds up like plaque. As it is power that is breaking down it attracts parasites and low-level beings that will try to break it down. It is a similar process to not putting out the trash: flies gather, smells happen, and bacteria starts to proliferate.

This is very apparent in some magical lodges and groups where the leaders or higher-ranking members become degenerate, parasited, and trapped in dead end ego trips. The grot slowly infects the whole group and eventually the picture becomes very messy.

Ensuring magic is composted is basic magical hygiene. It can be spotted in healthy magical systems where there are Underworld connections or restrictive or destructive powers working in balance with the creative ones: the deities and powers are reflected in the ritual.

When there is a religious element that only seeks to ascend, that only seeks the light, and the only Underworld element is one of redemption or resurrection, then that does not count as a composting element: it is seeking to reexpress itself, which makes it a creative and not a composting process.

As redemption and 'reaching up' are such strong elements of the Abrahamic faiths, and particularly in Christianity and Islam, the use of those religions in the magical pattern are particularly vulnerable to this mistake. Death, decay, and withdrawal are shunned in favour of rising up again, and once more the ego trap comes into play with the idea of *eternal life within life*.

Eternal life within life *is* a mystical element of magic, but it is so badly misunderstood that it serves to damage the magician rather than slowly reveal to them its Mysteries.

So now that we have looked at all these aspects of ritual and magical construction, it is time for you to move on to your practical work. Here you will apply these dynamics with critical thinking, so that you can begin to look closely at religious and magical acts to see what is actually going on, what the construction was like, what was it trying to achieve, and what, if anything, is missing or out of balance.

Because you will be looking at rituals that are close to people's hearts, look with discretion and common sense, and without emotive judgement. Everything is fallible in magic as it is constructed by humans, and looking closely at rituals can reveal hidden gems or gaping holes, both of which will teach you a great deal.

8.7 *Task:* Analysing some rituals

"An unquestioning life is no life."
—Socrates

The Lesser Banishing Ritual of the Pentagram

Look at the LBRP again in real depth, and answer for yourself the questions posed in this lesson. Think about the ritual in terms of its use by beginners in the Golden Dawn system, then adepts, and then also by someone not working directly in that system but picking and mixing for their own practice. Look at what types of groups use this ritual and why, and then think about how it would work within those contexts.

The Catholic Tridentine Mass

If you are interested in looking at ritual and magical acts embedded in religion, take a close look at the Catholic Tridentine Mass in English and Latin. Whenever you come across something that catches your eye in English, look up the meaning of the Latin words—and use a secular Latin dictionary, don't rely on a religious one. This is a bit of a job as it is a long ritual, but see if you can identify the various aspects of declaration, prayer, ritual, and magical acts.

Magical rituals available online

Look up magical rituals you can find on the internet—it's swamped with everything you can think of. Also look back at some of the ritual work you have done.

Questions to ask yourself

When you look at these different ritual forms, ask the same questions of all of them. Regardless of how they are presented today, if they are older rituals, ask yourself what was could have been their original purpose, and how their use today compares to it. Sometimes you will find that they have evolved forwards, and other times that they have degenerated. Both of these are normal over time: it is part of the magical evolutionary process.

8.8 Thinking

Though the concept of Divinity within you and everything is a very powerful one, think about how it can (and does) go wrong. What would the consequences of that be for a magician, both magically and for their mental health if this concept was poorly understood and yet used in magic? What elements could cause those consequences? How does the use of psychology affect magic for better and worse, and why? Many people who first step into magic see the world in terms of black and white, and have no understanding of the millions of shades in between.

Remember that these days most people have access to magic, which is a relatively new phenomenon in our history. What are the consequences of that for magic in general? What filters are in place in modern magic to protect the magic and to protect the person from themselves? Which filters work well and which do not? How does 'stupid' operate in magic?

This is all very relevant in ritual magic construction, as you have to assume with many rituals that lots of different people will use and access them.

None of this practical work requires you to write any essays: I want you to simply think your own thoughts without having to justify them in writing. I want you to come to your own conclusions, and not worry about being 'right or wrong': you can take notes for yourself so you can see, later on, how your opinion may have changed, but in general this research is purely for yourself and your own learning. Just don't skip it: it is an important process.

CPSIA information can be obtained at www.ICGtesting.com
Printed in the USA
BVOW10s0327251115

428362BV00022B/37/P